Red Pill, Blue Pill

How to Counteract the Conspiracy Theories That Are Killing Us

DAVID NEIWERT

Prometheus Books

Guilford, Connecticut

PB Prometheus Books

An imprint of The Rowman & Littlefield Publishing Group, Inc.
4501 Forbes Blvd., Ste. 200
Lanham, MD 20706
www.rowman.com

Distributed by NATIONAL BOOK NETWORK

British Library Cataloguing in Publication Information available

Library of Congress Cataloging-in-Publication Data
Names: Neiwert, David A., 1956– author.
Title: Red pill, blue pill : how to counteract the conspiracy theories that are killing us / David Neiwert.
Description: Lanham, MD : Prometheus Books, [2020] | Includes bibliographical references and index. | Summary: "A revealing trip down the rabbit hole of conspiracy theories-their appeal, who believes them, how they spread-with an eye to helping people deal with the alt-right conspiracists in their own lives. Conspiracy theories are killing us"— Provided by publisher.
Identifiers: LCCN 2020005105 (print) | LCCN 2020005106 (ebook) | ISBN 9781633886261 (cloth) | ISBN 9781633886278 (epub)
Subjects: LCSH: Conspiracy theories—United States. | Conspiracy theories—Political aspects—United States. | Right-wing extremists—United States—Psychology. | Radicalism—United States. | Political culture—United States. | United States—Politics and government—1989-
Classification: LCC HV6275 .N45 2020 (print) | LCC HV6275 (ebook) | DDC 001.9—dc23
LC record available at https://lccn.loc.gov/2020005105
LC ebook record available at https://lccn.loc.gov/2020005106

∞™ The paper used in this publication meets the minimum requirements of American National Standard for Information Sciences—Permanence of Paper for Printed Library Materials, ANSI/NISO Z39.48-1992.

CONTENTS

Prologue   v

1   Conspiracies and Theories   1

2   The Red Pilled   9

3   Sacrifices   29

4   Tangled Tales   49

5   A Brave New World Order   67

6   The Rabbit Hole   95

7   Chaos by Design   113

8   Everybody Get in Line   133

9   A Pill for Healing   147

Notes   181

Index   207

PROLOGUE

Somebody has to wake up the American public and get them to arm themselves. . . . Sometimes sacrifices have to be made.

—Gunman Stephen Paddock, three weeks before opening fire on a country music festival in Las Vegas, according to an informant

I used to be a "normal" American guy—I went to school, I got a good job, I had a house, a car, I used to love "stuff" . . . and I had everything: the electronic toys, the clothes, the gadgets, and all the accessories. I used to love movies: I had a massive movie collection. I used to love music: I had hundreds of gigs of music. I have a stack of concert ticket stubs and tons of concert T-shirts. My yard and house were very respectable, I spent time and money landscaping. I watched the news. I had debates with coworkers and family members about politics. I even had hobbies: coin collecting, woodworking, mountain biking, and surfing. I used to put on my good suit and go to church on Sunday and talk with all the other people there. I saw my career as a path toward upward mobility. I played politics in the company. I worked overtime. I got in good with the boss. I climbed the corporate ladder.

But, then, I started to really get into Conspiracy Theory (back like in 2012/2013). I went DEEP down the rabbit hole and came out the other side. I wanted to know EVERYTHING! I did days and weeks of research. I immersed myself completely. In 2016 I jumped into Pizzagate research with both feet. I devoured everything there was to know. Then, in 2017, I hopped on the QAnon bandwagon and went even deeper.

Something changed inside of me. I woke up! I no longer saw the world as I used to. I quit my job. I sold my stuff. I've downsized my entire life. I've been living off my savings for a few years now. I no longer see a point in participating in the "real" (fake) world. I know that everything I see is a lie. Everything that I've ever known is a lie. My whole world has been nothing but one giant lie from the start, and I can see that clearly now. So why bother? What is the point of perpetuating the corrupt system by playing along. Why bother pretending that anything matters? I have myself set up in a good situation financially. I spend very little money and I grow a lot of my own food. My expenses are minimal. I may never have to work again. I can just live on the bare minimum and avoid the fake world altogether.

The only people that I actually hang out and talk to are people who know the truth. I can't even interact with people who still believe the fake world is real. I just can't do it. Basically, I can no longer function in the fake real world. It pains me to play along with some stupid game that I know is fake. Now all I do is sit around here (and various other conspiracy forums) and look for news of "The Event." I'm waiting for that one trigger event that will end this whole corrupt system. I keep watching and waiting and praying. Maybe it will be a huge war? Maybe it will be a financial collapse? Maybe it will be some external event (aliens)? Either way, we're on the edge of the cliff and looking down into the abyss. It's only a matter of time before this whole thing blows up and ends.

Until then, I'm just going to drop out and mind my own business. I'm going to wait and learn as much as I can. Someday, when it all comes crashing down, a huge weight will be lifted off my shoulders and I will finally get to exist in the *real* world again.

Does anyone else feel this way?

—Anonymous contributor at Voat.com,
an Internet message board, October 2018

They call it "getting red-pilled." We all know the metaphor, the one from *The Matrix*: Morpheus holds out his hands to reveal two small pills: "You take the blue pill—the story ends, you wake up in your bed and believe whatever you want to believe. You take the red pill—you stay in Wonderland and I show you how deep the rabbit hole goes." Like the hypercool hero Neo in the films, true believers in the alternative universe of conspiracy theories are absolutely convinced that the epistemological bubble into which they have submerged themselves is the real reality.

The problem, of course, is that their version of reality isn't based in facts, sound evidence, or even logical reasoning, but rather is a complex farrago of conjecture, false facts and evidence, wild-eyed paranoia, and sociopathic authoritarianism. Rather than giving people who think they have "taken the red pill" a clear-eyed view of the world as it really is, conspiracism actually creates a crackpot version of reality in which the world is secretly run by a cabal of scheming Jewish globalists who control both the banks and the media, in which their planned one-world government is intent on disarming private citizens and putting them in concentration camps and in which Muslims work in cahoots with Marxists to destroy Western civilization.

It used to be that such people were few in number and mostly relegated to the fringes of society, their theories and claims the frequent source of amusement for some people. Now, the leading conspiracy theorists have audiences numbering in the millions, and their views are shared not just with the audiences on mainstream right-wing cable shows, but also by the president of the United States and members of his administration.

And it is killing us, both metaphorically and literally. Conspiracism is much of the fuel that feeds the rise of the radical right both in the United States and around the world, and its toxic effects on our communities and our democracy will be felt for many years to come. It feeds the scapegoating, fear, and eliminationism that in turn are the foundations of hate crimes and acts of domestic terrorism. More precisely, it has played an outsized role in fueling gun-related violence, particularly mass shootings: nearly every gun rampage in which large numbers of people have been killed in recent years has been perpetrated by men who have been radicalized on Internet forums devoted to conspiracy theories. Perhaps the most notorious of these was the mass shooter in Las Vegas in October 2017, who killed 58 people and injured another 851, driven by a belief in a government plot to take away Americans' guns.

This is where the very far end of the "red-pilled" spectrum reaches its apotheosis. The young people (mostly male) consumed by this radicalization call this "black-pilling": a bleakly nihilistic mindset in which the world's doom is seen as inevitable. The system is too rotten, the global environment poised for catastrophe, everything is too far gone. So violence becomes not just excusable, but a way of going out, paradoxically, with some kind of meaning, even if it's just the "score" you can roll up in a mass murder, glorified among your fellow trolls at 4chan and Reddit who have, horrifically, "gamified" these killings.[1]

Eventually, the online participants in all this "pilling" have evolved a whole pharmacopeia of variously colored pills that radicalize in different ways:

- Purple pill: A kind of "normie," or centrist, version of red-pilling that rejects both red- and blue-pilling, essentially acknowledging that the system is broken, but seeing possibilities for redemption and urging work toward it.
- Pink pill: A kind of female version of the "black pill," which is dominated by "involutary celibate" males (better known as "incels"), in which the people consuming it come to believe they'll never be accepted as attractive by males and, similarly, embrace nihilistic violence.

- White pill: A pill that embraces an optimistic view of whatever extremist "red-pilled" movement the person consuming it has joined. It's mostly an enhancement "pill."
- Bread pill: A dual-meaning pill: on the extreme right, it references people who have embraced traditionalist religious beliefs about gender and sex; on the extreme left, it signals an embrace of anarcho-communism.
- Green pill: As its name suggests, this means an embrace of radical environmentalism, but of a specifically far-right kind that blames many of the world's environmental ills on nonwhite people in third-world nations. This worldview is called "eco-fascism," and it encourages often viciously racist views directed at immigrants, refugees, and minority religions.[2]

The conspiracism innate to "red-pilling" is toxic on a personal and familial level, too. It affects interpersonal relationships when friends and family members refuse to clamber down the rabbit hole with them, since their refusal not only makes them, in the eyes of those who have swallowed it, certain sheep-like pawns in the vast conspiracy they see, but even potential conspirators. As the phenomenon spreads, thousands of families are being torn apart by the anger and fear the conspiracist industry generates, sometimes with fatal consequences.

Lane Davis's favorite song in high school, according to his senior yearbook, was "Loser." It seems fitting. The rest of his inscription featured offbeat aphorisms— "In the time of monkeys I was a chimpanzee" (a line from the Beck song), "Getting needles stuck through me and steel implanted," "Anywhere in life, make the best outta the situation. Keep it real while maintaining the front"—suggesting alienation and someone ill at social ease.

Blond with soft, heavy features, Davis looked large in these photos but really wasn't. He wasn't athletic, didn't play football like a lot of guys in rural Skagit County, Washington, where he grew up. Thumbing through the 2002 Burlington-Edison High *Tinas Coma*, you can spot him here and there but mostly lurking on the fringes—in the debate team room, posing with a Speedy Gonzales figure, looking skeptical and painfully hip in his senior photo.

He and his family—mom, dad, brother, and sister—lived out in the sticks, on Samish Island, which actually ceased being an island sometime in the early twentieth century when local landowners built a system of dikes that created a permanent causeway between the island and the mainland, so people drive on and off it across the main road at any time. But it is part of a cultural landscape populated with island communities, ferries, boats, and wildlife. Getting to high school each day entailed a thirty-minute drive across delta farmland.

Lane's dad, Charles "Chuck" Davis, was an attorney known around the community as "Mr. Samish Island." He organized all kinds of community activities, including sailing activities that taught young people how to handle a boat. He and his wife, Catherine, were pillars of the community, and their home was centrally located on a curve overlooking Samish Bay.[3] Their daughter Allison and son Peter were both considered bright, outgoing, pleasant young people. Their son Lane, not so much. He was, as polite Northwesterners put it, "difficult." Surly. Harsh. Highly intelligent and contemptuous of others around him.

When Lane graduated, he enrolled at the university on the other side of the state, Washington State, in the rolling Palouse farmland and began studying physics.[4] He washed out after only a year or so, though. After that he wandered quite a bit, career-wise. He worked in the software world around the Seattle/Redmond area for a few years, but nothing ever stuck. In 2009, though, he began finding his future: online.

That was the year Lane first popped up on YouTube under the nom de plume Seattle4Truth.[5] His first few videos were dabblings in health-related conspiracy theories, as well as Davis's theories about physics, which he eventually published on a dubious-science website called *The General Science Journal.* Titled "Quantum Cold-Case Mysteries Revisited," it was a series of ruminations on quantum physics that were, in fact, regurgitated and utterly discredited theories about perpetual motion. For most of the first year or so online, Lane's video output was along similar niche crackpot lines.

But then he began spreading out, creating videos that became increasingly imbued in far-right conspiracism. One video claimed the Oklahoma City bombing was a false flag, while another "exposed" the hoary conspiracy by the Jewish Rothschild family to control world banking and government. The 9/11 attacks were an insider "false flag" event. People who consume public drinking water are dosing themselves with mind-controlling lithium. In a media market where such videos were as common as seagulls at a fisherman's wharf, Lane's videos didn't make much of a mark.

He made his living by working at an aluminum smelter in Ferndale, an hour's drive from Samish Island, where he told friends he made a six-figure salary. He had a place of his own near Bellingham during those years but kept making videos. When he was laid off in 2014, he had to move back to Samish Island, where he took up a wing of his parents' home and tried figuring out other ways to make a splash online.

He struck online gold, finally, in 2015 with an epic three-hour-twenty-minute pastiche about the so-called Gamergate controversy, titled "#Gamergate: Actually, It's about . . ." Comprised mostly of clips arguing that discussions and seminars within the computer gaming corporations and the larger design community were part of a larger plot by "cultural Marxists" to make video games less "masculine"—that is, less structured around first-person-shooter architecture—as part of a larger globalist scheme to emasculate young white males.

Not only was it a massive hit, it brought him to the attention of some of the gods of the Gamergate world, particularly Breitbart News' tech editor Milo Yiannopoulos, who since 2012 had been generating an entire career as a political provocateur out of the toxic cauldron of that online controversy. Ostensibly a debate over the ethics of online-gaming journalism, in the fever swamps of Internet message boards, video chat rooms, and news comments sections, it turned mostly into an attack on feminists, especially those in the game-design community, featuring threats and at-home harassment and "doxxing," in which all of your personal information—your address, your Social Security number, everything—is published online for everyone in the world to see. It also became a recruiting ground for white nationalists and neo-Nazis and played an essential role in generating what became known as the "alt-right."

Davis's Gamergate video came to Yiannopolous's attention after he was adopted by a kind of feeder blog called *The Ralph Retort*, which specialized in right-wing conspiracism. Ethan Ralph, the site's founder and editor, began running Davis's videos and posts along with effusive praise for his "insanely good" research skills. He gave him the title of "senior political analyst" and wrote that "The things he's saying are true" and praised his "tireless efforts" and for being "proven right again."

Yiannopoulos snapped him up in late 2015 and added him to his "Project Milo" team. Davis worked as a speechwriter and ghostwriter on Milo's autobiography, *Dangerous*, the winter and spring of 2016. The problem was that Milo wasn't paying him. He wasn't paying anyone, for that matter; much of his organization was actually being operated by "volunteers" who were happy to be in his orbit and perform work for no pay.[6] At least, Milo seemed to think they were happy. Lane Davis wasn't. He asked Milo for a paying position in February. He got turned down. So in March, he handed a pile of emails to a *BuzzFeed* reporter, Joseph Bernstein, who turned them into a story exposing how Yiannopoulos was running a scam operation that ripped off the people working for him.

Milo did manage to land Davis a job at the right-wing Capital Research Center, praising him as "One of my most gifted researchers. Total autodidact . . . hugely smart."

Davis wrote a piece attacking the MacArthur Foundation that was published in May 2017 under a joint Yiannopoulos-Davis byline titled "MacArthur's Thought Police: A Foundation Helps Twitter and Other Social Media Enforce Left-Wing Ideology."

By then, however, Davis had moved on. Working more feverishly than ever for *The Ralph Retort*, he began pouring out videos focusing on the so-called

Pizzagate conspiracy theory, as well as a handful of associated conspiracies. One of these turned up at Alex Jones's *Infowars* website under a *Ralph Retort* byline (headlined "Big Brother: Top Soros Henchman Calls for Government-Run Social Media in Order to Stop Infowars and Breitbart") in May also. This meant he was rising steadily within the conspiracy theory ecosystem.

He had become increasingly obsessed with the conspiracy theory that there was a global pedophilia ring operating out of Washington and Hollywood that was the underpinning of the Pizzagate claims, which were predicated on emails stolen from Democratic National Committee (DNC) headquarters in 2016.[7] (Theorists claim that some of the emails contained secret code words indicating that there were children being held in a dungeon in a D.C. pizza parlor. In December 2016, one of the believers in these theories walked into that restaurant with an AR-15 and fired some rounds into a closet door he believed would reveal the opening to the dungeon rather than the janitorial supplies it contained.)

Lane often veered into violent, threatening language when discussing the supposed pedophilia ring. In a three-way video conversation with fellow *Ralph Retort* participants, he became enraged when one of them opined that same-sex restrooms were harmless. Lane accused him of hoping to spy on young girls in public facilities.

"Pedo Marxist piece of shit!" Lane screamed. "I'll stab your bitch ass if I ever see you."

Summer was getting into full swing on Samish Island, but Lane spent most of his time on his computer, creating and posting videos, nearly all of them variations on the Pizzagate theories, including a related theory that the unsolved death of a DNC staff member named Seth Rich was part of the lethal coverup of the pedophilia ring. Lane also posted a video arguing that all progressives and liberals were participants in the global pedophilia phenomenon.

"But what if I were to tell you that pedophilia is a basic tenet of the progressive ideology? You think hyperbole?" he told his audience. "Let's look to Germany, where the modern progressive ideology based on social sciences has its roots. In 2010, Germany's *Der Spiegel* newspaper published a three-part series on 'The Sexual Revolution in Children.' Part 1 was titled, 'How the Left Took Things Too Far.' Quote: 'Germany's left has its own tales of abuse. One of the goals of the German 1968 movement was the sexual liberation of children. For some time, this meant overcoming all sexual inhibitions, creating a climate in which even pedophilia was considered progressive.' . . . They felt they were doing nothing wrong, it was just scientific, progressive social science."[8]

There was a growing contempt and anger in his voice. He was primed and ready to explode.

Chapter 1

CONSPIRACIES AND THEORIES

[T]oday we live in a society in which spurious realities are manufactured by the media, by governments, by big corporations, by religious groups, political groups. . . . So I ask, in my writing, What is real? Because unceasingly we are bombarded with pseudo-realities manufactured by very sophisticated people using very sophisticated electronic mechanisms. I do not distrust their motives; I distrust their power. They have a lot of it. And it is an astonishing power: that of creating whole universes, universes of the mind. I ought to know. I do the same thing.

—Philip K. Dick, "How to Build a Universe That Doesn't Fall Apart Two Days Later"

The term "conspiracy theory" means many things—a technical definition might run something like "a hypothetical explanation of historical or ongoing news events comprised of secret plots, usually of a nefarious nature, whose existence may or may not be factual"—but in recent years, it also has become a kind of dismissive epithet.

Once a narrative takes on the taint of "conspiracy theory," the common response nowadays is to dismiss it out of hand as useless, if amusing, misinformation. (Unless you have been "red-pilled." Then, it's a very different story. Much more about all that momentarily.)

The majority of us who live well inside the mainstream of American society don't really have the time for conspiracist beliefs and the wild-eyed ranters who peddle them—shouters like Alex Jones and Michael Savage, the cartoonish scam peddlers whose mark on their true believers usually presages a kind of pathetic gullibility. (What's in those expensive vitamin supplements anyway?) We may count their marks among our friends, but their credibility is always . . . suspect, you know?

There's a problem, though. Real conspiracies do exist—and have through most of civilized history. In recent years, one need only point to an array of scandals—Watergate, which brought down an American president, or the COIN-TELPRO episode in which federal agents unleashed dirty tricks on American citizens for political reasons,[1] or the Reagan-era Iran-Contra scandal in which a web of conspirators shuttled money and weapons between Central America and the Middle East[2]—to demonstrate that conspiracies continue to weave their way into the fabric of American history. And truth be told, conspiracies as well as wild-eyed beliefs about them are deeply wired into our history and our national psyche.

A belief in conspiracy theories, more deeply, is reflected in very real problems in modern corporate-controlled media. After the American public eventually became aware that it had been gulled into supporting a travesty of a war in Iraq—an invasion of a foreign nation under the false pretenses that it possessed weapons of mass destruction—and more acutely realized the role that major journalistic institutions, including the *New York Times* and the *Washington Post*, played in foisting that deception on them, at great cost to the families of the soldiers lost there, a widespread mistrust of previously authoritative sources of information became not just a normal response, but a perfectly logical one.

Simultaneously, there's also become an increasing tendency to willingly consume and absorb conspiracy theories for generally partisan motivations. The so-called birther theories about Barack Obama's birth certificate circulated—and enjoyed a peculiarly obdurate half-life long beyond the expiration of any trace of factual grounding for the claims—primarily among partisan conservative Republicans. Donald Trump's defenders insist a Communist/globalist/far-left plot exists to remove him from the presidency for his multiple abuses of power with nothing but odd speculation about a "deep state" to support it.[3]

It's easy to dismiss discussion of actual conspiratorial behavior as conspiracy theories, especially in this environment. Recall, for instance, how discussion of the Bush family's dynastic wealth and its distant history of involvement with financing the war machinery of the Third Reich during the tenure of George W. Bush (2001–2008) was dismissed as "conspiracy theories" by mainstream conservatives, despite the factual grounding of the discussion[4] and the reality that the underlying subject—namely, the growth of wealth inequality and the concentration of power that resulted[5]—has remained a significant and very real issue on the American political landscape. Likewise, attempts to confront the involvement of Donald Trump's presidential campaign with Russian intelligence's interference in the 2016 election are still routinely dismissed as conspiracy theories and "fake news."

Indeed, "fake news" has become the more recent variation of this hall-of-mirrors distortion of journalism and the stream of factual information, one in which some of the most potent misinformation being injected into that stream deliberately is the claim that factually accurate information is false. It's a parlor trick that Donald Trump has mastered in his attempts to create chaos in the news coverage around his presidency, dismissing fact-checked *New York Times* investigative pieces as "fake" while embracing entirely false narratives about everything from immigrants at the border to Barack Obama's birth certificate.

The environment that is most conducive to conspiracy theories, at least initially, is one in which government operates with broad secrecy and in fact engages in deliberate deception and obfuscation, usually for short-term political motives rather than long-term nefarious intentions, but the latter instead becomes the preferred explanation. The government's handling of the unidentified flying objects phenomenon in the 1950s and 1960s is a classic example of the dynamic at work, producing a whole mini-universe of conspiracy theories about alien visitors and spacecraft that became such widespread cultural lore that they created whole genres of science fiction and fiction as well as in movies and television shows that indeed remain with us today, more popular than ever.

From this environment can emerge something unique to twenty-first-century America: an inability to determine, let alone agree upon, what is factual and real and what is not. This kind of chaotic soup is a prime environment for conspiracy theories to blossom like kudzu.

This sea change—the unmooring of even conspiracy theories from any kind of factual grounding whatever—has its origins in the conspiracy theory cottage industry that sprang up around the terrorist attacks of September 11, 2001. There was no shortage of speculation, suspicion, and questioning in the weeks immediately following the attacks, but even as it became established that they were the work of militant Islamists led by Osama bin Laden, fresh conspiracy theories began suggesting that the attacks were the product of an "inside job," perpetrated by the Bush administration, perhaps with the help of Israeli intelligence. The leader of this contingent, of course, was Alex Jones.

But these theories found an eager audience in no small part because the Bush administration attempted to stonewall efforts to investigate the disaster and, particularly, to form an official commission to examine its causes. From the outset, the White House put its thumb on the panel's scales by limiting its purview to the preparedness and response to the attacks, and in the end, the commission's report was completely lacking in any discussion of pre-attack warnings and the administration's response to it or lack thereof.[6]

The Bush White House all along was hostile to the commission, controversially naming Henry Kissinger its chair before he stepped down,[7] refusing to provide it with adequate funding and cooperation,[8] and then finally refusing additional time for the commission to complete its report.[9] Most of all, the report gave a truncated and, it soon emerged, entirely inaccurate accounting of the warnings the administration had received prior to the attacks. Some of this was because the White House refused to give key documents—especially the key presidential daily briefing of August 6, 2001, which included stark warnings of an imminent al-Qaeda attack—to the commission until late in its investigation.[10]

All of this led many millions of people to believe that the commission's final report was less than a full accounting of what happened, with reasonable cause. Most likely the whole point of the White House's secrecy was to cover what was later exposed (particularly by former National Security Director Richard Clarke, a few years after the fact) as its startling incompetence in responding to the clear and specific warnings it received before the attacks. But the coverup created a monster in which millions of people became susceptible to the broad menu of increasingly warped conspiracy theories about what *really* happened on 9/11.

> Reality is that which, when you stop believing in it, doesn't go away.
> —Philip K. Dick, *I Hope I Shall Arrive Soon*

Sorting out good information from bad has become seemingly an overwhelming task in the age of the Internet and social media. Some people have stopped trying. Others have embraced the abyss, as it were, by diving into the epistemologically malleable and manipulable world of conspiracy theories, a zone where normative rules of evidence and factuality need not apply.

Entering this zone can seem like wandering into a hall of mirrors designed by Philip Dick, in which it's difficult to distinguish reality from a kind of upside-down alternative universe where the rules of gravity are suspended. Some people veer sharply away, instinctively recognizing its toxicity, and avoid it altogether. Some wander into the hall of mirrors and never come out. Or, using a more popular metaphor, they vanish down the White Rabbit's gaping black hole.

This maze can be challenging enough for a person with balanced mental health and reasonable acuity. When persons dealing with mental illness enter into the conspiracy-theory alternative universe, there can be actual cognitive effects with extremely undesirable outcomes—making it difficult at times to ascertain what actions are fueled by conspiracy theories and which are products of mental illness.

What's incontestable, however, is that conspiracy theories have a powerfully toxic effect on people's sense of connectedness to others—to the point that many people drawn down those rabbit holes begin to cut off and fall away from all the friends and family with whom they once were close. Some of this is the logical product of the overarching narrative of conspiracy theories in general—namely, that ordinary people are up against forces so dark and nefarious and omnipotent that they have no real chance against them.

It convinces them that ordinary democratic participation—their votes, their caucusing, their phone-banking—is a joke. That you can't know who you can trust. Even your neighbors, your family, your old pals might be part of the conspiracy, if not its "sheeple" dupes. Eventually the logic of the conspiracist universe would have its adherents disconnect from all human contact and retreat to a cabin in the Montana woods.

Yet as harrowing and confusing as it can be to enter the world of conspiracism, it's actually easier than you'd think to distinguish between a real conspiracy and a conspiracy theory, beyond recognizing that the former has a reasonable degree of being real, while the latter is almost certainly a falsehood intended to scapegoat other people.

Real conspiracies, by their very nature (including their dependence on secrecy), have three major limitations:

- Scope: their purpose is usually to achieve only one or two ends, often narrow in nature.
- Time: their actions necessarily occur within a relatively short time frame.
- Number of participants: all successful conspiracies are the product of only a handful of people.

As the boundaries of all three of these limits increase, however, the likelihood of the conspiracy failing or being exposed rises exponentially. The broader the reach—if it attempts too much—the more likely it is to meet failure simply as a matter of raw odds and the nature of institutional inertia. The longer it takes, the greater the risk of exposure, not to mention the greater the risk of the conspiracy's components going awry. Similar issues arise when increasing numbers of people are involved in the conspiracy: both the likelihood of failure to complete their part of the conspiracy as well as the growing chances of exposure. And exposure is fatal to every conspiracy: once the secret is out, it's no longer a viable plan of action.

Conspiracy theories, on the other hand, almost universally feature qualities that contrast sharply with these limits.

- They are broad ranging in nature and frequently boil down to (or play key roles in) a massive plot to enslave, murder, or politically oppress all of mankind or at least large numbers of people.

- They are believed to have existed for long periods of time, in some cases for hundreds of years.
- They involve large numbers of people, notably significant numbers of participants in high positions in government or the bureaucracy.
- The long-term success of these conspiracies is always credited to willing dupes in the media and elsewhere.

Moreover, as Russell Muirhead and Nancy Rosenblum have explored in some depth, modern conspiracy theories have evolved sharply in the past two decades since 9/11 and are no longer what was once their central feature: evidence based.[11] Whereas JFK and UFO conspiracy theories always revolved around differing interpretations of varying pieces of evidence, conspiracists in the post-militia era primarily build their work around pure conjecture, speculation connecting odd factual dots with secret nefarious plots operating behind the scenes.

This "new conspiracism" represents, as Muirhead and Rosenblum explain, "a new destructive impulse: to delegitimate democracy":

> The new conspiracism is something different. There is no punctilious demand for proofs, no exhaustive amassing of evidence, no dots revealed to form a pattern, no close examination of the operators plotting in the shadows. The new conspiracism dispenses with the burden of explanation. Instead, we have innuendo and verbal gesture: "A lot of people are saying . . ." Or we have bare assertion: "Rigged!"—a one-word exclamation that evokes fantastic schemes, sinister motives, and the awesome capacity to mobilize three million illegal voters to support Hillary Clinton for president. This is conspiracy without the theory.[12]

Conspiracy theories are a problem for healthy democracies not only because they encourage people to disengage from their communities and abjure their political franchise by discarding it all as useless, but also because they represent serious pollution of the information stream. Democracies rely on robust debate, but that "marketplace of ideas" cannot function if the debate is founded on falsehoods, smears, and the wild speculations that all combine to take the place of established facts in any discourse with conspiracy theorists.

"The new conspiracists seek not to correct those they accuse but to deny their standing in the political world to argue, explain, persuade, and decide," write Muirhead and Rosenblum. "And from attacking malevolent individuals, conspiracists move on to assaulting institutions. Conspiracism corrodes the foundations of democracy."

Even beyond these broad social harms, conspiracy theories also inflict a host of smaller wounds that eventually have deeper ramifications, as political researcher Chip Berlet has explained. Among the casualties is a shared reality and sense of what truth is. "All conspiracist theories start with a grain of truth, which is then transmogrified with hyperbole and filtered through pre-existing myth and prejudice," Berlet writes.[13]

> Strange how paranoia can link up with reality now and then.
> —Philip K. Dick, *A Scanner Darkly*

In some ways, conspiracism is an understandable if not entirely rational response to conditions in the real world, particularly perfectly rational concerns about the quality and veracity of an information stream produced by a corporate-owned media apparatus. Moreover, those concerns are underscored when corporations and their figureheads are in fact caught conspiring to obtain political or profitable outcomes with some regularity.

"Conspiracist thinking and scapegoating are symptoms, not causes, of underlying societal frictions, and as such are perilous to ignore," says Berlet.[14] Indeed, one of the perils is that when legitimate grievances go unaddressed, the response of the aggrieved can be transformed to embrace illegitimate means, including violence.

Eventually, all conspiracism is a form of scapegoating, because all conspiracy theories construct narratives that blame specifically named targets (sometimes individuals, sometimes groups of people or even whole ethnicities and religions). And as Berlet observes: "Scapegoating and conspiracist allegations are tools that can be used by cynical leaders to mobilize a mass following. Supremacist and fascist organizers use conspiracist theories as a relatively less-threatening entry point in making contact with potential recruits."[15]

The toxicity unleashed by conspiracy theories—even when they do not center on Jews, people of color, members of the LGBT community, Muslim refugees, or other scapegoated groups—can create an environment where a panoply of bigotry, including misogyny, gay bashing, and anti-Semitism can flourish within our communities, often expressed as inchoate hate crimes and terroristic violence.

This gets to perhaps the most toxic aspect of conspiracism: it has a uniquely *unhinging* quality. Regardless of the direction of the theories, right or left or utterly idiosyncratic, the absorption of such beliefs into their worldview has a singular ability to separate people from their contact with reality.

In the real world, this means that angry young white men having romantic difficulties can blame a feminist conspiracy for ruining the world (as well as their video games) before embarking on killing rampages. It means another white man who has succumbed to conspiracy theories about black crime in America can walk into a church and systematically kill black congregants. It means a gun fanatic can come to believe that mowing down country music fans at a Las Vegas festival would somehow awaken Americans to the threat of a government conspiracy to take away their guns. It means young men living in their parents' homes can come to believe their own family members are participants in the conspiracies they loathe and fear and to strike out violently with swords and knives and guns.

As Berlet says: "People who believe conspiracist allegations sometimes act on those irrational beliefs, which has concrete consequences in the real world."[16]

So what can we do about it?

The answer is complicated.

Chapter 2

THE RED PILLED

Stephen Paddock didn't have a lot of friends. Those who knew him, though, all agreed that he had a thing about guns and the Second Amendment and a deep fear that the government would attempt to take them away.

They just didn't expect him to commit, on October 1, 2017, the worst mass shooting in American history.

Like most men of his generation—Paddock attended high school and college in California in the 1970s—Paddock was drawn into the world of conspiracy theories not through the Internet or social media, but from the alternative media ecosystem that emerged in the 1990s associated with the "Patriot" militia movement. These earlier conspiracists' main media then was the radio, including a variety of guerrilla broadcasts on underground networks, as well as mailings and email exchanges as the chief forms of communication.

Guns were the essence of the militia movement—most of its participants had multiple weapons and considerable stockpiles of ammunition. They showed them off to each other, and gun shows, which attracted a significant contingent of paranoid and suspicious people, were often where the militias themselves organized. Timothy McVeigh, the Patriot militiaman who killed 168 people in Oklahoma City in April 1995 with a large truck bomb, made a living for years traveling to gun shows and selling wares there. He would hand out copies of the white-supremacist race-war tract, *The Turner Diaries*, to people who bought guns out of the back of his car from him.[1]

It was this deep paranoia about the government confiscating their guns—set off by Bill Clinton's ill-fated ban on assault weapons passed in 1994—that was the meat and potatoes of what Patriot militiamen talked about, organized around, and prepared for. This fear in turn launched the career of the greatest megastar of the conspiracy-theory universe, Alex Jones.[2]

Many of the people who were radicalized by conspiracy theories in the 1990s never lost their conviction that there was a nefarious New World Order plot to enslave mankind. Among them was Stephen Paddock.[3]

When Adam Le Fevre, an Australian man who was in a relationship with the sister of Paddock's girlfriend, visited Paddock's suburban Las Vegas home in 2013, he was given a tour of the place, including the gun room.[4]

"Steve said 'bedroom . . . sitting room . . . and gun room . . .' Aah, gun room?" Le Fevre later told an interviewer.

The two of them got into a discussion about guns, and when Le Fevre expressed some skepticism about the need for Second Amendment protection of gun ownership, Paddock became emphatic.

"I raised that question with Steve and it's something that he came back at me with an incredible degree of vigor," Le Fevre recalled. "He was very strict and very firm on the fact that it's a right. It's the freedom of every American to participate, to own a gun and use it . . . when need be."

What most of his friends didn't know about Steve Paddock was that his father was one of the longest sought names on the FBI's Ten Most Wanted list, having escaped prison in Texas in 1969 and remaining uncaught until 1977. Though he had little contact with his father for most of his life (the old man died of a heart attack in 1998), they shared a set of personality traits: both men were described as highly intelligent, arrogant, and egotistical.[5]

People who knew Paddock in high school said that he was "a real brain" and "extremely smart," but also self-absorbed and narcissistic.[6] After getting a degree in business administration at Cal Northridge in 1977, he went to work as a postal carrier, then at the Internal Revenue Service, where he was an agent until 1984.

Family members later told reporters that part of his motivation for being a federal employee involved his desire to avoid paying taxes, which he loathed deeply: he "worked for the IRS in order to learn how to hide his income," his brother said.[7]

Multiple people, including a real estate broker with whom Paddock had dealings, described how he hated the government and hated paying taxes to it, even moving property ownership from California to Nevada in order to avoid them.[8] This did not change over the years: Adam Le Fevre described to another correspondent how Paddock was "animated about the government and the tax system" and "outspoken about the inadequacies and waste of the government."[9]

Though his behavior is consistent with a follower, it's unclear whether Paddock participated in the radical anti-tax movement of the 1970s and 1980s. This movement was affiliated with the conspiracist far right of the time, and many of its tenets and participants were foundational in establishing the Patriot militia movement of the '90s. Although it's likely he was exposed to the ideology, there is no evidence Paddock joined any of the anti-tax organizations of that period.

Telling people that he had figured out how to play gambling odds in a way that could sustain an income, Paddock quit work in 1984 and lived off his considerable real estate investments and gambling winnings. He began leading a more leisurely lifestyle, taking overseas cruise ship tours, settling into communities in Texas, California, and Florida before moving to the Las Vegas exurb of Mesquite in 2015.

Something went wrong with his finances in September 2015, according to Clark County Sheriff Joe Lombardo, who told reporters later that Paddock—who was profiled by experts as a narcissist obsessed with being part of the Las Vegas elite—lost "a significant amount" of money in his investments that month.[10]

He also began collecting guns and became increasingly paranoid about them. (Apparently he was also a fan of Donald Trump: "He was happy with Trump because the stock market was doing well," Lombardo noted.) Between October 2016 and the same month a year later, he purchased fifty-five weapons, most of them rifles, to complement what was already an arsenal of twenty-nine guns. Paddock also had a girlfriend, but in mid-September 2017, he sent her to her home country of the Philippines on a family visit—a surprise trip he sprang on her. When she arrived, he wired her $100,000 to buy a home there.[11]

At one point, he began scouting locations for what he had in mind. He visited several hotels overlooking popular music festivals, including what would have been the venue for the Lollapalooza rock music festival in Chicago.[12]

Back in Las Vegas, however, he had apparently taken up with a prostitute who later spoke on condition of anonymity. She told investigators she "would spend hours drinking and gambling in Las Vegas" with a "paranoid" and "obsessive" Paddock. "Mikaela," as the twenty-seven-year-old escort named herself, said Paddock would "often rant about conspiracy theories including how 9/11 was orchestrated by the U.S. government."[13]

Late in September, another witness told police she saw a man resembling Stephen Paddock with another white male at a Vegas restaurant three days before the shooting.[14] Both of them were ranting back and forth about the 1992 standoff at Ruby Ridge and the 1993 Waco siege, both important martyrdom dates for Patriot militiamen (McVeigh later told authorities the Oklahoma bombing was revenge for those two events).

These comport with a third unconfirmed witness's tale. This man—a former chef who was in the county lockup on a petty crime charge at the time of the mass shooting—told police he and Paddock had met at a Bass Pro Shop in Las Vegas two weeks before. The man offered to sell Paddock the schematics for making an auto sear: the kind of specialized mechanism that converts a rifle from semiautomatic to automatic, turning an AR-15 into a machine gun capable of mowing down crowds.

The chef described how Paddock would carry on about "antigovernment stuff" that included FEMA camps and Hurricane Katrina. "He asked me if I remembered Katrina," he said. "That was just a dry run for law enforcement and military to start kickin' down doors and . . . confiscating guns," the man quoted Paddock as saying.[15]

If this account is accurate, it is probably not a coincidence that Paddock had been stocking guns throughout the year preceding October 1, 2017. The 2016 hurricane season had been the worst on record, and the 2017 season was anticipated to be even worse (as indeed it was).

"He was kind of fanatical about this stuff; I just figured he's another Internet nut, you know, watching too much of it and believing too much of it," said the man.

The deal fell apart, though, because Paddock wanted the man not just to sell him the plans, but to actually make the auto sears for him. He offered him $500. The man turned him down, saying: "I'm too old to spend the rest of my life in federal prison." Paddock wasn't interested in the schematics.

He did, however, try to explain his motivations to the chef: "Somebody has to wake up the American public and get them to arm themselves.

"Sometimes sacrifices have to be made."[16]

Conspiracy theories are the one constant thread that runs through the backgrounds of every right-wing American domestic terrorist of the past half-century.

In 1984, the notorious neo-Nazi terrorist gang The Order went on a six-month criminal rampage in which they robbed banks and armored cars by the dozen, counterfeited money, and assassinated a radio talk-show host in Denver before being brought to ground by the FBI. They believed that white people were the victims of a nefarious Jewish cabal secretly running the government and the media, calling it ZOG, the Zionist Occupation Government.[17]

Timothy McVeigh believed a "New World Order" cabal was plotting to deprive Americans of their guns and round them up into concentration camps and that federal raids on right-wing extremists at Ruby Ridge, Idaho, and in Waco, Texas, were proof of that. He killed 168 people with a truck bomb outside the federal building in Oklahoma City in 1995.[18]

Eric Rudolph believed in a similar conspiracy theory, but with a decided religious twist in which abortion played a central role. Rudolph set off a backpack bomb at the 1996 Olympics in Atlanta, then pipe-bombed women's health clinics and a gay bar before leading authorities on a three-year manhunt in the North Carolina woods.[19]

These are only the most notorious examples. Right-wing domestic terror-ism in fact has been occurring at a steady but muted pace for most of the past three decades, embodied by armed standoffs and police officer shootings by so-called sovereign citizens (who believe in a convoluted but arcane and heav-ily document-oriented conspiracist version of government). Nearly all of these terrorists were recruited into their belief systems through relatively traditional means of recruitment—namely, exposure to printed material, underground ra-dio broadcasts, and face-to-face interpersonal proselytization, sometimes in the context of an organization. Rudolph was raised within an extremist Christian Identity church. Many of the terrorists were originally radicalized as members of the conspiracist John Birch Society.

Anders Breivik, however, was a different breed of domestic terrorist. A new breed. He was the first real Internet age terrorist.

Although the ideology that fueled Breivik's violence—eliminationist white supremacism—was what he had in common with those earlier terrorists, Breivik was very much a child of the Internet. He was mostly radicalized online. On the day he murdered seventy-seven people, he published online a fifteen-hundred-page manifesto, complete with video and multiple links, to the mostly American Islamophobes and white nationalists whose ideas he had absorbed.

Breivik grew up in the Norwegian capital of Oslo, a child of divorced par-ents who was raised by a mother who, according to one child psychologist who treated him as a child in the 1980s, "sexualized" him and berated him, telling him she wished he'd never been born.[20] As a teenager he dabbled in hip-hop culture and became a street graffiti artist, which got him into trouble with the law.[21] When he tried to join the Norwegian army, he was deemed "unfit for service" during the vetting process.[22]

In his early twenties, he would later claim, he embarked on a long-term plan to commit an act of terrorism.[23] In 2002, at the age of twenty-three, he founded a computer programming business that eventually earned him several million kroner. He moved back in with his mother after suffering financial setbacks, though he still retained a large nest egg of two million kroner, which he used to proceed with his plan.

In 2009, Breivik bought a farm operation in rural Hedmark County that mainly grew fresh produce of various kinds.[24] He moved to the farm, which had a small house on the acreage, in June 2011, and began buying lots of ammonium nitrate fertilizer. Being a farmer gave him cover.

The neighbors thought there was something "off" about Breivik. One de-scribed him as a "city dweller who wore expensive shirts and who knew nothing about rural ways." Still, there was nothing exceptional about him.

They didn't know that over the past year he had been assembling a private arsenal of weapons, including a Ruger semiautomatic rifle, purchased legally.

Breivik had traveled to Prague in 2010 in an attempt to purchase illegal guns but backed out when it became too hazardous. He also bought a Glock handgun.[25]

In the back of a large white van, he began assembling a classic McVeigh-style truck bomb: barrels of ammonium nitrate mixed with jet fuel, carefully stirred, and topped with detonators. It took him, he later said, a couple of weeks.

On the morning of July 22, he packed everything into the back of the van, then drove the ninety miles or so to Oslo. Just before he left, he hit "Send" on his computer, publishing his video on YouTube and launching his manifesto onto the Internet. He sent it directly via email to more than a thousand people.

Titled *2083: A European Declaration of Independence*, it rambled on for fifteen hundred pages of evidence intended to "prove" various conspiracy theories, all of which established the need for a new "Christian" crusade in Europe to drive out the invading Muslims.[26] It included a wealth of autobiographical information of often dubious value, though it does detail how he set out in 2002 with a nine-year plan, as well as how he trained for his attack on the youth camp by playing the video games *Call of Duty: Modern Warfare 2* and *World of Warcraft*.

The centerpiece of Breivik's manifesto was a conspiracy theory: namely, that the nefarious forces of "cultural Marxism" were colluding to destroy Western white civilization and to replace white Europeans with a polyglot population of brown people. Citing a range of mostly American anti-Muslim ideologues—notably Robert Spencer and Pamela Geller, both of whom he quotes multiple times—he propounds ad nauseam about the existential threat posed to traditional cultures by the influx of Muslim immigrants.

"Cultural Marxism" is a standout example of how conspiracy theories do the work of radical and often toxic political ideologies.[27] The general outline of this conspiracy, according to the progenitors of the theory, is fairly simple: a group of Jewish academics, all Marxists with a base of operations at the Institute for Social Research in Frankfurt am Main—known as the Frankfurt School—were responsible for concocting the ideas behind multiculturalism and "Critical Theory," which they saw as a means for translating Marxist ideals into cultural values. During the 1930s, the story goes, they moved from Frankfurt to New York and Columbia University, and their influence became so profound that it now dominates both academia and modern popular culture.

Indeed, as they tell it, nearly all of the modern expressions of liberal democratic culture—feminism, the civil rights movement, the '60s counterculture movement, the antiwar movement, rock and roll, and the gay rights movement—are eventually all products of the scheming of this cabal of Jewish elites.[28]

In reality, although the influence of the Frankfurt School is generally viewed by most political scientists to have had a considerable range within academia, especially regarding Critical Theory, this school of thought was directly in opposition to the theories promoted by "postmodernists," who are frequently themselves identified by right-wing ideologues as leading examples of "cultural Marxism."[29] Nor were its members leaders of any kind of international conspiracy to destroy Western civilization. Contrary to the characterizations of the conspiracy theorists, most of the "cultural Marxists" of the Frankfurt School were sharply critical of the modern entertainment industry,[30] which they saw not as a tool for their own ideology but as a kind of modern "opiate of the masses" that was antithetical to their values.[31]

Moreover, multiculturalism was not the product of Critical Theory but has much deeper roots in the study of anthropology, dating back to the turn of the twentieth century.[32] It became ascendant as a worldview in the post–World War II years after it became apparent (especially as the events of the Holocaust became more widely understood) that white supremacy—the worldview it replaced—was not only inadequate but a direct source of wholesale evil. The people who are widely recognized as the founders of multiculturalism—particularly such anthropologists as Franz Boas and Margaret Mead—were not members of the Frankfurt School (though both were affiliated with Columbia), and their work had long preceded the war.

The idea of "cultural Marxism" as a plot to destroy the West originated with a handful of far-right thinkers in the 1990s.[33] One of these was the conservative Jewish intellectual Paul Gottfried, who claimed in later years that he had identified with the right-wing bloc of the Frankfurt School and had first complained about cultural Marxism as an insider.[34] Gottfried (who is also credited with having helped coin the phrase "alt-right")[35] engaged in a debate with paleoconservative William S. Lind, an associate of far-right godfather Paul Weyrich and his Free Congress Foundation,[36] questioning whether or not such thinkers could be properly labeled Marxists. Lind concluded that they could and should be (Gottfried disagreed).

In short order, Lind began developing a cottage industry around his "cultural Marxism" theory, promoting the idea on the Internet, in speeches, and in videos. "Cultural Marxism is a branch of western Marxism, different from the Marxism-Leninism of the old Soviet Union," he wrote. "It is commonly known as 'multiculturalism' or, less formally, Political Correctness. From its beginning, the promoters of cultural Marxism have known they could be more effective if they concealed the Marxist nature of their work, hence the use of terms such as 'multiculturalism.'"[37]

Eventually, Lind propounded on the topic at a Holocaust denial conference in 2003, where he explained to the audience pointedly: "These guys were all Jewish."[38]

Weyrich, who had already promoted the idea of "cultural conservatism," also heavily promoted the idea, presenting it as the subject of a speech he gave in 1998 to the Civitas Institute's Conservative Leadership Conference: "Cultural

Marxism is succeeding in its war against our culture. The question becomes, if we are unable to escape the cultural disintegration that is gripping society, then what hope can we have?"[39]

This became the cornerstone in Weyrich's call for conservatives to join in a "culture war" against liberals, joining the ranks of such paleoconservatives as Patrick Buchanan, the former presidential candidate who in 1992 had originally issued a call for such a "culture war" at the Republican National Convention.[40]

Beginning in 2000, Buchanan picked up Lind and Weyrich's idea and ran with it, incorporating his attacks on "cultural Marxism" in his writings, and began giving a number of interviews in which he laid all of the world's ills at its feet. In his 2001 book *The Death of the West: How Dying Populations and Immigrant Invasions Imperil Our Country and Civilization*, Buchanan described it as a "regime to punish dissent and to stigmatize social heresy as the Inquisition punished religious heresy. Its trademark is intolerance."[41]

The book ascribes nearly superhuman powers to Critical Theory. "Using Critical Theory, for example, the cultural Marxist repeats and repeats the charge that the West is guilty of genocidal crimes against every civilization and culture it has encountered," Buchanan averred. "Under Critical Theory, one repeats and repeats that Western societies are history's greatest repositories of racism, sexism, nativism, xenophobia, homophobia, anti-Semitism, fascism and Nazism. Under Critical Theory, the crimes of the West flow from the character of the West, as shaped by Christianity. . . . Under the impact of Critical Theory, many of the sixties generation, the most privileged in history, convinced themselves that they were living in an intolerable hell."

In addition to Buchanan and the paleoconservatives, the theory was also quickly adopted by white nationalists who began promoting the theory assiduously. The most notable of these was the far-right publisher Roger Pearson, a retired anthropologist and prominent eugenicist.[42] Besides numerous eugenicist and supremacist books and journals, he published a book in 2006 by Frank Ellis titled *Marxism, Multiculturalism, and Free Speech* that laid out the basics of the cultural Marxism theory and claims. Ellis, a former Leeds University professor, claimed that "political correctness" could be traced to Vladimir Lenin and Mao Zedong and that it was designed as an attack on the principles of free speech.

Other white nationalists, notably Jared Taylor of American Renaissance,[43] academic Kevin MacDonald,[44] and Peter Brimelow of VDare, likewise made discussion of "cultural Marxism" central to their arguments. Taylor railed against it and multiculturalism at a Council of Conservative Citizens convention in 1999. MacDonald discussed "cultural Marxism" at length in his book *Culture of Critique* and discusses it frequently in interviews and in his magazine, *Occidental Observer*.[45] Brimelow mentioned the concept as early as 2003 and, all the way through 2017, was blaming it for the world's ills, including the cancellation of a VDare conference.[46]

It also gained wide play among right-wing conspiracy theorists led by Alex Jones, who featured guest conspiracist Alan Watt on air during a 2010 show. Watt told Jones: "People really have lost a sense of dignity and self-respect and definitely a common culture. That was part of the deep massive Communist move for multiculturalism. It wasn't to be nice to other cultures, it was to help you destroy your own cohesive majority."[47]

"Get rid of all other cultures and replace it with a corporate Borg culture," Jones surmised.

However, the concept also began moving into the mainstream of the conservative movement as early as 2008, mainly due to the contributions of Andrew Breitbart, the founder of the online news organization Breitbart News.

In his autobiography *Righteous Indignation*, Breitbart described his discovery, in about 2007, of "cultural Marxism" as his "awakening." He told an interviewer in 2012, shortly before his death, that the concept was like "putting the medicine in the sherbet. . . . My one great epiphany, my one a-ha moment where I said, 'I got it—I see what exactly happened in this country.'"[48]

Breitbart began holding forth at length in various venues about the evils of "cultural Marxism." He appeared on Fox News and told Sean Hannity and his audience: "For much of the latter half of the twentieth century, America dealt with Communism, which was economic Marxism. And what America was susceptible to during that period of time was cultural Marxism. Cultural Marxism is political correctness, it's multiculturalism, and it's a war on Judeo-Christianity."[49]

After Breitbart's death in 2012, the news organization bearing his name continued its tradition of obsession with cultural Marxism; the subject remains a popular keyword among the website's writers.

And, obviously, it had gained an ardent believer in Anders Breivik.

"We are sick and tired of feeling like strangers in our own lands, of being mugged, raped, stabbed, harassed and even killed by violent gangs of Muslim thugs, yet being accused of 'racism and xenophobia,'" he wrote.

"As we all know, the root of Europe's problems is the lack of cultural self-confidence (nationalism)," he continued. "Most people are still terrified of nationalistic political doctrines thinking that if we ever embrace these principles again, new 'Hitler's' will suddenly pop up and initiate global Armageddon. . . . This irrational fear of nationalistic doctrines is preventing us from stopping our own national/cultural suicide as the Islamic colonization is increasing annually . . . You cannot defeat Islamization or halt/reverse the Islamic colonization of Western Europe without first removing the political doctrines manifested through multiculturalism/cultural Marxism."[50]

His plan for doing so, according to the manifesto, entailed other true believers who also would participate in his "Christian Crusade." The video he posted on YouTube contained a plenitude of images of medieval knights in armor along with references to the "new Crusade." He claimed that other members of an organization called the "Knights Templar" were ready to spring into action with similar terrorist acts elsewhere—though none were ever named, and in truth none ever came to light.

Breivik saw himself as a white knight out to do his duty to save "his people." No doubt that image was in his mind as he drove the little white van into Oslo the morning of July 22, 2011.

––––––––

Anders Breivik, it later emerged, had had relatively few contacts with other white nationalist ideologues in real life, though he had exchanged emails with a number of others, particularly in the European scene. But the largest source of his inspiration, his manifesto made clear, was material he had found on the Internet.

This represented a marked shift. Conspiracy theories in the decades following the Red Scare of the 1950s, particularly in the 1960s and 1970s, were often spread slowly through organizations ranging from the John Birch Society to the Ku Klux Klan. People were recruited into the belief systems usually through exposure to the group's literature followed by face-to-face time in organizational meetings.

Some of the radical-right conspiracism of the 1990s was bolstered by the early stages of the Internet: white supremacist websites such as Stormfront began creating community spaces for like-minded bigots, and of course their main content involved a potpourri of conspiracist legends and theories. The email forwards of the 1990s—usually spurious, anonymous content alleging all kinds of nefarious behavior by godless liberals and their politicians—which were shared on listservs and among friends and family members, were especially effective in spreading conspiracy theories. And then there were radio shows, many of them "underground" broadcasts, but others reaching broad audiences like Alex Jones's show out of Austin, Texas—shows that specialized in spinning dubious tales of New World Order conspiracies, which as time went on and Jones's audience grew massive, in the 2000s, were renamed *globalist plots*.[51]

However, the arrival in the 2000s of a full-on digital culture changed the path of radicalization. Increasingly, people—young white men especially—were drawn to conspiracy theories in part because there was a deluge of them that began hitting the Internet in the latter part of the century's first decade, thanks primarily to the arrival of YouTube as a major source of media consumption, especially for younger users. On YouTube, thanks to algorithms that encouraged people to find "engaging" content, which often translated into "outrageously nutty and afactual" in reality, the conspiracy theories spread like kudzu.

Breivik was one of the first young men to emerge from the spiral of radicalization that the Internet can uniquely weave into being, and just as he hoped, his 2011 rampage became a model and inspiration for other young white men who tried to follow in his footsteps. Like Breivik, the funnel into which they were drawn was the seductive downward spiral of conspiracy theories like "cultural Marxism" that lead vulnerable minds down the rabbit holes of white nationalism and similarly hateful ideologies, including outright fascism.

Many of those who followed this path of online radicalization were a good deal younger than Breivik, who was thirty-two at the time he embarked on his terrorism plot. The archetype that developed was in most regards more closely embodied in two men who were both in their early twenties at the time they exploded: Dylann Roof and Elliot Rodger.[52]

Roof in particular left a social media crumb trail that was at once cryptic and clear. From his Facebook page, you could see that the twenty-one-year-old South Carolina man liked to visit historical sites. This was not a healthy thing: they tended to be sites from the slave-trading era, like Sullivan's Island, the largest slave disembarkation port in North America. He had black friends from school—despite dropping out after ninth grade—but he also hated black people generically.[53]

In his manifesto, he called black people "the group that is the biggest problem for Americans," but like most white nationalists, he also blamed nefarious Jews for creating it:

> Niggers are stupid and violent. At the same time they have the capacity to be very slick. Black people view everything through a racial lens. Thats what racial awareness is, its viewing everything that happens through a racial lens. They are always thinking about the fact that they are black. This is part of the reason they get offended so easily, and think that some thing are intended to be racist towards them, even when a White person wouldnt be thinking about race. The other reason is the Jewish agitation of the black race.[54]

Roof never joined any organizations, but in addition to spending inordinate amounts of time playing video games, taking Suboxone, and hanging out in Columbia with his friends, he also began hanging out on the chat boards at the neo-Nazi website the *Daily Stormer*—where "cultural Marxism" is conventional wisdom—as well as the old school website of the Council of Conservative Citizens (CCC).

It was at the latter site that, inspired by the case of Trayvon Martin, the young black Florida man who was gunned down by a white security guard, he began reading and absorbing the spurious statistics spewed there about black crime and particularly its effect on whites: Roof fully believed the CCC's assertion that 80 percent of white homicides are committed by black people. After all, a Google search had told him so.[55]

A ne'er-do-well whose last job had been a brief stint as a landscaper, Roof decided he needed to rescue the white race from extermination. That was why, on June 17, 2015, he set out on his mission, another knight off to save the world, like Anders Breivik:

> I have no choice. I am not in the position to, alone, go into the ghetto and fight. I chose Charleston because it is most historic city in my state, and at one time had the highest ratio of blacks to Whites in the country. We have no skinheads, no real KKK, no one doing anything but talking on the internet. Well someone has to have the bravery to take it to the real world, and I guess that has to be me.

Elliot Rodger, like Breivik and Roof, saw himself in a similarly heroic light, and likewise wanted to do battle with the forces of "political correctness." But his enemy was different: he hated women.[56]

Rodger was the well-to-do son of a Hollywood producer, and in most regards a good-looking young man. But he was deeply troubled. Smaller and slightly frail, he had always been something of a bully magnet in school and was known to spend his days alone: he later wrote that he "cried by myself every day." At Crespi Carmelite High in Los Angeles, he fell asleep at a desk one day, and other students taped his head to it.

He expressed himself at Elliot Rodger's Official Blog and on YouTube, where he mostly posted angst-ridden expressions of rejection and loneliness. At home, he received mental-health counseling and drug treatment by psychiatrists, although he never received a formal diagnosis of a mental illness.

Rodger also spent inordinate amounts of time online in chat rooms. The places he liked to dwell the most were some of the darkest corners of the Internet—in particular, among his fellow dwellers in the online "incel" culture.

"Incel" is short for "involuntary celibate," and the young men who participate in this universe invariably loathe women and feminists and blame them for the men's lack of receiving enough sex. Their solution: an "incel revolution" in which men take back the reins of society from women and put them back in their place with force. The revolution they envision is, of course, quite violent.[57]

After all, the problem in most respects is simple: these are men who for various reasons have difficulty sustaining a relationship long enough to have sex (often because they don't understand that, unlike in the world of pornography, most women are uninterested in sex with relative strangers). Put crudely, they can't get laid and blame women for that. In their view, it's owed them.

As incels imagine things, the world is mostly comprised of "Chads"—sexually competitive males, guys who are chosen for their superiority—and "Stacys," the sexually attractive and available women who get to do the choosing and who always choose Chads. Incels see themselves as noble-spirited rebels who stand outside that world.

Elliot Rodger was one of these young men. Posting at the misogynist site PUAHate ("The Forefront of the Anti-Pickup Artist Movement": this sector of the misogynist world had repudiated sex altogether), Rodger mused on both feminism ("If we can't solve our problems we must *destroy* our problems") and race:

> Today I drove through the area near my college and saw some things that were extremely rage-inducing.
> I passed by this restaurant and I saw this black guy chilling with 4 hot white girls. He didn't even look good.
> Then later on in the day I was shopping at Trader Joe's and saw an Indian guy with 2 above average White Girls!!!
> What rage-inducing sights did you guys see today? Don't you just hate seeing these things when you go out? It just makes you want to quit life.[58]

Rodger's mother was Chinese, but he saw himself as mostly passing for white. When an Asian male posted a query about whether a specific pair of shoes would help him "attract white women," Rodger responded: "White girls are disgusted by you, silly little Asian."

The Asian man replied by posting photos of himself with a white woman, which set Rodger off: "Full Asian men are disgustingly ugly and white girls would never go for you. You're just butthurt that you were born as an asian piece of shit, so you lash out by linking these fake pictures. You even admit that you wish you were half white. You'll never be half-white and you'll never fulfill your dream of marrying a white woman. I suggest you jump off a bridge."

Like many others in incel culture, he became a seething cauldron of frustration and anger toward women and feminists, though he often expressed vitriolic anger toward other men for outcompeting him. At other times he struck a genteel pose, naming himself "the supreme gentleman" and "the perfect guy."

Because the world failed to recognize him, though, he wanted to burn it all down. At PUAHate, he posted:

> One day incels will realize their true strength and numbers, and will overthrow this oppressive feminist system.
> Start envisioning a world where WOMEN FEAR YOU.[59]

Rodger drove a nice a car, a black BMW. On the evening of May 23, 2014, he walked out of his apartment near the University of California, Santa Barbara, campus, got into it, and drove away, leaving three dead roommates behind. He drove to a Starbucks, got some coffee, and sat in the car, uploading material to the Internet from his laptop.

Specifically, it was a manifesto, titled "My Twisted World: The Story of Elliot Rodger," with a meandering explanation for the violence he was about to commit. He also uploaded a video to YouTube. It was titled "Retribution."[60]

"On the day of retribution," he told the world, "I am going to enter the hottest sorority house of UCSB and I will slaughter every single spoiled, stuck up, blonde slut I see inside there."

Alek Minassian always had issues, even before becoming enmeshed in incel culture. In high school in Toronto, he was placed in a special needs program, where he was known for making cat sounds and hugging himself. Sometimes he tried to bite people, though otherwise was quite "harmless."[61]

In college, he studied software development and had an easier time fitting in as an adult, especially as he was able to cocoon himself in the more insular world of research technology. And that, seemingly, was when he was drawn into the world of incels.[62]

Minassian apparently fell into the culture while visiting the Internet message board 4chan, a popular website with massive traffic numbers built around an anything-goes approach to subject matter, including the open expression and promotion of white nationalist and other far-right beliefs.

The problem is that Minassian never could be identified with any previous comments or participation on incel threads, either at 4chan or Reddit (another popular incel gathering site) or websites specifically dedicated to the culture. Where and how he picked up the ideology is anyone's guess.[63]

In late 2017, he joined the Canadian military but washed out after two months and sought a voluntary release. Minassian "wasn't adapting to military life, including in matters of dress, deportment and group interactions in a military setting," a senior military official commented, noting that "there were no red flags" suggesting concerns about violence.[64]

The only thing anyone really knows about him is that on April 23, 2018, he rented a large white Chevrolet Express van from a Ryder agency and drove it into the heart of downtown Toronto, into the trendy North York City Centre shopping district on Yonge Street. He apparently parked it long enough to post a message onto Facebook.

Private (Recruit) Minassian Infantry 00010, wishing to speak to Sgt 4chan please. C23249161. The Incel Rebellion has already begun! We will overthrow all the Chads and Stacys! All hail Supreme Gentleman Elliot Rodger!

———————

Jeremy Christian had issues, too. But like Anders Breivik and Elliot Rodger, he never received an official diagnosis of mental illness. He was just, in the vernacular, "troubled."[65]

Mostly he was in trouble with the law as a young man. When he was a fifteen-year-old heavy-metal fan and skateboarder, he was caught breaking into a Goodwill clothing donation box in downtown Portland, Oregon. The police released him to his parents and there were no legal penalties. The next year he dropped out of high school and got a job in a pizza parlor, where he worked for the next four years, picking up a GED along the way. He also picked up classes at Portland Community College.

Christian argued with his parents a lot. So, at eighteen, he moved out of the family home and rented a room from the mother of a friend while continuing to work at Pietro's. Then, in 2002, at the age of twenty, it all went to hell when he decided to rob a convenience store.[66]

The attempt went sideways from the start, though Christian wore a ski mask. He threatened the clerk with a .38 revolver, then handcuffed him to a cigarette rack. Christian made his getaway with $1,000 and armfuls of cigarette cartons on a bike, and police caught him just a few blocks away, the ski mask sticking out of a pocket. He pulled out a gun, and the officer fired at him three times; one of the shots hit him in the right cheek. When they had him on the ground, he told the cops he wasn't aiming at them. He had intended to shoot himself.[67]

Christian had no criminal record, but he wound up spending the next seven years in prison, in part because the charges included kidnapping for handcuffing the clerk.

When he got out in 2010, he apparently fell into the everyday life of being a homeless street itinerant in downtown Portland. He was known to trade comics outside Powell's, the big local bookstore. He was also known for being loud and a little frightening.[68]

On his Facebook page, Christian began posting a variety of conspiracy theories. His politics swung wildly; he originally favored Bernie Sanders's 2016 candidacy for the presidency, but after the primaries, he swung to Donald Trump (for a while, at least) because his loathing for Hillary Clinton was deep, visceral, and violent. After the election, he ranted: "Death to Hillary Rodham Clinton and all her supporters!!! To be carried out by Bernie Supporters who didn't turn traitor and vote Hillary."[69]

As spring 2017 wore on, his posts became more openly violent, deeply Islamophobic and racist, not to mention voicing a weird obsession with circumcision, which he connected to a nefarious Jewish conspiracy.

"I want a job in Norway cutting off the heads of people that Circumcize Babies. . . . Like if you agree!!!" he wrote.

"If you support the cutting of babies genitals in sick tribal rituals in America get off my page," went another post. "I don't care if you are friend of family."

A law banning circumcision, he proposed another time, would "stop True Patriots from having to kill otherwise good doctors inside hospitals."

"F-- You if you say my body my choice but support circumcision," he declared.

Street artist Raymond Alexander, a sixty-eight-year-old black man, had known Christian for years from the streets. He told *Oregonian* reporter Allan Brettman that Christian had talked race with him, but "he didn't ever use the master race issue on me."[70]

"He went way back to Norway," Alexander said, "to some secret society that if they find out about this document that's never been exposed to the world then there's going to be mass chaos throughout the world. . . . [H]e was tied up in mythology, tied up in Viking blood lines."

That spring in the Portland area, a group of right-wing extremists who first organized as a kind of biker militia in nearby Vancouver, Washington, renamed themselves Patriot Prayer and began organizing pro-Trump street protests in Portland as a way of asserting their "free speech" rights—usually in the face of a militant far left/anarchist/black bloc contingent native to the city. Jeremy Christian was drawn to the conflict like a fly to garbage.

He showed up at one of Patriot Prayer's first events in Portland on April 29, a kind of street march in which about thirty people carrying American and Gadsden flags—in addition to the large Trump banner carried by Patriot Prayer leader Joey Gibson—traveled along a busy thoroughfare in the city's southeastern quadrant. A contingent of antifascists accompanied and taunted them, though no violence broke out.[71]

But Jeremy Christian got kicked out.

For most of the march he blended in with the other "Patriots"—a large American flag with the stars replaced by a "1776" logo draped over his back like a cape, a gray woolen ballcap reading "Wolverines" turned backward, shouting "Free speech! Free speech!" When they pulled up at a parking lot, though, Christian started getting into it verbally with some of the antifascists. He began yelling at one of them: "White nigger! You're a white nigger! You are a white nigger!"[72]

At that point, another "Patriot" intervened. "Hey, no language! No language!" He told Christian using the "N word" was "not appropriate": "Don't do that!" Christian later told others in the parking that being called a "Nazi" was "a joke! I'm a nihilist!" he shouted. Then, he started using a Nazi salute.

An antifascist counterprotester dressed in a clown hat, juggling balls and telling jokes, approached Christian and joked with him briefly. His name was Micah David-Cole Fletcher, a twenty-one-year-old Portland State student, and they would meet again, fatefully, a few weeks later.[73]

Finally, a larger group of "Patriots" stepped up and told Christian he was being ejected from the march. He started talking gibberish to them, and they stopped him: "No! No! You're giving the Nazi sign, you're using the N word! So please go away! I won't ask you again nicely."

Christian turned around and shouted to the gathered crowd. "I'm the only motherfucking free speecher here! Who will defend free speech?" Police then escorted Christian away from the scene.

Nearly a month later, on a late evening Portland MAX commuter train, Christian boarded and promptly announced that he was a Nazi and was looking to recruit others to join him. He shouted that he hated Jews, Mexicans, Japanese, and anyone who wasn't Christian.[74]

A black woman named Demetria Hester—the only person of color on the train—spoke up and told Christian he needed to keep it down.

"Fuck you Bitch!" he screamed at her, adding that she had neither the right to speak nor to be on the train.

"I built this country!" he shouted. "You don't have a right to speak. You're black. You don't have a right to be here. All you Muslims, blacks, Jews, I will kill all of you."

As the train pulled into Demetria Hester's stop, she stood up to leave. Christian made clear he intended to get off and began shouting loudly at everyone on the train that he didn't care if anyone wanted to call the police because he wasn't scared.

"I will kill anyone who stands in my way because I have a right to do this," he told them. He looked at Hester and seethed: "Bitch, you're about to get it now."

As she stepped off the train, Christian lunged at her with a Gatorade bottle and smacked her above the right eye with it just as she whipped out her can of mace and gave him a faceful. It knocked him down on the platform. She staggered away and awaited police, who finally arrived about twenty minutes later. Hester said the officers treated her as a likely suspect, even though witnesses pointed out Jeremy Christian—still washing pepper spray out of his eyes—standing feet away.

Christian wound up walking away from the scene and going home for the night. Police later blamed this on confusion regarding who the perpetrator was.[75]

The next day, he boarded another MAX train during rush hour. This time he had a knife.

Buckey Wolfe and his brother James were raised in the same home in Seattle's Fremont neighborhood and attended the same local schools, but they ended up on very different paths. After they graduated high school, James joined the army and served overseas. Buckey joined the Washington State Militia and became devoted to conspiracy theories.[76]

Everyone kind of knew that Buckey had mental-illness problems, though. He had a jittery, paranoid personality and was on edge a lot. Eventually, in his early twenties, he was diagnosed with schizophrenia and prescribed medication to cope with it.[77]

At the same time, he dove headfirst into the far right's rabbit holes. In addition to joining a militia group, he also participated in the events and drinking games with a local chapter of the Proud Boys—the far-right, pro-Trump, street-brawling organization that had been involved in a number of ugly riots along the West Coast in 2017 and 2018.

Wolfe also started watching conspiracy videos on YouTube. Initially, his video "likes" were a typical teenage boy's interests—lots of rock videos plus some fitness and personal motivation material. As he grew older, though, he was drawn into politics. Initially this came through "alt-lite" YouTubers, like Hunter Avallone, who specialize in making fun of "social justice warriors." Then he started liking weird science conspiracy theories about "free energy" and "Tesla's UFO," before he eventually became a full-time Alex Jones/Infowars fan. He later told friends that he had "watched every episode" of Jones on his massive YouTube channel.[78]

After that, all of Wolfe's video likes revolved around the far right, especially Proud Boys founder Gavin McInnes and his cohorts, as well as Milo Yiannopoulos, Steven Crowder, and "Sargon of Akkad," all figures in the so-called alt-lite. Unsurprisingly, he then began liking videos from openly white nationalist sites such as Red Ice.

"I'm a proud Western chauvinist and I refuse to apologize for creating the modern world," a Facebook post read, closing with the Proud Boys' slogan: "Uhuru!!!"

A Facebook post from a Proud Boys member in March 2018 showing the twenty or so members of the Seattle chapter standing outside a local light-rail station making the mock-white-nationalist "OK" sign and holding up a "Trump 45" shirt featured a comment from Buckey Wolfe, who appears in it: "My face [is] covered by hands lol. Last night was awesome I had a great time!"

Finally, Wolfe reached the apotheosis of this journey when he became an ardent supporter of the "QAnon" conspiracy theories—a sort of meta-conspiracy theory involving Donald Trump, Robert Mueller, Hillary Clinton, and the same global pedophilia ring featured in Pizzagate. "It's coming, and it's gonna be good!" Wolfe commented on YouTube. "Y'alls are gonna get your just dues. I will be so happy, you have no idea."[79]

While circulating in that world, Buckey also became enamored of David Icke's theory positing that world leaders are in fact a species of lizard aliens from outer space who are able to disguise themselves.

In November 2018, he posted a rant: "If I start talking about the iluminati and you role your eyes at me you have been successfully indoctrinated. The ilimunati is VERY real, the CIA agrees with my asurtion, this is straight from the CIAs website!!! I erge you DO YOUR RESEARCH BEFORE YOU BLOW ME OFF!!!"

Two of his fellow Proud Boys chimed in to support him. One replied: "I didnt believe in Zionist till I watched a rabi speak about rothchilds being their Zionist leaders."[80]

Wolfe's family became concerned, especially after a long late December 2018 rant that he posted on Facebook about humans being replaced by alien lizards that ended with a plea not to ignore him. His brother James chimed in to try to calm him down. An aunt who lived in Ohio asked him if he was okay but said that she couldn't understand what he was talking about. This aunt, who had lost a son the year before, added that she loved him.[81]

Buckey replied: "I know you don't cus you've been taken, don't think I didn't notice when you got back from your cruise your eyes had changed!!!! You will be made in to dust lizard!!!!!"

Brenton Tarrant had a perfectly unremarkable upbringing in the town of Grafton, Australia, located south of Brisbane and the Gold Coast in New South Wales.[82] He worked for a few years as a personal trainer after graduating high school and then began traveling widely.[83]

Around 2016, at the age of twenty-six, he became obsessed with the long-simmering conflict between Serbs and Muslims in Kosovo after visiting the Balkans extensively.[84] He began posting Balkan nationalist material, defending the Serbian military as "Christian Europeans attempting to remove these Islamic occupiers from Europe," as he later put it in his manifesto. Investigators believe that he met far-right extremists in Europe on his travels and became deeply influenced by them.[85]

The manifesto explained that he "dramatically changed my views" between April and May 2017. He felt that a "series of events . . . revealed the truth of the Wests current situation." He decided at that time that a "violent, revolutionary solution" was needed.[86]

The key event, he said, was the April 7, 2017, truck attack by an Islamist radical in downtown Stockholm that killed five people and injured another eleven. Tarrant said he was visiting Western Europe at the time, playing the tourist in France, Spain, Portugal, and other countries at the time of the attack. Among the dead was an eleven-year-old girl named Ebba Akerlund: "Young, innocent and dead Ebba," he wrote.

At this point, he said, he began planning his own attack, initially from his home in Melbourne. Sometime in 2018 he moved to the town of Dunedin, on New Zealand's South Island, just a five-hour drive down the eastern coast from Christchurch. It's a quiet town, at one time a famed whaling station, now best known for its college campuses, with students accounting for about a fifth of the population.

Tarrant rented a place in the suburb of Andersons Bay. His neighbors said that he was quiet, polite, and reserved—indeed, they scarcely ever encountered him in person. No one had any idea he even had guns.[87]

Like Breivik, whom he celebrated in his manifesto, he was obsessed with "white genocide" and changes in ethnic demographics. "It's the birthrates. It's the birthrates. It's the birthrates. If there is one thing I want you to remember from these writings, its that the birthrates must change," Tarrant wrote. "Even if we were to deport all Non-Europeans from our lands tomorrow, the European people would still be spiraling into decay and eventual death."

However, he claimed he was "not a direct member of any organization or group, though I have donated to many nationalist groups and have interacted with many more."

He said "no group ordered my attack. I make the decision myself. Though I did contact the reborn Knights Templar for a blessing in support of the attack, which was given."

Tarrant's attitudes about the left were also clear.

> To Antifa/Marxists/Communists
> I do not want to convert you, I do not want to come to an understanding. Egalitarians and those that believe in heirachy will never come to terms. I don't want you by my side or I don't want share power.
> I want you in my sights. I want your neck under my boot.
> SEE YOU ON THE STREETS YOU ANTI-WHITE SCUM

He titled the manifesto "The Great Replacement," and delivered it via email to thirty recipients at around noon Friday, March 15, 2019. He was in downtown Christchurch, a good two hours north of Dunedin, sitting in a car, and he had several guns with him: two semiautomatics, two shotguns, and a lever-action gun. He also had a GoPro camera strapped to his chest.

Chapter 3

SACRIFICES

There are always those little "sacrifices" that "have to be made" when it comes to the conspiracist mindset of mass killers. Little people. Ordinary people. People you and I and everyone else knows, somewhere, who become their victims.

The killers don't know these people. To them they are "sheeple," hapless pawns in the vast conspiracy ruling the world. They might as well be conspirators themselves. Maybe some of them are.

Something like that was what Stephen Paddock, whose contempt for the "sheeple" was remarked by several people who knew him, was thinking the night of October 1, 2017, as he surveyed the crowd that gathered for the huge, week-long country music festival taking place next to the Sunset Strip, right below the suite of rooms he had rented three days before in the Mandalay Bay hotel.[1]

It was quite a view. In fact, he could take it in from two entirely different angles from the two adjoining rooms.

———

At first, Jenna thought someone had tossed out some firecrackers in the middle of the Jason Aldean performance. An obnoxious drunken guy who had been annoying the hell out of her suddenly dropped to the ground. She thought he had just passed out. He hadn't.[2]

Then there were more pops, and she could see people falling in front of her, one after another.

"I don't know how long it was, but I didn't put the two together," she recalls now. "To me they were separate situations. Someone threw firecrackers, which was annoying, and then the drunken man fell. And no one was screaming. I would say people were kind of looking around, but Jason Aldean did not stop singing.

"And then there was the second part when he shot again, and many more people fell. You could see the crowd and they looked like little dominoes going down.

"That's where Jason Aldean stopped singing."

Jenna and her childhood friend Sammi were not first timers at the Route 91 Harvest country music festival in Las Vegas that October 1. They had attended the same three-night event two years before. In between, Jenna had given birth to a little blond-haired baby girl, a bright-eyed chip off her mama's block, who was now ten months old, and in the care of her grandmother back home in Tacoma, Washington.

Like Jenna, Sammi had graduated college and moved on to the working world, too. The week in Vegas had been a chance to taste their old lives again, maybe one last time. So Jenna left the baby, Camden, with her own mother, and flew off for an autumn music fling.

"Sam Hunt was who I really wanted to see, and then Eric Church," she recalls. "So we had already seen them the previous nights. So Sunday night we were only there to see Jason Aldean."

Before the show, they hit a couple of casinos. Sammi's gambling luck changed everything and may have saved their lives. "We first went to the Luxor where there's this fish game that she just loves," Jenna recalls. It was just across Sunset Boulevard from the concert venue.

"She said she just wanted to put $10 in and then we can go over there, because every night we had gotten up right close to the stage—not that we could touch him, but maybe four rows back. And $10 turned into $100, and we were there for over an hour.

"So we showed up probably fifteen minutes before he started, and that's why we ended up kind of farther back," she says.

Now, people were falling in front of her, some not far away, and the popping sounds kept coming. "I just kind of looked at Sammi and I was like, that's a fucking gun," she remembers. "Someone's shooting people. And it finally occurred to me what we heard thirty seconds prior was a gun, too, so this is someone shooting, twice now. And I knew it was not like a pistol. I knew that it was something automatic and big.

"People around us had hit the ground. At that point, everyone kind of went down. Some people just ducked. Other people had fallen or gotten hit.

"I just went down. Because that's your human instinct, I guess, to get closer to the ground."

Her lifelong friend then probably saved her life again: Sammi made her get up and flee. "She said, 'We need to run.' And I said, 'I don't think we should run.' And she said, 'We have to fucking run.' And I was super scared. I didn't want to run because at that point, it seemed like the shooter was among us, so I didn't want to run into him. I couldn't tell—which way is he coming from?

"People all over are falling, so I don't know if he's over by us. Someone got shot right by us. But then I could see people screaming on the other side of the stage, so I had no idea where the gunfire was coming from.

"So I said, 'I don't think we should run.' And she said, 'We will fucking die here.' And I said, 'Okay.'" Jenna got up and they took off away from the stage, toward the back of the venue.

"Basically the only reason I ran is that she started to. I was like, 'Well, I don't want to die alone, I guess.'"

Ironically, it was mere moments after the two of them start running away that they were separated. They had played soccer as teammates since grade school and into high school, and both were good athletes, though Jenna was known as the slower of the two. Running with the crowd away from the gunfire to the right and past the concessions, Jenna sprinted through the pack. "I just booked it a little bit faster I guess," she says.

A woman who had been running alongside her suddenly took a shot through the neck in front of Jenna. She "whipped around and went down," as though someone had cut the strings on a marionette.

"It was literally like it just went through and whipped her whole body around and she went down. And I was just thinking, 'I just have to keep running, just have to keep running.'"

She ran outside the venue over a cyclone fence that had been toppled by panicked concertgoers as they fled. Out on the street, however, she instinctively took cover behind a five-foot-high transformer that shielded her momentarily. She pulled out her cell phone and called her mother back in Tacoma, who promptly picked up.

"After I saw that girl fall, I was like, I'm probably not going to survive this," she says. "I don't even know where I'm running to. So I called her when I was definitely behind the transformer. And I said, 'I need you to take care of Camden. I need you to let her know that I love her.' And she was kind of confused: 'Well, where is the shooter? Or, where's Sammi? What's going on?'

"And I said, "I can't explain everything but I need you to know this. And I don't think I'm going to . . . I don't know where to go. But I don't know if I'll make it.' Because at that point I'd seen . . . I mean, there were just dead bodies everywhere, some of them just when I was running past—I don't know if they were dead or just lying there.

"And so it was in mind—I still have a ways to run, to where I don't know, or if I'm going to get hit here, but I need to at least get this out of the way. For me, I just had a real urgency—like any parent, I'm sure—there was a sense of urgency to tell my mom to take care of Camden. In hindsight, it's like, of course she would have. But it was the most important thing, just to get confirmation that she will take care of her and that she'll raise her to know that I loved her.

"And for me, once that was done, I was able to start thinking a little more clearly. OK, now let's see if we can survive this."

Across the street from the transformer was the local Hooters franchise, and she dashed over to it and inside. That's when it hit her that Sammi was not with her and nowhere in sight. So she called her mother again, and told her she didn't know where her friend was. But her mother calmly reassured her: "No, we've heard from Sammi."

"Tell her to come to Hooters, it's the closest place," Jenna answered.

Jenna wandered through the first-floor casino at the restaurant, which was a vacant madhouse of toppled machines and tables. Finally, she found refuge in a walk-in cooler in the kitchen. What she did not know was that by this point she was herself drenched in blood from the head down, none of it her own.

"So I ran because they were holding the kitchen door open as an access door, and I ran in and they were kind of shuffling people into the freezer. And the woman next to me was holding a woman next to her who had a cut or had been shot. And that was kind of shooting blood, too." A woman there asked Jenna where she had been hit; she answered, "I don't think I've been hit."

The scene was fraught with the lethal unknown and all the wild misinformation that accompanies it: Death had descended on all of them from some place they could not see and they had run, but none of them believed there was only one gunman. The shots rattled around the plaza and they came from different angles, and Jenna thought it seemed as though a team of terrorists was shooting at the crowd. Her perception was widely shared.

Once inside the restaurant and locked down in the walk-in cooler, the panic began to set in. Misinformation was running rampant—people inside the cooler believed there was an active shooter inside the hotel. "Every time someone came into the kitchen, they thought it might be the shooter and there was a big commotion," Jenna recalls. "And that's when I kind of had a moment where I could think: 'OK, if the shooter does come in, we're all sitting here like a little bunch of ducks. This isn't a good hiding spot.'

"So I announced, 'I'm leaving.' And I remember, the lady next to me was kind of motherly. She was, 'No, you can't leave, you can't go out there.' And I was, 'I can't stay here.'" Jenna left and returned to the vacant casino floor, trying to find a hiding place.

It turned out that Sammi had hit Hooters running and fled to the upper floors immediately, finding refuge in one of the rooms on the fourth floor, and her mother texted Jenna that she could find her friend there. At first she couldn't get an elevator because they had stopped working and she was advised not to take the stairs, but after a while, the elevators returned to service and she was able to get to the fourth floor.

Jenna ran down the halls screaming her friend's name: "Sammi!" No one answered. Then, a man opened his door and told her, "Okay, you need to get in here. There's a shooter out there." Jenna began: "Is my friend in your room? Her name is Sammi and—" The man stopped her: "No, but you need to get in here, there is a shooter in this hotel." So she went in, he closed the door behind her, and she joined the fifteen or so people who had already taken refuge in the ordinary little room.

"Everybody had these injuries, and so all of a sudden these women start coming up to me and begin taking off my dress and stuff. And I'm like, 'What are you doing? Stop!' They're saying, 'No, honey, you've been hit. We need to figure out where you've been hit. She's a nurse.' But I told them, I haven't been hit." They persisted: "You're in shock, you've been hit."

"So they take me into the bathroom, and at that point I knew I had been hit, because I looked in the mirror, and I look like Carrie. There's blood on my face and stuff and everywhere else. So suddenly I'm just thinking, OK, maybe I am hit. Even though it feels like I've been down in the lobby for an hour and I never felt like I was hit.

"And so anyway, they get me in the shower, and they're literally spraying me off with my dress on, and I'm thinking, this is lovely." The women washed her down and found a wound in her leg—a graze with flecks of shrapnel in it that they removed and cleaned. But it wasn't large enough to have drenched her in blood. The man whose room they were hiding in gave her some warm socks.

They were safe, but in the swirl of panic and misinformation, the hysteria became relentless. Someone in the room tied the sheets together so people could climb down to a courtyard below in the event the shooter came to their door. Everyone was certain that killers were roaming the hallways of the Hooters Casino Hotel.

Jenna finally managed to connect with Sammi, who was hiding in another room on the same floor. Their respective hosts accompanied them to a halfway point, and then Sammi came back to the room where Jenna had found refuge.

"And that's the first time that I felt like we might get through this," Jenna says, "because I was sure I'd never see Sammi again, regardless whether it was her or me. So when I saw her, I felt as though, OK, there might be the light at the end of tunnel. And so this was probably an hour and a half in and there was still nothing on the news. And then, finally, we got the news on the TV and they started to give kind of a report. And that's when it felt like, 'OK, they're taking care of this.'"

As the night went on, it became evident that the shooting had ceased and that police had the situation largely under control—not to mention that much of what they had been hearing throughout the night had been misinformation that only heightened the chaos. The local media had also contributed to it, spreading unconfirmed rumors, including a report of bombs in the basements of the hotels.

"It's just crazy because really I was only in danger two minutes, basically. But I felt in danger for three hours . . . just sure I was going to die. Like saying my goodbyes to my family. In hindsight, I think that's one of the hardest parts of the process—realizing you didn't have to be panicked for that long."

The sheer chaos and terror of the scene had spread confusion like wildfire, including among police, who had great difficulty figuring out where the gunfire was coming from. There were reports it was coming from the Luxor casino resort, the great glass pyramid that is next door to both the Mandalay Bay resort and the concert venue; other reports suggested it was coming from the festival grounds. Finally, police had observed the flashes of gunfire that were emanating from the thirty-second floor of the Mandalay and dispatched a tactical squad to put an end to it.[3]

Stephen Paddock had already had an encounter with a Mandalay security guard named Jesus Campos, who had gone to the thirty-second floor in response to an open-door alert and promptly found he couldn't enter through an access door because Paddock had screwed it shut with a metal bracket. Entering through another door, Campos went to the door of the room where Paddock was waiting with his arsenal of fourteen AR-15s equipped with bump stocks that enabled him to fire them like automatic weapons, along with eight AR-10s, a revolver, and multiple one hundred–round magazines loaded with ammunition. When Campos knocked, Paddock opened fire through the door.[4]

One of the rounds caught Campos in the thigh, and he took refuge in an alcove. Inside, Paddock took a hammer and bashed out the windows of both suites he had rented. A Mandalay maintenance man named Steve Schuck approached his door about that time and barely evaded another round of gunfire. Campos, from his alcove, warned him to take cover, which he did. Then Schuck got on his radio and warned the hotel's security office about the shooting on floor thirty-two.

Ranging from room to room with his weapons, Paddock had unleashed a relentless fusillade of more than eleven hundred high-velocity rifle rounds into the audience gathered below him. Then, just as suddenly, he had stopped. When the tactical team came to his door about ten minutes after he had first opened fire, the gunfire had ceased; when the team broke through an hour later, he was already long dead from a self-inflicted gunshot.[5]

Fifty-eight people died at the Route 91 festival that day, thirty-six of them women. Another 851 people were injured, about half of them with gunshot and shrapnel wounds. Hundreds more were injured in the scramble to escape—broken legs, torn ligaments, deep cuts.[6]

There were thousands of survivors that day. They all endured the same trauma—and all of them are still in various stages of recovery. Many, like Jenna, receive therapeutic treatment for post-traumatic stress disorder.

Despite the shooter having been taken out, the chaos continued for hours afterward as reports poured in of shooters at other hotels, including the Hooters where Jenna and Sammi had taken refuge. Eventually, as the morning light grew brighter outside and it became clear that things were safe again, the two of them wandered back downstairs, out of the casino, and onto the streets again. They navigated their way back to their hotel, showered and changed, then caught the 11:00 a.m. flight home to SeaTac airport just as they had planned all along.

Camden was waiting for Jenna. It was a heartfelt embrace, but it took Jenna a while before she could hug her daughter for as long as she wanted. In her mind, she had already died and left her little girl behind, and now it felt like a betrayal for which she could not forgive herself.

That was just the beginning of her journey back. Three years later, she is still traveling it.

"Now I live thinking it's going to happen everywhere," Jenna says. "I don't think I'm entirely wrong. I think that because of the way that things have been going, people just shoot other people in Walmarts these days. So I don't go to Walmart. I do avoid Walmart."

She says she still finds herself affected "in strange ways," adding that she keeps wondering if or when things will start getting better. "He didn't take away a day, he didn't take away a week—he's taken so much joy from my life, and that's the hardest part.

"I drive by the school where kids are playing and I can't have a nice thought like, 'Oh, I can't wait to drive past this elementary and see Camden playing out there.' No. I have to think, 'Oh, it would be so easy for someone to hop the fence and just kill all those kids.'

"That's what I've been robbed of. It's hard—like just having nice thoughts, it's hard to have nice thoughts to think they get ruined by such a horrible thing. I think that's what is the hardest part.

"I can walk through what happened with anybody; it's not traumatic to go through that for me anymore. It's what I've been left with that's so destructive."

Even having the blessing of a happy-go-lucky toddler in her life becomes a kind of curse: "I mean, I think it helps to have [Camden] in my life, but I think that she is also a source of my worry. I think I'd have less worry if it was, 'Oh, if I get shot in this movie theater, my parents will be sad, my brother will be sad, but no one needs me.' So I think having someone that needs you almost makes it worse because you're thinking, 'Someone needs me out there.'"

As is so often the case with trauma, it actually hits the hardest at quiet moments when she's not busy and it blindsides her. "I don't look forward to lying in bed at night," Jenna says. "After this, I would never want to go to bed and not go to sleep for an hour because I don't want that time alone with myself to think about things because I know where I'm going to go. So I'll either read or watch TV to the point where I can barely keep my eyes open. So then I don't even have the ability to sit there and have some sort of deep thought.

"Because if I start thinking—why do these things happen in the world? It's just too much. Because there's no answer."

In an ironic twist, the survivors of the Route 91 massacre, as well as the families of the victims, soon found themselves victimized a second time by the same universe of conspiracy theories that had fueled the mass death in the first place.

Misinformation had been rampant throughout the night, and it continued into the next day and then into the following week. A thread at the alt-right-friendly 4chan /pol/ message board misidentified the shooter, describing him as a registered Democrat;[7] this misinformation quickly spread to other right-wing sites, such as Gateway Pundit. A fake news site called Your News Wire reported a second gunman firing from Mandalay's fourth floor.[8] A Russian news agency, Sputnik, falsely reported that the FBI had identified the shooter as part of a terrorist group;[9] still other false reports indicated the shooter was a member of the antifascist movement.[10]

But that was just the beginning.

The conspiracy theories about what happened in Vegas that night began spreading widely through the usual rumor mills, particularly Infowars and its dozens of YouTube imitators whose ability to attract audiences usually depends on their ability to be outrageous. Soon, the narrative in conspiracy land was set: this was a false flag operation by government agencies designed to provide the government an excuse to take away their weapons.

They couldn't have known that this was precisely the same narrative that Stephen Paddock believed—namely, that his attack would inspire an extreme government crackdown that would reveal its tyranny.

The day after the massacre, Alex Jones speculated that it had been perpetrated by his usual menu of favorite villains: Islamic State, antifascists, leftists, Communists, and globalists. On his Infowars show, Jones went even further, warning his audience that liberals were going to be killing them.[11]

> The enemy's engaging us. Everybody needs to be packing, like I told you on Friday and on Sunday. Get ready—Democrats are going to be killing people, a lot of folks. And obviously, just like you don't

see conservatives going out and doing mass shootings, they don't want to blame the Second Amendment, they don't want to go out and kill people.

It's almost always drug-head Democrats, devil worshippers, you name it. That's their M.O. The Democrats know when they mass kill now, they know to not say they're Democrat operatives. They just want to use that to get the Second Amendment and get a civil war going.

According to Jones, the whole event was part of a scheme to cow the American public into accepting sweeping gun controls: "With this event and this attack, the leftists, the globalists, the social engineers are going to use those dear lives of those poor people who were snuffed out to try to wound what's left of our republic and complete our journey into disarmament," he warned, claiming that comments after the shootings by Michelle Obama and Hillary Clinton were proof that they intended to start a "race war in America."

Although Jones had promoted the idea of a looming civil war for decades, his projection-fueled rhetoric reached stochastic terror levels as the broadcast continued:

This is a leftist Democratic Party operation, with mainstream media, corporate media hyping the climate of "kill the Republicans, kill the white people."

They've gotten so radicalized with their own propaganda that they're believing all this stuff. And then when their folks go out and kill, they cover it up, and they blame it on the victims.

. . . They're getting ready for war! And in full spectrum dominance, they're going to carry out the attacks, and then they're going to turn around and blame us and say our rights and our freedoms are to blame! Get it? That's twenty-first-century warfare. You carry out the attack, and then you blame your enemy, who you just killed.

Near the end, he concluded with a red-faced rant warning his audience that their "globalist" enemies intended to round them up in concentration camps and murder them en masse, with a flourish worthy of Slim Pickens:

You think you're hunting us? We're going to destroy you politically. And we're going to hold our fire. But you watch, they're going to false flag even bigger now. They're going for total broke to break your will. And if they do that, then they're gonna put fifty million people in forced-labor camps. That's mainstream news. And they can't wait to give every one of these little Communists time with your wife and kids in some dungeon. 'Cause that's what they want.

> I'm not kiddin'. They're comin'. You wanted to see the fight for
> America, you're living it, 2017, baby! This is it! Toe-to-toe combat
> with the globalists, politically.[12]

The conspiracy theorists immediately began claiming that the victims weren't really victims but instead paid "crisis actors" working on behalf of a "globalist" conspiracy. That's when the death threats started.

Braden Matejka, a thirty-year-old from British Columbia, caught a bullet in the back of his head that night when he and his girlfriend, Amanda Homulos, turned to run away. However, he was lucky: the shot only grazed his skull and knocked him down. He found himself in a hospital room recovering the next week, and TV crews visited. Both he and Homulos gave interviews describing how happy they were to be alive and how fortunate they felt.[13]

Soon there were supportive posts on Facebook, but then everything took a turn to the dark side. Strangers began showing up in the comments making threats and accusing the couple and their family of being liars.

"Obviously a TERRIBLE CRISIS ACTOR," wrote one named Samantha. "HE'S SCAMMING THE PUBLIC. . . . This was a government set up."

"YOUR A LIAR AND THEFT PIECE OF CRAP," wrote another named Karen.

"You'll pay on the other side," said a user named Mach. Others called Braden a "LYING BASTARD," "scumbag govt actor," and "fuckin FRAUD," while one user named Josh wrote: "I hope someone comes after you and literally beats the living fuck outa you."

"You are a lying piece of shit and I hope someone truly shoots you in the head," a commenter wrote to Matejka on Facebook. "Your soul is disgusting and dark! You will pay for the consequences!" said another.

"There are all these families dealing with likely the most horrific thing they'll ever experience, and they are also met with hate and anger and are being attacked online about being a part of some conspiracy," Taylor Matejka, Braden's brother, told the *Guardian*. "It's madness. I can't imagine the thought process of these people. Do they know that we are actual people?"

"It makes you angry," said Rob McIntosh, fifty-two, who suffered chest and arm wounds at the massacre yet was subsequently accused of faking his injuries. "You've already been through something that's traumatic and terrible, and you have someone who is attacking your honesty. You don't even have the opportunity to respond."[14]

Taylor Matejka said nothing seemed to work when he tried responding to the conspiracy theorists in person: "I'd be happy to talk to these people, but it seems there's no reasoning. A really sad part of this is that a lot of these people think they're fighting the good fight and exposing truth."

Jenna encountered similar people in her mother's social circle on Facebook. "It wasn't like a conspiracy group, but they were just saying like, 'what's the funniest conspiracy that you believe in?' And . . . some of them were funny. Like—oh—'I believe reptiles run the government' and it's like . . . 'the Titanic was switched.' It's . . . kind of fun. And then it started to get into 9/11, and Sandy Hook, or Vegas, or Holocaust deniers.

"And I got so heated—like to the point where I was shaking and crying—because it was these whackadoodles who believe the craziest things. They don't believe Sandy Hook happened and basically were saying the same thing—that everyone there was paid actors. And I lost it.

"So someone said, 'Oh, the Las Vegas shooting didn't happen the way they said. No one was up in the hotel. The shooter was down below.' And that it was all government driven—that there were multiple shooters, there's proof.

"I understand where people get worked into these beliefs, but this person insisted that the victims were paid actors. And I said, 'Okay, well, I can tell you that it wasn't. I definitely was not paid anything. So I'm still waiting on that check.'" The woman remained insistent, though, eventually concluding that "we'll just never know what really happened.

"It was just so frustrating. You can't even reason with someone like that. And when they get enough people to believe it, then they just feed off each other, it seems like."

Jenna used to dabble in conspiracy theories a little herself, just for fun. Now she runs away from them, because she knows firsthand that they arise in a vacuum of ignorance. "These people who believe like Sandy Hook or Vegas didn't happen—I doubt any of them have spoken to anyone that was there. So they can say whatever they want: 'Oh, well, it's because everyone's a paid actor.' And I'm, 'Talk to me, I'm right here.'

"I just don't think they want to know the truth—or it's not that they don't want to know the truth, I think it's that they think they know the truth, and it would be hard to be faced with something else that then they would be able to reconcile with the story that they've created."

The official investigation took ten months, but in the end, it provided no resolution for the victims, the survivors, or their families. Las Vegas Metro's official report in August 2018, despite the abundance of evidence of Stephen Paddock's conspiracism, was unable to determine any kind of motivation. It pointed to his lack of organizational affiliations, the absence of any kind of manifesto, and no evidence of a conspiracy before concluding: "What we have been able to answer are the questions of who, what, when, where and how . . . what we have not been able to definitively answer is why Stephen Paddock committed this act." The FBI's report five months later likewise concluded that "there was no single or clear motivating factor."[15]

That meant that the deadliest mass shooting by an individual in American history was committed for reasons that law enforcement officials couldn't explain—to the victims, their families, the survivors, or to the public. The conspiracy theories that Paddock believed in, in this calculus, could not count as a motive. And so his victims just became the inert things Paddock himself conceived them as.

"Sacrifices."

———————

The six hundred or so teenagers who had gathered in late July 2011 for summer camp on Utoya Island—an idyllic twenty-six-acre getaway on Lake Tyri, about twenty-four miles northwest of Oslo, where the Norwegian Labour Party's youth wing, the AUF, had for years held its annual summer training sessions for up-and-coming young political leaders—were in the kind of place where violence, especially hate-filled, relentless lethal violence, did not seem even remotely possible. It was so peaceful. So beautiful. The atmosphere at the camp, as always, was convivial and uplifting.[16]

All of which is a large part of why Anders Breivik chose Utoya Island as his target. It seemed so inconceivable. Certainly, what happened was.

The kids at Utoya were the nation's future political elite, and that too is why Breivik targeted them. A number of prime ministers had attended the camp, crediting the camp with shaping their careers, and were known for returning and giving speeches. That morning of July 22, former prime minister Gro Harlem Brundtland addressed the kids. Breivik originally wanted to target the camp while she was there—his plan was to behead her on video then post it on the Internet—but encountered a hitch in his plan when his departure from downtown Oslo was delayed.[17]

Then again, when he departed Oslo that morning, the city was in utter chaos because he had set off the truck bomb he had created in the Volkswagen Crafter van at his farm in the center of the government office district, near prime minister Jens Stoltenberg's offices. It was a McVeigh-size blast that killed eight people.[18]

Most of them were government workers, including Anne Lise Holter, a fifty-one-year-old senior consultant to Stoltenberg. There was Hanna Endresen, sixty-one, a receptionist in the security department; Jon Vegard Lervag, thirty-two, a lawyer in the justice department; Ida Marie Hill, thirty-four, an adviser to the ministry of justice; Hanne Ekroll Loevlie, a thirty-year-old senior government worker originally from rural Tyristrand; twenty-six-year-old Kjersti Berg Sand, who worked on international issues in justice. A couple of random passersby—Tove Ashill Knutsen, fifty-six, who was on her way to a subway station, and Kai Hauge, thirty-two, who owned a nearby bar and restaurant—also were killed. Another 209 people were injured, twelve of them severely. However, none of the government main ministers was among the injured, including Stoltenberg.[19]

Many of the teens on Utoya that day had parents who worked in Oslo's government district, so when word of the bombing reached the island, the camp suspended activities so attendees could contact their parents. In the meantime, they were told that a police officer from the mainland was on his way over on the small ferry that serviced the camp.

That officer was actually Breivik, dressed in a police uniform with tactical armor and carrying high-powered rifles in cases.[20] He had driven to Utoya in his mother's vehicle and arrived at the ferry dock, requesting it be summoned to fetch him, telling them his name was "Martin Nilsen." But camp director Monica Bøsei became suspicious on the ferry ride back and summoned security director Trond Berntsen when they reached shore. When Berntsen asked to see some ID, Breivik pulled out his pistol and dispatched both Berntsen and Bøsei on the spot.[21]

It was done out of view of the teenagers, however, so when Breivik walked up to the open field where they were assembled, he asked them to gather around him so he could debrief them on the bombing in Oslo. When they had encircled him, he opened fire with one of the high-powered rifles. The kids screamed and scattered, and when the open space had cleared a minute or so later, there were only tents and fallen teenagers who had been shot as they fled.[22]

Breivik then walked into the camp's café/canteen, where thirteen teens had taken refuge. He burst in the doors and announced: "You will die today! Marxists, liberals, members of the elite!" Then he began shooting all of them, first with a pistol, then finishing them each with a shotgun blast to the head. Afterward, he went outside and finished off the teens who had fallen in the open field outside in identical fashion.[23]

For the next hour or so, Breivik conducted a systematic search for camp attendees around the rest of the island. He tried getting into the schoolhouse building and found it was locked; after firing a couple of rounds through the lock without it budging, he moved on to the kids hiding in the woods. His rifle was loaded with special hollow-point bullets designed to cause the most damage to his victims' internal organs and body tissue.[24]

As he walked along, he shouted: "You're going to die today, Marxists!" And when he found them—often clustered together in protective huddles—he cold-bloodedly opened fire. As he reached the island's edge, he found more of them similarly clustered beneath rock outcroppings, at which point he simply mowed them down.[25]

Many of the teens decided to try swimming for it. Breivik began firing at them from shore, shouting as he did so. Others swam back to shore when they realized they couldn't make it, only to encounter Breivik walking up to them there and firing off more rounds from his rifle.

Police had been desperately trying to reach the island, but a variety of bureaucratic snafus prevented them from reaching Utoya until ninety minutes or so after Breivik's arrival. When they got there, Breivik freely surrendered, smirking and telling them that all would become clear soon.[26]

They also found seventy-seven dead teenagers. Another 110 were injured, 55 of them with serious wounds and lifelong consequences.

"Sacrifices."

———————

Dylann Roof very nearly didn't go through with it after meeting and spending an hour or so in Bible study with the people he had targeted for death. They were "so nice," he later told investigators that he almost changed his mind and called off what he called his "mission."[27]

His primary target was the senior pastor of the church—Emanuel Baptist AME in Charleston, South Carolina—whose Bible study sessions he had joined the evening of June 17, 2015. The pastor's name was Reverend Clementa Pinckney,[28] a man who had gained renown as national civil rights leader and had recently been in the news advocating for the use of body cameras by police officers in the wake of a highly publicized shooting of a black man in Charleston.[29] Roof told investigators later that he picked Emanuel because of its long significance in the history of civil rights.

Roof entered the church around eight in the evening, dressed in a long-sleeve gray shirt and jeans with a fanny pack rotated in front, as the gathered congregants broke into groups for Bible studies. He asked for Reverend Pinckney by name and then sat next to him. For the next hour or so, a pleasant conversation about scripture commenced, and Roof appeared to be enjoying himself. But at some point around 9:00 p.m., his countenance changed, survivors said, and he suddenly pulled a pistol out of the fanny pack and shot Reverend Pinckney point-blank in the head, killing him instantly.[30]

Then he aimed at the eighty-seven-year-old woman across the table from him, Susie Jackson. Her nephew, twenty-six-year-old Tywanza Sanders, was seated next to her and began speaking in a calm voice to Roof, telling him he didn't need to do this.[31]

"Yes I do. I have to do it," Roof replied. "You rape our women and you're taking over our country. And you have to go." Sanders dove across the chair to protect his aunt, and Roof shot him next, then Susie Jackson. Then he systematically went around the room, shooting everyone in it, shouting: "Y'all want something to pray about? I'll give you something to pray about." Two survived by pretending to be dead. Roof left one person alive to act as a witness to the carnage then tried to shoot himself, but, after reloading five times, he had run out of ammunition. So he walked out of the church and into the night. He was arrested the next day in North Carolina.[32]

"Sacrifices."

———————

The first victims of Elliot Rodger's rampage were two roommates with whom he shared an apartment in Isla Vista and one of their friends. It's not clear what set the final spark, but that day—May 23, 2014—Rodger lay in wait at the apartment as each of them returned home, where he ambushed them with a large knife. He left the bodies of the roommates—Weihann "David" Wang, twenty, and Cheng Yuan "James" Hong, twenty—in their bedrooms and the corpse of their nineteen-year-old friend, George Chen, in the bathroom.[33]

Rodger appears to have waited several more hours in the apartment before setting out in his black BMW with his Sig Sauer P26 pistols on what appears to have been a meticulously planned mass killing. Except, of course, that it went awry almost immediately.[34]

The initial plan, after all, called for him to "enter the hottest sorority house of UCSB" and then to "slaughter every single spoiled, stuck up, blonde slut I see inside there." That was what he said, anyway, in the "Retribution" video he uploaded to YouTube as he drank his vanilla latte at Starbucks that evening.

That didn't work out. He did indeed walk up to the front door of the Alpha Phi sorority house near the UCSB campus and knock on it at about 9:30 p.m. No one answered. It was getting dark.[35]

However, there were random people nearby on the lawns of neighboring sororities, so he began shooting at them instead—wounding three women from the Delta Delta Delta sorority, two of them fatally—before getting back in his car and peeling away.

The short remainder of Rodger's life consisted of a mobile gun rampage from inside his car through Isla Vista. He shot and killed a man standing in front of a nearby market and then continued shooting: a man and woman standing outside a residence a short distance away, a woman waiting at a crosswalk, another woman walking along a sidewalk. He also used his car to intentionally strike several pedestrians, as well as a man riding a bicycle, all of whom were injured but survived.[36]

When sheriff's deputies cornered him at an intersection, they exchanged gunfire, and Rodger suffered a wound to the hip. Still careering madly through the streets, he whipped around and took out one last bicyclist before shooting himself in the head—at which point his car veered off to the side and crashed to a halt.

All told, in addition to Elliot Rodger, there were six people killed in Isla Vista that day, and fourteen more injured, several severely.

"Sacrifices."

———————

Yonge Street is the main artery in downtown Toronto, and it's usually packed with traffic, especially in the tony North York City Centre, where Alek Minassian drove his van and parked long enough to post his Facebook message praising the incels.

For Minassian, however, traffic was no object. Starting up the big van, he hopped the curb at Yonge and Finch Avenue and began driving at a high rate of speed down the sidewalk, mowing down every pedestrian he encountered.[37] He remained on the sidewalk for several more blocks, a trail of bodies in his wake. He seemed to be aiming especially for women. One witness said that Minassian appeared to be like someone playing a video game, trying to kill as many pedestrians as possible.[38]

At one point the sidewalk became too narrow and he was forced back onto Yonge Street, where he remained for a couple of blocks, still careering along at high speed but without hitting anyone, until he reached Park Home Avenue. Veering back onto the sidewalk, he again began mowing people down as he encountered them.[39]

Minassian's van had struck so many people that its front end was badly damaged, and it finally lurched to a stop just as he turned a corner onto the sidewalk on Poyntz Avenue. He sat inside until a police officer reached the van. When he got outside, he had something in his hand, which he pointed at the officer, screaming: "Shoot me in the head!" The officer, gun in hand, instead patiently talked him down and arrested him. Minassian still awaits trial, scheduled for November 2020.

The scene behind him: bodies strewn along the avenue, shrieking sirens, and aid workers trying to rescue the victims. There were shoes randomly tossed in the street and torn pieces of clothing and briefcases.[40]

The final toll: ten people killed and fifteen injured, many critically. Eight of the ten dead were women, as were twelve of the injured.

"Sacrifices."

———————

When Destinee Magnum and her Muslim friend boarded the Green Line MAX train in downtown Portland on May 26, 2017, it was just an ordinary early rush-hour ride at around 4:00 p.m. The two teenage girls, one black and outgoing and the other shy and wearing a hijab, managed to find seats out of Union Station and were quietly chatting with each other when they pulled into the station at the Lloyd Center.[41]

That was where Jeremy Christian got on board.

Unlike the night before, when he had harassed Demetria Hester, this train was full of people. But that didn't stop Christian. No sooner had he boarded than he spotted Destinee and her friend, immediately standing in front of them and shouting at them about how they didn't belong in Portland. That Muslims should die, because they had been killing Christians for hundreds of years. That the girl in the hijab should go back to Saudi Arabia.

The girls got up and fled to the back of the train, seeking another seat. Christian followed them, still shouting.[42]

Three men, regular commuters who had been watching the scene unfold, stepped between Christian and the two women. One of them—Rick Best, fifty-three, a Portland city employee—stood closest to Christian and tried using reason: "I know you are taxpayer, but this is not OK. You're scaring people." Christian kept shouting that it was about his free speech.

As they neared the next stop, Taliesen Myrddin Namkai-Meche, twenty-three, pleaded with Christian: "Please get off this train."

Another of the trio, Micah David-Cole Fletcher, twenty-one, recognized Christian from the alt-right march the month before, when he had marched with the counterprotesters and Christian had made a scene. He tried pushing himself between Christian and the women.

"You fucking touch me again and I'll kill you," Christian snarled at him. At that moment he lost his balance and fell back; when he came back up, he had a knife in his hand, and he plunged it into Rick Best's neck, then turned to Namkai-Meche and Fletcher and did the same to each of them. Then he ran from the train and away from the Hollywood station. The two dark-skinned girls fled the train, too, leaving their belongings behind.[43]

Rick Best bled out before help could arrive and was declared dead at the scene. Namkai-Meche, who told everyone who stopped to help that he loved them, died in the intensive-care ward at the nearby hospital. Only Fletcher, who remained in the hospital for a month recovering from his wound, survived the attack.

At his arraignment on murder and attempted murder charges—but, mysteriously, no hate-crime charges—two days later, Christian ranted behind the glass for the benefit of the press.[44]

"Free speech or die, Portland!" he shouted. "You got no safe place. This is America! Get out if you don't like free speech!"

After hearing the official charges being read, he shouted again: "Death to the enemies of America! Leave this country if you hate our freedom. Death to antifa!"

"You call it terrorism, I call it patriotism!"

"Sacrifices."

Buckey Wolfe had made himself a kind of crude sword that he kept in the mother-in-law apartment at the back of his parents' home in Seattle, where he lived. It was a two-edged piece of steel about four feet long, which had been sharpened at the tang end to a fine point with razor edges.[45]

The evening of January 6, 2019, his brother James paid a visit. They chatted for a while, and their dad handed them some food before they retreated to Buckey's mother-in-law's apartment.

At 6:40 p.m., Buckey called 911 and told the dispatcher that he had killed his brother by ramming the crude sword into his head.[46]

"Kill me, kill me, I can't live in this reality," he said and rambled on: "God told me he was a lizard," he added.

When police arrived, they found James Wolfe dead inside the apartment, fatally wounded by the sword. Buckey was gone, but police found him shortly afterward, walking through the neighborhood about a mile away.

When detectives interviewed him at police headquarters, he told them "that their eyes and mouths were changing and asked if they could see lizards in the room," according to court records.[47]

The Proud Boys shortly afterward issued a lengthy statement claiming that Buckey Wolfe had never been a member of their organization, claiming he had "never made it past our strict vetting protocols."[48] But in fact, nearly a year before, Wolfe had posted the certificate on his Facebook page that verified his "first degree" membership, along with multiple group shots with other Proud Boys out on the streets.[49]

The judge ordered Wolfe detained without bail, agreeing with prosecutors that he posed an extreme danger to the community. He awaits trial in Seattle, having been found mentally competent by the court in July 2019.

"Sacrifices."

Brenton Tarrant had the ultimate alt-right massacre in mind: livestreamed, like a first-person shooter video game.[50]

After sending his manifesto out into the world from the car parked outside the Al-Noor mosque in Christchurch, he got out of the car and began livestreaming from the GoPro strapped to his chest. He told viewers: "Subscribe to PewDiePie!" Everything that happened during the next seventeen minutes was broadcast live on Facebook.[51]

And it was a horror show. Tarrant walked up to the door of the mosque and was greeted there by a worshipper who smiled and said, "Hello, brother." He was the first to die.[52]

Tarrant then could be seen systematically walking through the mosque and gunning down dozens of worshippers there for Friday prayer. Viewers could see him aiming his weapon—an apparently modified semiautomatic high-powered rifle, though at other times he could be seen using both a pistol and a shotgun. All of them were being fired at people who then fell over and died.[53]

Most disturbingly, the videos engendered by this livestream—which were then shared globally over the Internet and became a kind of forbidden fruit after being outlawed in a number of countries, including New Zealand—were almost live-action re-creations of first-person shooter games, which often present the world to video-game players (as Tarrant himself was) from precisely this perspective.[54] Tarrant clearly set up the camera perspective with the chest-level GoPro with exactly this in mind.[55]

When he was done at Al-Noor, Tarrant jumped in his car and headed out in a necessarily roundabout route to the city's other mosque, with police cars screaming toward the Al-Noor mosque passing him along the way. When he finally reached the Linwood Islamic Centre, five kilometers away, about eight minutes had passed.

However, he apparently had done a poor job of scouting this location and approached it from a back door, where he was unable to gain entry. So he began firing at people through the window there, striking a number of worshippers inside.

Tarrant ran out of ammo, though, and returned to his car to fetch another weapon. When he did so, one of the Islamic Centre congregants—a forty-eight-year-old father of four named Abdul Aziz Wahabzada—whose four children were inside the mosque—ran out of the mosque with an electronic card reader the size of a small adding machine and threatened to bash Tarrant with it.[56] Startled, Tarrant pulled out a gun and fired at Aziz, who ducked between cars to avoid the string of gunshots. Eventually Aziz was able to retrieve a gun that Tarrant had abandoned when his second gun ran out of ammo. Gun in hand, Aziz chased Tarrant to his car and threw the gun through one of the car's windows. Tarrant hit the ignition and the gas and drove away. Police arrested him a few blocks away; they believe he was on his way to a third target.[57]

Tarrant killed fifty-one people that day: forty-two at Al-Noor and another seven at Linwood; two of the Al-Noor wounded later died at the hospital. The slain ranged in age from three to seventy-seven. Another thirty-six were treated for gunshot wounds, a number of them life-threatening, though most survived. Fourteen others suffered shrapnel injuries.[58]

"Sacrifices."

Chapter 4

TANGLED TALES

It was clear that, even though the army colonel was trained in public relations and handling a crowd, he was up against something completely different.

"When we have a federal government that cannot tell the truth, how do we know that what you're saying is true?" asked one of the commission judges, reading from an audience questions card. The overflow audience of about five hundred people packed into the Bastrop County Commission chambers in Texas cheered loudly.[1]

The officer, Lieutenant Colonel Mark Lastoria of U.S. Army Special Operations Command, was there to try to explain to his rural audience how and why the largest training exercise in the army's history, code-named Jade Helm 15, was scheduled to take place over the course of two months in a broad swath of the nation's countryside, mainly in seven states in the Southwest and interior West, that summer of 2015.

"We're truly invested in everybody's personal rights and their privacy," Lastoria told the audience. "That's what we live for, to support the Constitution of the United States and that's what everybody wants to protect. . . . We're not going to be interfering with people's livelihoods, or negatively impact their farms. Some of these counties that we're going to be in, they're very concerned that we're going to disrupt recreational activity. It's not going to happen."

The first questioner came to the microphone, introduced himself, then asked: "In spite of people's overwhelming opposition to this program, would the commission consider rescinding their invitation to these guys? And would the court be offended if I told the colonel that I didn't believe a single word that he just said?"

There was more raucous applause.

Someone then told Lastoria that Jade Helm appeared to be nothing more than "a preparation for martial law."

"It is not a preparation for martial law," the colonel answered.

"That's what you say," his interlocutor replied. Again, the crowd cheered.

"It has nothing to do with martial law, period. We are Title 10 forces, not Title 32, nothing like that. No martial law in any way, shape, or form. We basically simply want to train United States Special Operations forces for future operations overseas. That's it," Lastoria explained.

No one in the audience seemed convinced. Notably, there were large numbers of Infowars T-shirts among the people voicing the most skepticism, and indeed the questions reflected claims that Alex Jones had been making on his nationally broadcast conspiracy theory program.[2]

According to Jones, Jade Helm was tantamount to martial law. He told his listeners that because the special operations forces from four branches of the U.S. military would be blending in with local populations, they were in fact secretly training for an eventual battle to disarm Americans.

"Jade Helm 15 is more than just a military exercise, it's also an exercise of the new field in geospatial intelligence using human domain analytics to map the politics and thoughts of any nation, state, city, right down to the individual," he told his audience.

Jones had been circulating similar theories for a while. The previous year he had claimed that a much smaller army training exercise involving a mockup of an urban invasion zone actually was intended to prepare armed forces for an attack on American citizens, labeling it part of "a giant buildup for war with the American people."

All along, army officials dismissed these claims, particularly as Jade Helm came under attack. The exercise, they asserted, was nothing more than "routine training to maintain a high level of readiness for [special forces] since they must be ready to support potential missions anywhere in the world at a moment's notice." Lastoria told reporters that "the concerns expressed center around misinterpretations.

"Unofficial sources providing inaccurate information on Jade Helm want people to believe that it's something other than a training exercise," Lastoria said.

The theories even spread to Fox News, where Megyn Kelly described the conspiracy theorists merely as "critics": "Well, conspiracy theories are running wild tonight about the army's plan for a multistate training exercise this summer called 'Jade Helm 15,'" she told her audience. "While the military says they're just training soldiers for the realities of war, critics say the army is preparing for modern-day martial law."[3]

What apparently drove the theorists to leap to the conclusion that the exercise was nefarious in intent was a map that had been leaked in connection with the army's mock strategy for the exercise showing that Texas and Utah, as well as parts of California, had been designated "hostile territory." Jones and others immediately claimed this reflected the Obama administration's view of those states and suggested that this was more preparation for martial law.

"Training with the police, training with locals in plainclothes, quote, doing suspicious activities, is to train the police to work with the military in covert operations, and to condition the military to accept it, and to condition the public to accept it, and then when we cover it and talk about it, they practice a psyop in real time, putting out this information," Jones claimed.[4]

Infowars was hardly alone. Some right-wing radio talkers from Texas began making similar claims. Next News Network, a right-wing website with a history of regurgitating propaganda from Russian websites, also chimed in with a series of reports on Jade Helm. In one video, an announcer intoned: "This is without doubt the largest public-conditioning exercise in American history. This, as the public watches Cheyenne Mountain reopening in anticipation of an EMP attack, and key operations of the New York Federal Reserve moving to Chicago in the event of a natural disaster. Now the event that is truly on the horizon is anyone's guess, however, one thing is for sure: troops will be ready and trained to take over your town when it happens."[5]

One of the men who questioned Lastoria in Bastrop was particularly keen to know if a memorandum created by the Department of Homeland Security in 2009 describing how right-wing extremists might target military veterans for recruitment—and citing certain conservative causes, including gun rights and abortion, as among the issues around which radical terrorists might act—had any role in the army's designations of the area as "hostile."

Infowars interviewed him afterward. "I think what concerns me the most is, I am a student of history, and I know that governments go tyrannical," the man said. "And I know that our government, through Homeland Security, has labeled people like the kind of people that live in Bastrop that are conservative gun owners, libertarians, veterans, the government's labeled those people as potential terrorists. And so I do see an odd correlation between a huge military buildup and a hostile designation for the state of Texas in this area."[6]

Conservative Texas politicians echoed this paranoia. Representative Louie Gohmert of Texas released a statement on Jade Helm, noting, "When leaders within the current administration believe that major threats to the country include those who support the Constitution, are military veterans, or even 'cling to guns or religion,' patriotic Americans have reason to be concerned."[7]

U.S. Senator Ted Cruz, who was gearing up for a run as a presidential candidate that year, blamed it on President Obama: "When the federal government has not demonstrated itself to be trustworthy in this administration, the natural consequence is that many citizens don't trust what it is saying."[8]

Shortly after the Bastrop gathering, Texas's governor, Greg Abbott, sent a letter to the commander of the Texas State Guard ordering his men to monitor the Jade Helm operations. "During the training operation, it is important that Texans know their safety, constitutional rights, private property rights and civil liberties will not be infringed," he wrote. (It later emerged that much of the hysteria regarding Jade Helm was in fact the product of a Russian disinformation campaign intended to sow chaos among American voters and disrupt an American military exercise.)[9]

That afternoon before the Bastrop commission, Lastoria tried to reassure the crowd by appealing to their patriotism. "I'd like everyone to not confuse apples and pumpkins, OK?" he told the audience and pointed to his army patches. "This institution has been around for 240 years. You may have issues with the administration, OK? So be it. But this institution has been with you for 240 years. Period."

However, what soon became clear was that his very presence there was interpreted by the conspiracists who packed the room as powerful evidence of a psychological operation, or "psyops," as it's known in the conspiracy world, by the army.

"It appears that the psyops are taking place right now," one questioner insisted. "And psychological operations, meaning psychological warfare, that would be a weapon being used against citizens if you're talking about blaming it, obtaining information, all that sort of stuff."

Lastoria, of course, patiently denied this: "One, there's not a psyop campaign going on associated with that. This is an information brief, and it has nothing to do with private citizens. . . . That's not normally part of a training exercise."

Another asked if, by blending in, the soldiers participating would be gathering information on people in the community "that they'll come in later and pick everybody up."

Lastoria repeated: "Everybody truly wants this to be something that it is not. All we want to do is make sure that our guys are trained for combat overseas. That's it."

The more he sounded persuasive and reasonable, the worse things got.

"My question is, why is it not reasonable for me as a private citizen who just questions things—maybe some conspiracy theories, but some of us just have questions," one man asked. "Why is it not reasonable for me to see this as absolute training for a domestic rendition program where eventually, worst-case scenario, in a potential battle, good folks like yourselves who swore an oath would go after Alex Jones, Joe Biggs, Jakari Jackson—why is it not reasonable, sir, for me to be scared of that?"

"There's a reason that people have problems with this," an elderly woman interviewed by Infowars said afterward. "It's not irrational fears. It's well-founded fears."

Later that summer, as the exercise actually got under way and every locale in which it was supposed to occur came to realize that the whole operation was very low-key and designed not to create problems, much of the paranoia simmered down. However, in the mind of conspiracy theorists, the very lack of such evidence is actually proof that something nefarious is occurring, and so a number of the dedicated "Patriots" worked into a lather by Infowars began taking matters into their own hands.

In August, gunshots were fired for two consecutive days near the Camp Shelby Joint Forces Training Center in Mississippi's Perry County, where 4,600 National Guard and Army Reserve troops were participating in the exercise. No one was arrested, but Mississippi Governor Phil Bryant ordered some of the military personnel to be armed as a precaution.

A few days later in North Carolina, federal agents assigned to the Joint Terrorism Task Force in Charlotte arrested three men, including a previously convicted felon, on a variety of conspiracy and firearms violations. The trio had purchased assorted high-quality military gear and ammunition and were making homemade explosives in anticipation of interacting with Jade Helm troops, charging documents claimed.[10]

Walter Eugene Litteral, fifty, Christopher James Baker, forty-two, and Christopher Todd Campbell, thirty, expressed "their disapproval of the Jade Helm military exercises" to an FBI informant, their federal criminal complaint said.

At trial, it emerged that Litteral had been building an arsenal of explosive devices, including tennis-ball bombs and a variety of pipe bombs, as well as simple bombs using coffee cans, gunpowder, and ball bearings. He even had figured out how to make a dummy grenade into a live one.

Litteral, prosecutors said, "believed that the United States government intended to use the armed forces to impose martial law, which the conspirators planned to resist with violent force."

The suspects also discussed a ninety-nine-acre "base camp" near Clover, South Carolina, where they intended to plant booby traps and lure government forces in and "kill them."

All three men pleaded guilty. Litteral was sentenced to twenty-two months in prison, while Baker and Campbell each received twenty months.

When Jade Helm wrapped up in September 2015, it was almost as if it had never happened as far as the communities where it was held were concerned.[11] But following the uproar around it, the army has not attempted a similar exercise of that scale again.

Conspiracy theories used to exist in a universe almost wholly separate from the real world of policy and politics. That's because, for most of their history, conspiracies have been offered as counternarratives to the official explanation for a range of historic real-life events—that is, they usually have come after the fact, and they rarely if ever have changed anything. In the new age of conspiracism, the theories have taken on a life of their own that, as with Jade Helm, are fatally infecting real-world policy and even military outcomes.

There is a long and colorful history of conspiracy theories infecting popular culture and discourse—indeed, much of American history is interwoven with them. For the most part, that effect has been diversionary at worst, but there always has been a dark side to them, closely related to their central function, which is to scapegoat.

One of the oldest conspiracy theories—perhaps the Ur-smear—is what is commonly known as the "blood libel": namely, the claim, originating in the mists of antiquity, that Jews used the blood of Christian children, obtained ritually from sacrificed abductees, to leaven their matzo dough. Over the years, there have been about 150 recorded cases of Jews being tortured and murdered by mobs because of this belief.[12]

Around the twelfth century, the legend became so widespread and thoroughly believed in the English countryside that there were massacres of Jews in London and York, and the Jewish delegation attending the coronation of Richard the Lionhearted was attacked by the London crowd.[13] A Benedictine monk penned an "investigation" of a boy's murder in 1144 that claimed that a secret international council of Jews oversaw the annual ritual killing of a Christian boy at Easter time and had selected England that year.[14] By 1255, when another boy named Hugh of Lincoln was found in a well (the story is even recounted in Chaucer's *Canterbury Tales*),[15] the hysteria became so widespread and extreme that King Henry III—who also stood to gain considerably financially by having his debtors executed—intervened and ninety-one Jews were arrested and taken to the Tower of London, eighteen of whom were put to death, and issued edicts banning Jews from commerce with other Britons. His successor, Edward I, took the final step and ordered the expulsion of all Jews from England in 1290. The ban remained in place until 1655.[16]

Over the centuries, of course, a number of real-world plots and conspiracies affected the course of European politics, and the reality of these conspiracies led also to a number of theories about them that turned out, in fact, to be completely bogus. As with the blood libel claims, these theories not only were hyperventilating nonsense, they often created scapegoats of an entire class of people. The most notorious of these was the "Popish Plot" of seventeenth-century England, when a cleric named Titus Oates composed a manuscript claiming that there was a massive conspiracy by the Catholic Church to assassinate King Charles

II. The ensuing three-year panic after its 1678 publication led to the execution of twenty-two men, most of them Jesuit priests. Five Catholic lords were imprisoned in the tower, and the king ordered the expulsion of all Catholics from London. Eventually, Oates was exposed as a fraud and convicted of perjury, for which he spent three years in prison.[17]

Then there were the Bavarian Illuminati, whose legacy remains very much with us. Between 1776 and 1785, this clandestine collection of highly educated civic and intellectual leaders met in secret with the intent of overpowering the prevailing monarchist rule in Europe and replacing it with an Enlightenment-based society opposed to superstition and religious influence over political life.[18] Led by a Bavarian professor of philosophy named Adam Weishaupt, they essentially plotted to take over the world through secretive methods, because they had good reason to believe that monarchists were too ruthless for them to attempt such a massive political change in public view.[19]

The Illuminati started out small in number but gradually grew to somewhere between 650 and 2,500 members, many of them elite politicians and people in positions of authority and influence. Much of their recruitment came from within the ranks of another secret society, the Freemasons, who similarly shared Enlightenment ideals.[20] Initially, it was very popular within the more educated circles of aristocratic society, but then it ran afoul of the ruling aristocracy, as well as the pro-monarchic sect within the ranks of Freemasonry known as the Rosicrucians. In 1785, Charles Theodore, the elector of Bavaria, banned all secret societies, with a particular eye on the Illuminati. Weishaupt lost his teaching position and was exiled to a remote Germanic duchy, where he lived out his years still teaching philosophy.[21]

The lasting influence of the Illuminati, however, lies in the fear that they created due to their secretive and subversive nature, and particularly in the way they challenged the ruling monarchical order. Notably, a few years after the group's demise, a conspiracy-minded Jesuit priest with a fondness for defending the authorities in power named Augustin Barruel published a 1793 text claiming that the excesses of the French Revolution's Jacobins were the fault of the Illuminati and its machinations. He also claimed that the conspiracy's design in fact was eventually to destroy Christianity and the church.[22]

A Scottish professor named John Robison lustily joined in, publishing a tract titled *Proofs of a Conspiracy against All the Religions and Governments of Europe, Carried on in the Secret Meetings of Freemasons, Illuminati and Reading Societies*. Robison's claim was that the Illuminati had first penetrated the Freemasons and then gone on to twist and pervert the civic institutions the same men had led. He described Weishaupt as "a human devil" and his mission as pure malevolent destruction.[23] The tract was widely read and influential; George Washington replied in correspondence after reading the book that he doubted the Illuminati's reach had become deep into the United States but that it had been attempted, he said, "is too evident to be questioned."[24]

The anti-Catholicism of the old English Popish Plot hoax was revived in the 1840s in the United States as an entrenched belief about Irish and Italian immigrants—namely, that they were "papists" whose first loyalty was to the Pope and the Vatican and Americans only secondarily.[25] The most prominent progenitor of this view—which came to call itself "nativism," referring to the descendants of the original thirteen colonies' occupants—was the inventor of the single-wire telegraph and its code system, Samuel F. B. Morse. In the 1830s, Morse began railing against the "invasion" of the country by rough-necked Irish Catholics.[26]

Morse published a text titled *Foreign Conspiracy against the Liberties of the United States and Imminent Dangers to the Free Institutions of the United States through Foreign Immigration*. He warned his readers that America's democratic institutions were viewed as a threat by European despots, many of them allied with the Catholic Church, itself a type of gigantic despotism in Morse's view. They were sending their secret minions to undermine and destroy those institutions, he claimed, in the person of those immigrants.[27]

"You are marked for their prey," he warned ominously, "not by foreign bayonets, but by weapons surer of effecting the conquest of liberty than all the munitions of physical combat in the military or naval storehouses of Europe." The only way to save America, Morse insisted, was to shut off all immigration.

Morse's book helped spawn the nativist movement, and the results were brutal: in New York, nativists battled Irish immigrants in violent riots in which scores were killed.[28] In 1844, a series of Philadelphia riots resulted in churches being burned to the ground and dozens of homes destroyed, as well as several dozen deaths and many more injuries. It also led to the creation of a political party—the Know Nothing Party, which, after it won seats in Congress in 1854, renamed itself the American Party—dedicated to combating the "Romanist" plot to subvert American liberty, and fundamentally anti-Catholic, anti-immigrant, xenophobic, and prone to violence.[29]

———

The nativist movement and its anti-immigrant paranoia concocted another conspiracy theory with lasting consequences: the "Yellow Peril."[30] This was the racial animus that began rising against immigrant Chinese laborers in the American West in the 1870s after the great intercontinental rail lines were completed and the imported laborers suddenly were no longer welcome. The white supremacists of the era began warning then that Asians threatened to overwhelm Europeans and Americans with their sheer numbers.[31]

During the successful drive to exclude them—culminating in the Chinese Exclusion Act of 1882—popular prejudices of the nativist variety came into full play, such as a labor organizer's screed warning of "China's Menace to the World":

> MEN FROM CHINA come here to do LAUNDRY WORK. The Chinese Empire contains 600,000,000 (six hundred millions) inhabitants.
>   The supply of these men is inexhaustible.
>   Every one doing this work takes BREAD from the mouths of OUR WOMEN.
>   So many have come of late, that to keep at work, they are obliged to cut prices.
>   And now, we appeal to the public, asking them will they be partners to a deal which is only one of their many onward marches in CRUSHING OUT THE INDUSTRIES OF OUR COUNTRY from our people by grasping them themselves. Will you oblige the AMERICAN LAUNDRIES to CUT THE WAGES OF THEIR PEOPLE by giving your patronage to the CHINAMEN?[32]

It took on a special life, however, when Japanese began emigrating to the United States in the mid-1890s, in many regards taking the place of Chinese laborers on rail lines. Mostly this went unnoticed until Japan's victory in the Russo-Japanese War in 1905, an event that shocked the reigning white supremacist worldview, since it marked the first time a nonwhite nation had managed a military victory over a white European power. Suddenly Japanese immigration was not just racially distasteful, but a perceived threat.[33]

Japan's victory and the Treaty of Portsmouth sparked imaginative fears among white supremacists of a looming Asian world domination. California newspaper magnate William Randolph Hearst adopted the "Yellow Peril" as a major storyline and began widely disseminating the theories around them through the *San Francisco Examiner*, which in 1907 published a two-part Sunday supplement titled "Japan May Seize the Pacific Coast," which reported that "the Yellow Peril is here."[34]

Popular literature, too, contained similar motifs. Homer Lea's bestseller *The Valor of Ignorance*, published in 1909, prophesied a great war between the United States and Japan, and even published maps showing the likely routes of an invading imperial force on the western American coast.[35]

The theory underlying the Yellow Peril posited that the Japanese emperor intended to invade the Pacific coast and that he was sending these immigrants to American shores as shock troops to prepare the way for just such a military action and to lay the groundwork for acts of sabotage and espionage when the signal was given. As California politician James Phelan put it in 1907, the Japanese immigrants represented an "enemy within our gates."[36]

Phelan—who served a single term in the U.S. Senate and was the mayor of San Francisco—was probably the single most prominent figure in California on the issue of Japanese immigration. In 1906, then-Mayor Phelan denounced Japanese immigrants in a speech: "They now occupy valleys in California by lease or purchase of land to the exclusion of not only whites but Chinese, and if this silent invasion is permitted by the federal government, they would at the rate at which they are coming, a thousand a month, soon convert the fairest state in the union into a Japanese colony. If they were naturalized they would outvote us.

"But California is white man's country, and the two races cannot live side by side in peace, and inasmuch as we discovered the country first and occupied it, we propose to hold it against either a peaceful or a warlike invasion."[37]

Phelan was of course part of a much larger movement, embodied in such groups as the Asiatic Exclusion League, which in its May 1905 newsletter pronounced the following:

"As long as California is white man's country, it will remain one of the grandest and best states in the union, but the moment the Golden State is subjected to an unlimited Asiatic coolie invasion there will be no more California."[38]

Then the *Examiner* got into a Bay-area newspaper war with the *San Francisco Chronicle*, the latter of which began trying to out-jingo its rival by running sensational headlines:

The Yellow Peril—How Japanese Crowd Out the White Race

Japanese a Menace to American Women

Brown Artisans Steal Brains of Whites[39]

Eventually, this agitation led to the passage of Alien Land Laws, forbidding Japanese farmers from owning land. There were also national bestsellers that supported these sentiments, such as Madison Grant's *The Passing of the Great Race*, published in 1916, which asserted:

> We Americans must realize that the altruistic ideals which have controlled our social development during the past century, and the maudlin sentimentalism that has made America "an asylum for the oppressed," are sweeping the nation toward a racial abyss. If the Melting Pot is allowed to boil without control, and we continue to follow our national motto and deliberately blind ourselves to all "distinctions of race, creed, or color," the type of native American of Colonial descent will become as extinct as the Athenian of the age of Pericles, and the Viking of the days of Rollo.[40]

A few years later, his fellow eugenicist Lothrop Stoddard published an accompanying tome, *The Rising Tide of Color: The Threat against White World-Supremacy*, which concluded:

> "Finally perish!" That is the exact alternative which confronts the white race. For white civilization is to-day conterminous with the white race. The civilizations of the past were local. They were confined to a particular people or group of peoples. If they failed, there were always some unspoiled, well-endowed barbarians to step forward and "carry on." But today there are no more white barbarians. The earth has grown small, and men are everywhere in close touch. If white civilization goes down, the white race is irretrievably ruined. It will be swamped by the triumphant colored races, who will obliterate the white man by elimination or absorption. What has taken place in Central Asia, once a white and now a brown or yellow land, will take place in Australasia, Europe, and America. Not to-day, nor yet to-morrow; perhaps not for generations; but surely in the end. If the present drift be not changed, we whites are all ultimately doomed. Unless we set our house in order, the doom will sooner or later overtake us all.[41]

In December 1941, when Japan attacked the American naval station in Pearl Harbor, Hawaii, a public conditioned to tales of sneaky immigrants posing as farmers while lying in wait to spring an invasion on the Pacific coast was swept up in a wave of hysteria that was inflamed by military officials who encouraged their fears, as well as a sensational press.

For a war-happy press anxious for a local angle on the conflict, the prospect of a West Coast invasion made great-selling copy. The *Los Angeles Times* ran headlines like "Jap Boat Flashes Message Ashore" and "Caps on Japanese Tomato Plants Point to Air Base."[42] Pretty soon, everyone was getting into the act. Reports of "signals" being sent out from shore to mysterious unknown Japanese boats offshore began flowing in. One widely circulated legend came from someone in Hawaii who heard a dog somewhere along the Oahu coast and thought it was barking in Morse code to an offshore spy ship.[43]

In the Seattle area, the stories were similarly ridiculous. "Arrows of Fire Aim at Seattle" shouted the front-page headline of the *Seattle Times* on December 10. It told of fields in the Port Angeles area, between Seattle and the Pacific Ocean on the Olympic Peninsula, that had been set afire by Japanese farmers in a shape resembling an arrow when viewed from the air; ostensibly, the arrow pointed to the Seattle shipyards and airplane-manufacturing plants, a likely target for incoming bombers. The Seattle *Post-Intelligencer* blared a similar front-page story the next morning. Neither paper carried any subsequent stories about the fires—which investigators soon determined had been set by white men who were clearing land.[44]

Lieutenant General John L. DeWitt, the elderly commander of the West Coast forces, encouraged these fears when he wasn't insisting on them. However, his clamorous appeals for devoting badly needed troops for the defense of the West Coast were dismissed by War Department officials who knew better; to the planners there, preparing an offensive army for operations in Europe and the Pacific, such requests were self-indulgent wastes of their time.[45]

This did not slow DeWitt, who began leading a charge to have all persons of Japanese descent removed from the Pacific coast. As it happened, West Coast politicians were eager to follow suit, and after congressional hearings were held, it was decided that every Japanese person on the coast would be rounded up and shipped to a new location in the interior. The decisive factor was a report issued by DeWitt, who declared the need to do so a matter of national security:

> It therefore follows that along the vital Pacific Coast over 112,000 potential enemies, of Japanese extraction, are at large today. There are indications that these are organized and ready for concerted action at a favorable opportunity. *The very fact that no sabotage has taken place to date is a disturbing and confirming indication that such action will be taken.*[46]

Two months later, every Japanese American along that corridor—indeed, some 110,000 of them—had been rounded up and placed in a concentration camp for the duration of the war.

***

Shortly before Russia's defeat in the Russo-Japanese War, a pamphlet republishing a series of articles purporting to be the minutes of a late-nineteenth-century gathering of world Jewish leaders began appearing in Moscow and elsewhere. Titled *The Protocols of the Seven Elders of Zion*, it claimed to reveal a massive plot by Jews to gradually seize control of the world and destroy Western civilization.

It was a hoax concocted by czarist secret police for the purpose of whipping up hatred of Jews and pogroms against them, since monarchists blamed Jews for their defeat at the hands of the Japanese. In fact, the text was a confabulation of previous texts, some of it straight-up plagiarism of a satire by Maurice Joly titled *Dialogue in Hell Between Machiavelli and Montesquieu*. But it was ingenious in its construction, just vague enough to lack verifiability, but specific and counterintuitive in ways that made the text seem real to gullible readers. And as it emerged, there have been millions of those.[47]

Among them was Henry Ford. Already having demonstrated an inclination toward anti-Semitism, in 1920 the car-making magnate ordered the Michigan newspaper he owned to begin publishing the *Protocols* in serialized installments titled "The International Jew." When it was finished, he collected them into a five-volume set with the same title and sold them for $5 each at Ford car dealerships. He sold thousands of copies.[48]

Ford's sponsorship of the text created a global demand for it, and translations appeared throughout Europe, including in Germany, where it was promptly adopted as a core text of the young National Socialist Party, better known as the Nazis. Adolf Hitler, the party's leader, cited the text regularly in his speeches and later wrote in his book *Mein Kampf* that even though the *Times of London* had exposed the *Protocols* as a hoax as early as 1921, "the important thing is that with positively terrifying certainty they reveal the nature and activity of the Jewish people and expose their inner contexts as well as their ultimate final aims."[49]

Hitler's anti-Semitism was a central aspect of his fascist politics, and as his regime became further entrenched in power in the 1930s, the more actively it pursued his goal of eradicating Jews from German and European society altogether. Combined with his program of *lebensraum*—seizing territory from other European states and "liquidating" its occupants in order to create more "living space" for pure white German Aryans—the end result became known as the Holocaust, the mass killing campaign that used both deadly mobile assassination units and concentration camps to manufacture death on a genocidal level. By the end of World War II and Hitler's defeat, he had killed more than six million Jews, along with a couple million more members of other targeted ethnic groups, particularly Roma, as well as homosexuals and political opponents of the fascist regime.

After the war, the *Protocols* became a banned text in most of Europe and elsewhere, though it could continue to be found in dark corners of the American publishing world where laws prevented it from being banned, but shame had driven it underground. It remained a core text of the remnant far-right movements in the United States, particularly the Ku Klux Klan, the American Nazi Party, and later far-right groups such as the Aryan Nations and the National Alliance.

By the 2000s, even these ideologues were willing to acknowledge the *Protocols* as a forgery, but as with Hitler, that fact seemed irrelevant to them. Ku Klux Klan leader David Duke acknowledged in 2014 that the *Protocols* were fiction, though true like other great novels like *1984* and *Brave New World*: "Although the characters and storyline in both those works are 'fiction,' the idea which underlay both those books was most certainly fact. Thus, they were works of 'fiction'—just like the Protocols of Zion."[50]

It was going to be just a routine business flight. When Kenneth Arnold took off from the airport in Chehalis, Washington, with his little CallAir Model A airplane on June 24, 1947, en route to Yakima on the other side of the Cascade Mountains, things were business as usual until he neared Mount Rainier and spotted a row of flying objects.

They appeared to him to be tracking his rate of speed, about 100 miles per hour, and at times well outpaced him. He later described the objects as being like "flying discs" or "saucers." When he reached Yakima, he told everyone he could about what he had seen, and soon the story was in all the papers around the country. Headlines dubbed them "flying saucers."[51]

Thus began the enduring mystery of unidentified flying objects, aka UFOs. For much of the 1950s and 1960s, the objects spotted by Arnold suddenly were seen seemingly everywhere else in the world as well, by people whose stories were usually less credible and more fantastic with each sighting. People produced photos of "flying saucers" that later turned out to be thrown hubcaps or simply bad retouching jobs.[52]

The sensation spread to Hollywood, which produced science-fiction thrillers like *The Day the Earth Stood Still*, in which an alien emissary arrives on a mission of peace in a disc-shaped spaceship, or conversely *Earth vs. the Flying Saucers*, in which aliens from a dying planet attack Washington, D.C., but are eventually defeated. The airborne saucers remained a sci-fi stereotype for decades afterward, with featured roles in television series like *The Invaders* and *Lost in Space* in the 1960s, and even into the 1990s in the alien-invader movie epic *Independence Day*.

The mystery surrounding the flying saucers never subsided, and speculation about their possible origins not only grew outsized, but eventually metastasized into conspiracy theories, especially as government officials continued to deny their existence and to debunk the claims of their existence with regularity. Combined with random reports that government officials had in fact encountered aliens, or perhaps had alien corpses or other evidence of their existence held in secret, the legend grew into a cottage industry devoted to "exposing the truth" about UFOs.

A key component of the legend included the idea that a cadre of government agents who wear dark business suits and sunglasses as their uniforms—known generically as "men in black"—was primarily responsible for suppression of this "truth." Eventually, Hollywood made use of this as well, with sci-fi television series like *The X Files* and movie franchises like *Men in Black* depicting the exploits of these same government agents in a mostly heroic light.

Another infamous public event—the assassination of President John F. Kennedy in 1963—had similarly sparked a raft of conspiracy theories, especially after the official investigation into the event concluded it had been the act of a single man, despite seemingly contrary evidence. The high levels of uncertainty were piqued by the intense speculation about who was behind the death, with suspicion coming to rest on everyone from the CIA and J. Edgar Hoover of the FBI, to mob bosses angry about Kennedy's anti-gangster policies, and seemingly everything in between. Many of these conspiracy theories were laden with similar tales of sunglasses-wearing men in black suppressing evidence and quietly "suiciding" people who spoke up.[53]

The industry around the UFO phenomenon never entirely went away. The conspiracism it engendered on radio programs like Art Bell's nationally syndicated *Coast to Coast AM* show and in multiple pseudo-documentaries and sensational books readily blended over into other theories suggesting that nefarious government or corporate forces were secretly conspiring to harm or enslave the public in other, often health-related, ways. In particular, the belief that the government had secret cures for cancers locked away and deliberately suppressed or that it was engaged in a variety of plots that were slowly poisoning the population—through fluoridation of the water supply, various food supplements, vaccinations, or even in chemicals in the contrails left behind by jets—became part of the same industry, and often their theories intersected with those involving UFOs or even old anti-Semitic theories.

In the 1980s, for instance, a conspiracy theorist named William Cooper, who in addition to publishing books ran a radio show based in Arizona, published a kind of all-encompassing, hypercomplex metatheory titled *Behold a Pale Horse*. It proposed that JFK's assassination, along with a number of other infamous mysteries, were secretly the doings of Illuminati—who, moreover, were not people at all, but nefarious invading aliens from another planet who were able to disguise themselves by appearing to be human. It also proposed that the *Protocols* were produced by the Illuminati and that one could easily read them as a manual for an alien takeover of the Earth.[54]

Cooper's book and radio show, as it happened, are credited with playing a major role in the early development of the "Patriot" militia movement of the 1990s.[55]

There was another major conspiracy-minded movement of the 1950s that had a lasting impact, though it was aligned politically with the far right of American politics from the beginning: namely, the anti-Communist movement that emerged from the aftermath of World War II and the ensuing "Red Scare" led by Senator Joe McCarthy of Wisconsin.

An earlier Red Scare, between 1917 and 1920 that arose in the wake of the Russian Revolution, was similarly constructed around fears of an international Bolshevik conspiracy with designs on American democracy.[56] It had produced several notable outrages against the Constitution, particularly the passage of the Sedition Act of 1918, which targeted immigrants as potential terrorists, and the so-called Palmer Raids, in which federal authorities rounded up and deported suspected leftist radicals from the Italian and Jewish communities. However, it had been rather short-lived, cooling down especially after the attorney general for whom the raids were named issued a national warning about an attempted coup against the government on May Day 1920 that turned out to be completely false.[57]

The Red Scare that reverberates in American politics even today began taking off in 1947, shortly after Russia and the United States ended their wartime alliance and began the series of mutual hostilities that soon came to be known as the Cold War. This time, there was a round of public hysteria generated in the press about possible Communist spies handing over American military secrets, particularly the recipe for a nuclear bomb. This fear intensified in 1949, when the Soviets successfully tested their first such weapon, and then became feverish in 1950, when a State Department employee named Alger Hiss was arrested and convicted of spying for Russia and a physicist associated with America's own nuclear bomb was exposed for passing key information to the Soviets. The couriers included an American couple named Julius and Ethel Rosenberg, who eventually were executed for spying.[58]

The same year, Senator McCarthy spoke to a gathering of Republican ladies in Wheeling, West Virginia, and brandished a sheet of paper upon which, he declared, were the names of known traitors working for the U.S. government: "I have here in my hand a list of 205—a list of names that were made known to the Secretary of State as being members of the Communist Party and who nevertheless are still working and shaping policy in the State Department," he told them.

The remarks sparked a flurry of national headlines for the senator and thrust him into a leading role among the demagogues who began making hay from the hysteria, which included congressmen like Richard Nixon of California, who served on the House Un-American Activities Committee. Almost overnight, McCarthy became one of the best-known politicians in America and began using his new fame to smear his targets and political opponents. He campaigned that fall for a Republican challenger to one of his Democratic Senate colleagues, claiming that the incumbent—who went on to lose by forty thousand votes—was "protecting Communists" and "shielding traitors."[59]

In 1953, McCarthy became chairman of the relatively mundane Senate Committee on Government Operations, but he managed to twist the investigatory powers of one of its subcommittees into a stage-managed investigation of Communists operating within the U.S. government. He hired a ruthless attorney named Roy Cohn as his chief counsel, and they set about making life hell for a number of government employees, first at the federally owned Voice of America radio network, then at the State Department. Meanwhile, a blacklist produced by the House Un-American Activities Committee condemned hundreds of people working in the entertainment industry in Hollywood, including a large number of well-known actors, directors, and screenwriters, to nearly a decade of unemployment.[60]

McCarthy met his Waterloo, however, when he set out to investigate the U.S. Army in 1954. His Senate subcommittee's hearings were broadcast live on national television, which was still in its infancy. Though McCarthy exploited the heavy exposure for the opportunity to accuse a number of people of aiding the Communist Party, in the end it did not serve McCarthy well: the more people saw of him, the more they came to see him as a reckless bully and a liar.[61]

The culminative incident generally credited with ending his career as a demagogue came when the army's lead attorney, Joseph Welch, responded angrily to McCarthy's insinuation that a young Boston lawyer was also a Communist by saying: "Let us not assassinate this lad further, Senator. You've done enough. Have you no sense of decency, sir, at long last? Have you left no sense of decency?"[62]

At the end of the year, the Senate voted to censure McCarthy. Afterward, he became a pariah in Washington and in the press, especially as he began to drink more than he already had. He died in 1957 from liver failure attributed to his alcoholism.

However, the legacy of the Red Scare remained vibrant and active for the better part of the 1950s and even into the 1960s, as the Cold War proceeded apace. The paranoia, in particular, took on a life of its own thanks to the rise of organizations like the John Birch Society.

Founded in 1958 by candy magnate Robert Welch, the JBS—or "Birchers," as they became better known—immediately picked up McCarthy's cudgel and began beating a broad range of American politicians with it, accusing them of being "soft" on Communism or even "card-carrying members of the Communist Party," as Welch was fond of labeling his opponents, including President Dwight D. Eisenhower, who he described as "a dedicated, conscious agent of the Communist conspiracy."[63]

However, the smears were only the tip of the scapegoating spear that was the Birchers' main enterprise: the real heart of the organization was its conspiracism, which distinguished it from other anti-Communist conservatives, particularly the William F. Buckley contingent that denounced the Society and ridiculed them as "far removed from common sense."[64]

According to Welch, "both the U.S. and Soviet governments are controlled by the same furtive conspiratorial cabal of internationalists, greedy bankers, and corrupt politicians. If left unexposed, the traitors inside the U.S. government would betray the country's sovereignty to the United Nations for a collectivist

New World Order, managed by a 'one-world socialist government.'" Birchers developed a fixation with the UN, whose "real nature," they claimed, "is to build a One World Government." All around the nation, particularly in areas where the society was popular, billboards sprung up with bright blue letters: "Get US Out! of the United Nations."[65]

The society became one of the earliest progenitors of health-related conspiracy theories. First, in the 1950s, many Birchers became involved in protesting the use of fluoride in public water supplies (a health measure that was just then gaining prominence). They argued that it was a secret Communist conspiracy that would surreptitiously inflict a host of ills on an unsuspecting American public.[66]

Perhaps the most incisive portrayal of the John Birch Society's mindset was delivered in a brutal black-comedic satire, Stanley Kubrick's 1963 film *Dr. Strangelove: Or How I Learned to Stop Worrying and Love the Bomb*, about a Bircherite general who sets off the end of the world because of his paranoid beliefs. Trapped in his offices with a hapless British attaché played by Peter Sellers, the cigar-chomping General Jack D. Ripper (Sterling Hayden) explains why he sent an entire wing of nuclear-armed bombers to attack Russia: "I can no longer sit back and allow Communist infiltration, Communist indoctrination, Communist subversion and the international Communist conspiracy to sap and impurify all of our precious bodily fluids." Fluoridation, Ripper explained, was "the most monstrously conceived and dangerous Communist plot we have ever had to face."

The society revived that tradition in the 1970s, when it began promoting claims that an apricot-seed derivative called laetrile was a secret cure for cancer that had been deliberately suppressed by the Federal Drug Administration. The reality was that not only were there no known clinical benefits for cancer patients using the drug in tests, but consuming it actually put them at risk of poisoning from cyanide, which laetrile can release in humans when digested. Nonetheless, the JBS became involved in pro-laetrile campaigns in at least nine states, while the pro-laetrile organization "Committee for Freedom of Choice in Cancer Therapy" had a board almost entirely comprised of people with official ties to the society.[67]

Through the 1960s and 1970s, the society—which largely remained on the fringe of the national conversation due to their marginalization by mainstream pundits—mostly recruited new members with surreptitious evening dinners that ended with filmstrip presentations and literature, often of leading local businessmen, with varying degrees of success. It was a slow recruitment strategy.

Their numbers didn't flourish, but the society's quiet influence remained steady over the years, particularly in rural areas. By the 1980s, they had largely vanished from the political scene—but the roots they had created in the preceding decades came springing back to life in a new form: militias.[68]

Chapter 5

A BRAVE NEW WORLD ORDER

The Militia of Montana was always kind of a low-tech operation. John Trochmann, the founder and chief guru, liked it that way. Their meetings were generally held in little community meeting halls, granges, schoolrooms, small venues with a few dozen people in attendance. Although it was the 1990s and computers with PowerPoint were still years away, Trochmann in any event preferred using old-style overhead projectors that used full-page transparencies, and he would shuffle through them one by one, laying out his case.[1]

The room was always darkened, and the glow from the projector below gave Trochmann's face an ominous appearance, which fit well with the mood of his presentation.

Trochmann's top page read: "Enemies, Foreign and Domestic: Part I—The Problem." The next sheet was the cover of a military journal with a story about international armed forces cooperating under United Nations auspices, the illustration showing a number of nations' flags, including the Stars and Stripes, all subordinately positioned beneath a UN flag.

So would begin a sojourn for the audience that approached two hours in length, as Trochmann trod through 190 pages of "documentation," each page a strand in a web the bearded man spins, all pieces of a puzzle Trochmann claimed as proof of a conspiracy to destroy the United States. It was not uncommon to hear snoring from the frequently elderly audience. The message Trochmann was trying to convey seemed shocking enough, but the delivery often turned into a drone.

The New World Order, he told them, is a shadowy one-world-government group that conspires to put an end to the U.S. Constitution by subsuming it under the "Communist" United Nations. Conspirators included the president (then Bill Clinton), the speaker of the house, and most financial and political leaders around the world.

The nightmarish world government Trochmann envisioned would be a population-controlling totalitarian regime. Guns would be confiscated. Urban gangs like the Bloods and the Crips would be deployed to conduct house-to-house searches and round up resisters. Thousands of citizens would be shipped off to concentration camps and liquidated, all in the name of reducing the population.

The conspirators' evil designs, he said, had already surfaced in significant ways:

- Gun control. "What is it about the word 'infringe' they don't understand?" Trochmann asked, referring to the Second Amendment, which he believed completely protects people's right to own any weapon they want—even a missile launcher or tank.
- The botched federal police raids at Ruby Ridge, Idaho, and Waco, Texas, in 1992 and 1994 respectively. "These things prove our government is out of control," he would say. Moreover, Trochmann claimed they were harbingers of a future government crackdown on law-abiding citizens.
- Troop and equipment movements throughout the country. Trochmann flashes pictures of armored vehicles, tanks, missiles, all kinds of military hardware—some marked with UN symbols or lettering, some with red Russian stars. These pictures are sent in from all over the country, Trochmann says, and the government can't explain them.
- "Unconstitutional" executive orders. These range from the inclusion of U.S. troops among UN forces in Somalia, Haiti, and Bosnia under Presidents Bush and Clinton to seemingly innocent preparations for disaster under the Federal Emergency Management Administration (FEMA). All, says Trochmann, are meant to undermine the U.S. Constitution.
- Black helicopters. Reports of these black, unmarked choppers with seemingly nefarious intentions, harassing and striking fear into the public, were becoming more common than UFO sightings, and Trochmann had dozens of grainy photographs he'd show his audiences. These choppers, he said, were being used for training now. What they're training for, he said, was rounding up citizens and putting them in . . .
- Planned concentration camps. Trochmann came up with a list of about two hundred sites around the country where he claimed such mass detention centers were being constructed under the authority of the Federal Emergency Management Administration and made a map for his audiences. They would nod sagely.
- Floods, hurricanes, and other natural disasters, he said, were manmade. Government conspirators are manipulating the world's weather (using, Trochmann claimed, technology at an Alaska radio project called HAARP), causing

all these horrible weather patterns that affect crop production around the world. The intent, he said, is to induce food shortages, which would become a pretext for imposing martial law. That, he'd say, is when they'll start rounding people up.

"It's going to end up like this," Trochmann told his audiences. "The most mild and calm of scenarios will be: 'Would you like to eat today? Give me your guns. Would you like your children back from school today? Give me your guns.' That's the mildest of versions you'll see."[2]

Trochmann toured the Pacific Northwest and the Inland West for much of the 1990s, delivering these talks in a fairly uniform fashion, traveling to places like Mount Vernon, Washington; Klamath Falls, Oregon; Orem, Utah; or Jordan, Montana—anywhere that had a base of active "Patriots" who would invite him to speak at their local community centers. He'd collect a nominal speaking fee and then sell books and survival gear and T-shirts at the tables set up around the speaking venue.

What was essential, however, was getting people to sign up for Militia of Montana (MOM) catalogs. Once he had them on his mailing list, he was able to sell even greater mounds of gear and goods through the catalogs themselves, which featured a buckskin-clad sniper firing from a treetop with an ancient rifle. It fit with Trochmann's fantasy of a guerrilla resistance in the manner of old colonial-era combatants, duking it out with the federal government from their mountain retreats in the West, which he sold relentlessly to his readers.

Inside the catalogs, Trochmann's first few pages were often devoted to the dozens of VHS videos he sold to his fellow Patriot movement true believers, featuring lectures given by himself and dozens of other leading movement figures, men such as Mark "from Michigan" Koernke, MOM spokesman Bob Fletcher, and even mainstream political figures like Representative Helen Chenoweth, the Idaho congresswoman who toured the far-right "Patriot" chicken-dinner circuit speaking on behalf of the "Sagebrush Rebellion" in the years before she first won election in 1994.

The following pages featured a full library of books, including a variety of "survival" manuals that suggested forming independent "sovereign" communities even before the apocalyptic downfall of society they all expected to happen soon. Some were simple army survival manuals. Other books detailed conspiracy theories, such as the claim that the Federal Reserve Bank was the nexus of the New World Order plot, or another detailing the satanic origins of Planned Parenthood, or the book devoted to Hillary Clinton's witch's coven. And at the back of the catalog were various kinds of survival gear, including gas masks and hazmat suits of dubious provenance, as well as food-preservation systems and other items designed to come in handy during an apocalypse.

I also encountered Trochmann's beliefs in weather manipulation when I interviewed him in Montana at a little roadside log-cabin café. Federal conspirators, he assured me, had already put the mechanisms in place for the big coup. "Most of this Emergency Powers Act that we've been studying that they put together. . . . They have to have a replacement for war to get down to those levels and still retain the legitimacy of power. What might that be? Catastrophes to deal with? We know that electromagnetically, they control our weather now. There's all kinds of documentation of that. We've got documentation right from the United Nations that say that people have to get a permit to change the weather somewhere."[3]

On the big-screen TV behind us, pictures from a national broadcast showed a hurricane slamming into Florida, and an announcer displayed the storm's path on a map.

Trochmann looked at the owner of the café, and they exchanged knowing glances. "See the hurricane?" Trochmann asked him. "Boy, that's really late, isn't it?" The owner nodded.

You mean, I asked, this is part of the weather-control pattern?

"Sure," Trochmann said. "Naples, Florida, got hit at the same time Naples, Idaho, did."

Coincidence, maybe?

"Yeah, right," he said. "And I have another bridge for sale for you."

This kind of selective credulity—a willingness to believe the most insane, cockamamie nonsense if it fits with or, better yet, helped open another dimension on the nefarious nature of the conspiracy—became the trademark of the 1990s Patriot movement and how the world of conspiracy theories was transformed by it. Evidence—the real, factual, hard evidence that was the meat and potatoes of JFK and UFO conspiracy theories—was replaced with conjecture whose main value was not in its plausibility but in how it further deepened the universe of conspiracies. Over time, this conjecture grew ever wilder and ever less plausible.

However, the movement suffered a permanent and nearly fatal setback in April 1995 when a Gulf War veteran and avid Patriot named Tim McVeigh set off a truck bomb in front of the federal Murrah Building in Oklahoma City on the anniversary of the botched Waco raid, killing 168 people, including toddlers in a day-care center. The next summer, another Patriot terrorist, Eric Rudolph, set off a backpack bomb at the Atlanta Olympics then, as the FBI and investigators barked up numerous wrong trees, went on a bombing spree over the next two years that included a gay bar and two abortion providers.[4]

The militia movement before then had spread like wildfire through rural and exurban America. Trochmann's operation was the best known and most prominent, and it sold the three-pack of conspiracies, ideology, and gear through its catalog as it circulated mailing lists around the United States. Militias were especially strong in the Midwest, around Michigan and Mark Koernke's organizing, and they were readily adopted as a concept by enthusiasts of the neo-Confederate ideologies in the South and the nativist border-watching movement building slowly in the Southwest.[5]

But after 1995, it went into a steep decline, in large part because of its association with domestic terrorism. However, the new brand of conspiracism it engendered remained very much alive, thanks in large part to a singular Patriot movement adherent and former John Birch Society member with a little radio show out of Austin, Texas, named Alex Jones.

Jones first cut his radio chops doing Art Bell–style broadcasts focusing on theories about the Waco raid, which he naturally declared to be evidence of a looming police state. After the Oklahoma City bombing, he shifted gears into fresh territory, promoting the claim—first suggested to me by John Trochmann when I called him up the day after the bombing, even before McVeigh's arrest—that McVeigh's act had been a "false flag" operation designed to give the government an opportunity to crack down on the Patriot movement.[6]

Jones continued to run with this theory, along with a number of others, mostly regarding the United Nations and its programs for the next several years. What he actually specialized in was regurgitating Trochmann's old theories: first it was the FEMA concentration camps (which Jones still promotes to this day), and then he picked up Trochmann's HAARP weather-manipulation theories and ran with those; again, he still trots these out from time to time.

Most of all, he tuned in to a number of Bircherite theories about the health industry and cancer cures, along the lines of the old laetrile claims but now updated to reflect new trends in cancer treatment and understanding of consumer demands. These included theories about the introduction of toxins into the atmosphere from jet contrails (renamed "chemtrails") deliberately tainted by government conspirators with carcinogens and other body-altering chemicals.[7] Some of these, according to one of Jones's later theories, are turning frogs gay.[8]

As the 1990s drew to a close, he and many others on the far-right conspiracy fringe began pumping apocalyptic fears about the coming year 2000, primarily focused on a supposed bug inherent in all software that would result in massive data corruption at the stroke of midnight December 31, 1999.

This "Y2K bug" was a real thing, and software companies around the world scrambled to fix it. But in the meantime, a plenitude of theories—mostly along the lines that the fixes would fail and all of America's banking and electrical infrastructure would fail and the world would shortly erupt in the flames of mass chaos—began proliferating, particularly on the Internet. Helping lead that charge, of course, was Alex Jones.

As the clock wound down toward New Year's Eve, Jones's broadcast became increasingly frenetic, not to mention driven by patently (and proven) false information, all seemingly aimed at drumming up a fever pitch of hysteria.[9] The chief demon in all this, the leader of the New World Order, according to Jones, was none other than Russian president Vladimir Putin:

> Cash machines are failing in Britain and now other European countries. They're finding large amounts of explosives in France. Vladimir Putin, who is known as Vladimir the Ruthless, using all his profanity on national TV, you name it. We won't read the profanity here but we've got it—this person is on an unbelievable power trip and resembles a demon. He is a creature of the IMF and the World Bank and International Communism. He is a former KGB head and this information is vital, ladies and gentleman.
>
> We're seeing the New World Order really come out in full force. More wars than have been in the past fifty years are going on right now. The war in Chechnya is raging in Rosney with reports of hundreds to thousands dying.
>
> Twenty to forty thousand civilians trapped in the city. Russian hinds are being shot down, tanks are being blown to bits. Massive grad unguided rocket attacks are being launched from the city indiscriminately right now. Air and artillery bombardments as well. It's absolutely out of control, it is pandemic, ladies and gentlemen.

That wasn't all. The whole FEMA camps thing was coming true, he told his audience.

> The occupational government in Washington, D.C., has set up a huge $50 million command bunker hooked into all the FEMA boxes that can take over all the shortwave broadcast and commercial AM and FM stations, as well as television broadcast stations. And we hope they do not activate that, ladies and gentlemen.
>
> Police and military are on high alert, running around, looking for supposed boogie men and terrorists under every rock. Military are highly visible now. Yes, ladies and gentlemen, there are trains of military equipment moving into Austin. Two nights ago, on Wednesday night, Fox News reported that the airport will be used as a massive holding facility for troublemakers or rioters here in Austin—that has no history of riots.[10]

Not a word of this, of course, was true. And on January 1, 2000, everyone woke up and went to work and brushed their teeth and their electricity was fine and the traffic signals were fine and their bank accounts were fine and everything mostly went along as normal, since the software companies had done as promised and fixed the bug.

Meanwhile, the people who had listened to Alex Jones and John Trochmann and the multitude of Patriot cohorts and had followed their advice to prepare for the upcoming apocalypse by salting away stores of beans and rice and water and other foods (especially the expired canned military rations that Trochmann specialized in) were left wondering what the hell to do with them now.

The reputation of Jones and his "Prison Planet" radio operation—soon to be renamed "Infowars"—lingered in a kind of twilight zone until September 11, 2001, when the worst terrorist attack on American soil in history was perpetrated in New York and Washington, D.C., and more than three thousand Americans were killed, which also opened up a brand new dimension for the world of conspiracy theorists.[11]

Jones, naturally, was among the first to leap into the breach, claiming that it was all a false flag, perhaps perpetrated by Israeli intelligence, perhaps by the Bush administration itself—who knew?—but they, Jones and his army of followers, had to investigate! Within hours—and before the dust from the collapsing twin towers had even settled—the theories about the secret perpetrators of the attacks began to mount and swell into a mind-boggling pile-on.[12]

Over the next several years, Jones became the leading peddler of theories generated by what they called the "9/11 Truth Movement," but who became known best by their short handle, Truthers. Initially the ranks of the movement were filled with a large number of far-left conspiracists who wanted to blame the Bush administration for the attacks, but these voices over time were minimized and drowned out by the Infowars and other far-right conspiracists who blamed the New World Order, for whom Bush and his White House were merely pawns.[13]

As time went on, the theories became more elaborate: There were no planes that crashed into the Pentagon; that was an illusion the conspirators created to cover for the bomb that actually was dropped on the place. The towers in New York couldn't have collapsed because the melting point of steel is much higher than burning jet fuel could have created. Over time, as they multiplied and turned inward upon themselves, often feeding a frenzy of competition among the theorists, the name "Truther" became the essence of ridiculousness.[14]

Certainly, mainstream conservatives—despite taking on a starkly authoritarian strain to their rhetoric as well during the invasions of Afghanistan and then Iraq, particularly—maintained a deep divide from conspiracy theorists like Jones, since Infowars' biggest target at the time was George W. Bush. Infowars' audience kept building during these years to numbers in the multimillions. But pundits like Rush Limbaugh and Bill O'Reilly—the real voices of the conservative establishment—made their loathing of the Alex Joneses of the world unquestionably clear during the Bush years. It took the candidacy, and then the presidency, of a black man to change all that.

In the meantime, the nativist elements of the American Right, many of them with deep connections to those same mainstream Republicans, were busy building their own alternative universe of conspiracy theories about immigration down on the American borderlands. This world, too, involved militias, mixed along with classic nativist rhetoric about an "invasion."

The idea of a citizens' border watch grew out of the longtime embrace by the radical right of vigilante violence, à la the Ku Klux Klan. Indeed, the very first such operation was organized in 1977 by David Duke and Tom Metzger, both longtime figures in the Klan of the 1970s and beyond.[15]

They called it "Klan Border Watch," and all it really amounted to was a photo opportunity featuring a couple of carfuls of white men in Klan robes driving around the border crossing at San Ysidro, California, and Duke vowing that vast numbers of men now would begin patrolling entire stretches of the border under his command. No such force existed, of course, and no one heard about Duke's outfit again, though Metzger continued running racist stunts along the border for decades afterward.[16]

The concept gained new life in the 1990s with the rise of the small cell militia concept as part of a larger "leaderless resistance" against the federal government. The main progenitor of the concept was a California man named Glenn Spencer, who ran an outfit called American Patrol that claimed Latinos wanted to reclaim the U.S. Southwest for Mexico as part of *Reconquista*—that is, to revive the legacy of Spanish conquerors.[17]

The whole thing, of course, was an elaborate conspiracy theory spun, as so many such fantasies are, out of a thin thread of factual truth woven with reams of fabricated nonsense: A small claque of Hispanic radicals in the 1960s had suggested creating a new Latino homeland they called "Aztlan" and even made maps outlining their dreams, which then faded mostly into the mists of history until Glenn Spencer discovered them and began trotting them out to his fellow nativists as proof that all these Latino immigrants represented a conspiracy to invade the United States surreptitiously and then take it down at a given signal. (Japanese immigrants of the 1920s certainly were familiar with these kinds of suggestions.)

In 1999, Spencer put it like this: "The consul general says Mexico is reconquering California. A Mexican intellectual suggests that anyone who doesn't like Mexicans should leave California. What else do you need to hear? RECONQUISTA IS REAL. . . . EVERY ILLEGAL ALIEN IN OUR NATION MUST BE DEPORTED IMMEDIATELY. . . . IF WE CAN BOMB THE TV STA-

TION IN BELGRADE [in the former Yugoslavia] WE CAN SHUT DOWN [U.S. Spanish-language stations] TELEMUNDO AND UNIVISION."[18]

Around the same time, Spencer's Voices of Citizens Together (VCT) released a video titled *Bonds of Our Nation* hawking this conspiracy theory: a Mexican invasion is racing across America "like wildfire," Spencer told his viewers, lamenting that there were now drugs in Iowa and gang takeovers in Nevada, not to mention "traitors" in the Democratic Party, the Catholic Church, and among the "corporate globalists," which many Patriots were now using as the euphemism for the New World Order.[19]

The video is a litany of vile racist tropes dating back to the nineteenth century: these immigrants—Latinos from south of the border this time—were bringing crime, drugs, squalor, and "immigration via the birth canal," threatening to overwhelm white people and decent American civilization with their impure filth, their disease, their stupidity, their laziness. Mexicans, he warned, are a "cultural cancer" from which Western civilization "must be rescued." They are threatening the birthright left by the white colonists who "earned the right to stewardship of the land."

And this invasion, he claimed, was not any accident. It was a well-planned conspiracy to bring America to its knees. Working in league with Communist Latino activists and their allies in America, Spencer claimed, Mexico was secretly deploying a little-known but highly effective stratagem "to defeat America." Spencer claimed these conspirators had already succeeded in seizing control of California.

Spencer named this conspiracy the "Plan de Aztlan."

"Some scoff at the idea of a Mexican plan of conquest," the video's narrator says, then warns that a "hostile force on our border" engaging in "demographic war" against the United States threatens to overwhelm whites with sheer numbers: "Mexico is moving to capture the American Southwest."

Spencer sent every member of Congress a copy of this videotape and had it delivered to a number of congressmembers by Betina McCann, the fiancée of his friend neo-Nazi Steven Barry.[20]

"If the Border Patrol had done its job, using the technology that is available to us, we could stop these people," Spencer said in an appearance on the *Donahue* show. "This is an invasion of the United States!"[21]

Spencer moved his operations to Arizona in the early 2000s and renamed it American Border Patrol. That was when things started to take off for him and his border-militia concept. Taking Spencer's cue, Casey Nethercott, another Arizona resident, started a border-watch operation called Ranch Rescue. They developed legal problems in short order.

Nethercott, who had done prison time in California for assault in the 1990s, and some of his fellow Ranch Rescue members in 2003 assaulted two Salvadoran migrants who had crossed the border on foot and wound up on a ranch where the nativist border watchers operated. The migrants were held at gunpoint, and one of them was pistol-whipped and attacked by a Rottweiler. With the assistance of the Southern Poverty Law Center (SPLC), the migrants sued their attackers and won a $1 million civil judgment against Ranch Rescue.[22]

A California schoolteacher who had migrated to the Arizona desert town of Tombstone, finding employment as an actor in the daily reenactment of the gunfight at the OK Corral in the town's tourist center, decided to join the action. In 2002 he announced he too was organizing a border militia, hoping to stop illegal border crossings in the area south of Tombstone. His name was Chris Simcox, and initially he named his outfit the Tombstone Militia, but after a while he adopted a more media-friendly name: Minuteman Civil Defense Corps.

What really motivated Simcox, he was eager to tell you, was border security: his belief that more 9/11-style terrorists were secretly sneaking over our borders with Mexico because, as anyone could see, it's actually very easy to do so if you don't mind hiking for dozens, if not hundreds, of miles in open searing desert. He believed "globalists" were conspiring with government officials to leave the door open for this Trojan horse disguised as immigrant workers.[23]

What was also clear was both Simcox's overweening paranoia, as well as the potential for real violence that ran as an undercurrent in everything he did. Simcox was insistent that immigrants were providing cover for terrorists crossing the border.

"It is frightening to think that just one terrorist hiding among thousands of illegal immigrants who come across the border each day could easily carry chemical, biological or even nuclear materials into the U.S.," Simcox told a reporter in 2005. "At this point, it's not a question of 'if' but of 'when.'"

Naturally, translating this paranoia into government action was the entire purpose of his organization. "While officials are talking, Minutemen are acting," Simcox pronounced. "They need to put our money where their mouth is, and start doing something about our borders."

Simcox's paranoia also made him volatile: "Take heed of our weapons because we're going to defend our borders by any means necessary," he told an audience in 2003. "There's something very fishy going on at the border. The Mexican army is driving American vehicles—but carrying Chinese weapons. I have personally seen what I can only believe to be Chinese troops."[24]

This became the cornerstone of the right-wing belief—eventually mainstreamed by the Republican Party—that national security is utterly dependent on immigration police and that border crossers represent a significant potential terror threat.

For Simcox and the Minutemen, the rubric of reason for the "citizen border watches" they organized all revolved around "national security"—at least when the TV cameras were on. When they were off, it was a different story: Minute-men border watchers were fond of explaining in private to people they thought were fellow participants that the best solution to stopping "the invasion" (as they liked to call it) of Latino immigrants they hoped to catch in the act was to start shooting one or two of them.

One of them even explained it on camera to a documentarian once: "No, we ought to be able to shoot the Mexicans on sight, and that would end the prob-lem. . . . After two or three Mexicans are shot, they'll stop crossing the border. And they'll take their cows home, too."[25]

In 2004, a California nativist named Jim Gilchrist heard Simcox being interviewed on a right-wing radio program and got the idea to make the border watch a national callout that would last for a month on the border. He contacted Simcox and the Minuteman project was started.[26]

It all came together in a big media event in April 2005 that really only lasted about a week but drew tons of national TV coverage in the border area south of Tombstone. About the third week into what was supposed to be a month-long affair, everyone had pulled out. Simcox and Gilchrist, it turned out, hated each other and barely were able to maintain a façade for the first couple of weeks. Near the end of it, the Minutemen founders announced they were splitting into two separate organizations.[27]

There was always an obvious problem with the claim that the Minutemen were about "border security": if that was their chief concern, then why weren't they focusing their efforts on the three thousand–plus miles of border the country shares with Canada? After all, when it comes to terrorists crossing our borders with intent to bomb—not merely entering the United States via airport with false papers, as the 9/11 plotters did—the only known case fitting that description was on the Canadian border: in 1999, when "Millennial Bomber" Ahmed Ressam was caught in Port Angeles, Washington, with a carful of bomb-making material and plans for striking Los Angeles in hand. The Ressam case is particularly instructive, because it revealed that—in contrast to Mexico, where no al-Qaeda cells have been known to exist—there exists an established network of Islamist operatives in Canada.[28]

Simcox, of course, had an answer for that: within a year of the Minuteman Project's national debut, he would be organizing citizen watches along the Ca-nadian border, as well, most notably in Washington State near the crossing at Blaine. That didn't turn out too well, either.[29]

It was, first of all, a mere smokescreen, as reporters found when they ven-tured out to the Canada border watches. No one was out to catch terrorists sneaking over the border (which, after all, comprised only a six-foot-wide ditch in some places); they were there to catch reporters who would dutifully repeat their "border security" schtick—which in turn became the common way for nativists to describe their chief concern when it came to immigration. It sounded innocuous and devoid of ethnic xenophobia, when it was in truth neither.[30]

Because if you spent any time with these Canada border watchers, you pretty quickly ascertained that what had them agitated was not skilled white Canadian laborers sneaking over the border through the ports (which is actually fairly common) but Latino immigrants sneaking over the Mexico border. Those were the "illegal immigrants" they were out demonstrating against.

"Border security" was just a verbal façade pasted over the real source of these nativists' anxieties. It was a coded phrase for the underlying intention: "Keep out the brown people."

Strikingly, this rhetoric gradually became embedded both in conservative rhetoric and later, under a Donald Trump administration, into official government policy. Republican politicians during the tenure of President Barack Obama refused to advance comprehensive immigration reform—the only sensible long-term solution to the problem—on the dubious grounds that such reform needs to wait until after the border is fully and completely secured. It's a familiar saw: "We need to secure the border before we can pass reform."

Moreover, it will at best put only a dent in the problem. That's because about 40 percent of all undocumented immigrants come here legally to begin with, through various kinds of visas, and then simply never leave. Another significant percentage of them arrives through human smuggling operations that are not deterred by fences.[31]

As Representative Henry Cuellar, D-Texas, told a *Forbes* reporter: "Simply stated, a fence is a 14th century solution to a 21st century problem."[32]

Moreover, insisting on emplacing "border security" before providing a sane and legal path to citizenship for millions of immigrants is a classic case of putting the cart before the horse. Border security is realistic only when one's borders are not overwhelmed, and it can't be achieved until the conditions that overwhelmed the Mexico border—particularly the trade policies that damaged the Mexican economy and drove millions of people out of work there, along with antiquated immigration laws and policies ill-suited for a modern nation competing in a twenty-first-century global economy—are brought under control.

Current immigration laws and policies, however, are both chaotic and manifestly inadequate, and that's because the toxic brand of politics practiced by the Minutemen led inevitably to the failure of the existing system. The border-militia movement itself also foundered, split in the years after the big 2005 Arizona demonstration by its own innate toxicity, amid egotistical turf wars and accusations of financial fraud and mismanagement. It finally crumbled apart after a movement leader named Shawna Forde (who first joined during those Canada border watches) led a home-invasion robbery on the Arizona border that resulted in the murders of an Arivaca man and his nine-year-old daughter in 2009.[33] Other Minutemen and border watchers have, since then, been embroiled in even more criminality and mayhem, including another murderous rampage in 2012 in which a neo-Nazi border-watch leader in Arizona gunned down his girlfriend and her family.[34]

Perhaps the final fitting coda for the whole Minutemen episode came in 2015, when Chris Simcox himself was arrested and eventually convicted on multiple counts of child molestation involving young girls under the age of ten, one of them being his own daughter. So much for keeping American families safe.[35]

It didn't take long for the white supremacists to come crawling out of the woodwork after Barack Obama announced his candidacy for the presidency in February 2007. By June, a Ku Klux Klan leader named Railston Loy (he went by "Ray Larsen") warned that the black senator from Illinois was a likely target for assassination: "Well, I'm not going to have to worry about him, because somebody else down South is going to take him out," he said. "If that man is elected president, he'll be shot sure as hell."[36]

Neither Obama nor the rest of the country took those warnings much to heart, and he was indeed elected president a year or so later. As his candidacy had gained momentum, however, so did a kind of parallel reaction among far-right conspiracists, who—failing any actual successful plots against Obama—turned to their old standby weapon: conspiracy theories.

Both the Internet and right-wing media—particularly Fox News—became riddled with the spurious claims about Obama that had been circulating well before he had even announced his candidacy, including charges dating back to 2004 that he was secretly a Muslim. Not only did these old smears resurface, new ones were generated partially from them: accusations that Obama was actually a black radical, beholden to an extremist black Chicago pastor named Jeremiah Wright, got full airings not just on Fox News but on CNN and every other mainstream network. Eventually, it became clear there was no truth there.[37]

To the eternal frustration of the people generating them, that proved true of pretty much every other conspiracy theory cooked up during the 2008 campaign to prove Barack Obama a crook or a fraud or a radical Muslim. For a while, theorists claimed that Michelle Obama had used the word "whitey" in a talk that was taped—though no such tape ever surfaced.[38] A photoshopped image that was nonetheless widely believed and distributed made Barack into a cigarette-smoking Black Panther. He was rumored to have refused to say the pledge or to wear an American flag pin, none of it true.[39]

It was during these years that Alex Jones's Infowars operation—which was control room central for the conspiracy-theorist world—came into its own as an online media giant. In 2011, it was estimated that, with the website's ten million monthly viewers, its reach exceeded that of established firms like *The Economist* and *Newsweek*, not to mention that the reach of his radio show now outdid both Rush Limbaugh and Glenn Beck.[40]

The spread of anti-Obama conspiracism was bolstered by the arrival on the cultural scene of the Tea Party: an ostensibly "grassroots" conservative resistance to the Obama administration that, for its first six months or so of existence, was actually propped up by a combination of right-wing corporate organizing funds and extremely heavy promotion on Fox News and other right-wing media, which led to mainstream news organizations dutifully following suit. Initially Tea Party gatherings helped the right gum up the works on health-care reform (with, predictably, such conspiratorial claims as Sarah Palin's accusation that Democrats were planning to create "death panels" to decide who lived and who died), but once that effort failed and Obama's signature Affordable Care Act was passed, the corporate money withered away, and the TV interest dried up, too. The Tea Party notion of an organized resistance to the Democratic presidency—already festooned with "Don't Tread on Me" banners lifted straight from the Patriot movement of the 1990s—became a more genuinely grassroots movement, spreading into the rural areas, away from the TV cameras, where the far right was already well organized.[41]

Within a year or so, the Tea Party had evolved into a new, even more reactionary phenomenon: the revival of "Patriot" militia movement ideas.[42] Outside groups such as the Oath Keepers—who recruit veterans and law enforcement officers into an organization built around conspiratorial claims about imminent government takeovers and gun confiscations—and the "Three Percenters," who see themselves as the vanguard of a "second American Revolution," attached themselves to the Tea Party at its national gatherings and brought a disturbing militant edge to the events.[43]

After being largely dormant during the George W. Bush years, the Patriot militia movement began to reemerge even before Obama took office: after hitting a post-9/11 low of 131 militia groups counted by the Southern Poverty Law Center in 2007, they suddenly returned to life in 2009 with 512, ultimately reaching an all-time high of 1,360 such antigovernment groups in 2012.[44]

So even after Obama was inaugurated as president, the conspiracism didn't slow down—and actually became worse. The belief that Obama was secretly a Muslim simmered among Republicans quietly during the next eight years, gaining popularity especially among the party's evangelical Christian bloc. By the end of his tenure in 2016, some 70 percent of Republicans believed it.

This belief was also burnished by what became the eventual centerpiece of the web of conspiracy theories built around Obama's presidency: the "birther" theory, which arose from the bogus claim that the birth certificate the candidate had presented to both federal officials and later to the press proving his birth in the state of Hawaii in 1961 to an American mother was somehow inadequate (even though it was the same form any other candidate from Hawaii would present as proof of birth on American soil, a constitutional requirement). They claimed it was merely the "short form," and began demanding to see the "long form."[45]

Underlying the birther theory was similarly spurious information suggesting that Obama had actually been born in Kenya (his father's homeland) or that he had forsaken his American citizenship while attending school in Indonesia as a boy (also false). Yet despite each of these theories being sequentially disproven, the legend lived on, along with demands that Obama reveal his true, long-form birth certificate. The signs demanding this document were commonly seen at Tea Party gatherings.

Into this breach stepped Donald Trump.

Trump really had only peripheral contact with the sketchy world of conspiracy theories before 2011, but as with everything else the publicity-hungry tycoon did, he leapt aboard the birther conspiracy bandwagon that year with remarkable gusto. With little previous reference to interest in the subject—but a March poll showing him leading among potential Republican candidates—that April, he told reporters he had "looked into" the questions about Obama's birth certificate and that he now believed "there is a big possibility" the president was in violation of the Constitution.[46]

"I'd like to have him show his birth certificate," he said. "And to be honest with you, I hope he can."

When there was a backlash to the remarks, he doubled down and began talking about sending investigators to Hawaii to "look into it." It made him a hot guest on all the TV news talk shows, and he disingenuously proceeded as though there was no racial component to his challenge of the president's credentials, in spite of the claims about Obama's previously presented birth certificate being entirely spurious.

It became such a hot topic, both on network talk shows and on the Internet, that President Obama—who at the time was working furiously to get a budget resolution passed through the House—requested Hawaii officials to release his "long form" certificate, which showed exactly the same information as the short version but with some more details, including the hospital in Honolulu where he was born.

Of course, this was not enough for the conspiracists. It never is enough. In a matter of hours, Alex Jones and his cohorts were publishing claims that the long form, too, was in fact entirely bogus. Within days, their verdict had spread through most of the hard-core Obama-hating right, and it became accepted wisdom. Trump, meanwhile, harrumphed—after being humiliated by Obama at the White House Correspondents dinner a few days following the long form's release—that he still "wasn't sure" that it was real. Within a week or so, he too was claiming it was bogus.[47]

What few people realized at the time, however, was that in addition to the kooky conspiracist right all leaping aboard the birther bandwagon, they were simultaneously being joined by most of the extremists on the racist radical right, particularly white nationalists and neo-Nazis. These racist elements, as time went along, became some of the most ardent and virulent promoters of the theories, particularly at racist forums like Stormfront, as well as emerging open message boards like 4chan and Reddit, where open white nationalists could post at will without fear of censorship. And it was in these realms that the movement that became known as the alt-right was born.

Trump ultimately chose not to run for president in 2011 and more or less lay low for the next three years, occasionally popping up to promote his friend Sheriff Joe Arpaio's bizarre Arizona-to-Hawaii "investigation" of Obama's birth certificate, as Arpaio kept insisting he had proven the long form a hoax, which of course he never actually had.[48]

Nonetheless, Trump's name kept turning up high in polls speculating about possible presidential candidates in 2015, and when he announced his candidacy in June of that year, he did it with his usual race-baiting gusto: denouncing Mexican immigrants as "rapists" and vowing to deport them all, he almost immediately attracted the support of the nativist anti-immigrant factions, as well as many of the white nationalists who had attached themselves to that movement. Indeed, nearly every SPLC-designated hate group (there were about twenty of them) that supported Trump during the 2016 presidential campaign actually announced their fervid support for his candidacy within a month after he had announced, in August 2015, his initial, draconian deport-all-twelve-million-undocumented immigration policy (its language was later softened for general-election consumption).[49]

Conspiracism was reaching a fever pitch that summer, too, with Alex Jones playing no small role. The hysteria over Jade Helm reached its height in mid-July that year, and it seemed to just fit with the mood of the times.

Certainly, Trump's campaign positively bubbled with conspiracism: Hillary Clinton, his nemesis, was portrayed as part of an "elite" who hated the white voters Trump cultivated, and he frequently referenced conspiracies to "rig the election." At one point, he appeared on Alex Jones's Infowars program and embraced him verbally: "Your reputation is amazing. I will not let you down," Trump told him.[50]

As the election rolled along, Jones's conspiratorial fanaticism reached extraordinary levels. Late that summer, he went on a rant claiming that Clinton and Obama were, in fact, demons from hell, quite literally. He told his audience that they reeked of sulphur and that others couldn't stand to be around them. Hillary, in particular, inspired his visceral, purple-faced loathing.

"That's a frickin' demon!" he screamed. "We're gonna have President Linda Blair, people, and I'm not gonna go along with it!" He looked like the veins in his neck were going to burst.[51]

Near the election's end, conspiracists poring over a raft of stolen emails from Clinton campaign official John Podesta's computer and released in late October by Wikileaks discovered what they claimed were clues of an elaborate child kidnapping-and-sex ring being run by a powerful cadre attached to the Democratic Party and Clinton, as well as Obama. According to these alleged clues, this global pedophilia ring—which purportedly traded stolen children and transported them around the world so that powerful people could have sex with them and then dispose of them afterward—was run by Hillary and her evil cohorts out of a dungeon that happened to be located in the basement of a pizza parlor in Washington, D.C., called Comet Ping Pong.[52]

This became known as the Pizzagate conspiracy theory, and it spread like wildfire among the Hillary-hating right, despite the fact that she had lost the election and was no longer a serious political threat to them.

Naturally, there was no dungeon at Comet Ping Pong, nor even a basement, as a gunman from North Carolina who insisted he was only there with his semiautomatic rifle to "personally investigate" the restaurant during lunch hour one day in December 2016 discovered when he blasted several rounds into a locked door in hope of finding it. It turned out to be a broom closet. The man was arrested.[53]

This certainly did not stop the theory from spreading. Indeed, each round of evidence that the theory and claims of a global pedophilia ring are utter fictions, fantastic concoctions of right-wingers' fevered (and projection-prone) imaginations, only produced another round of theories and further doubling down on the belief, spread largely through media, of the pedophilia ring's existence.

Indeed, it was only beginning. Pretty soon, the QAnon "Storm" would make Pizzagate look like tiddlywinks.

———

In an online universe where conspiracy theories not only sprout like kudzu but attract bigger audiences the more outrageous and strange they grow, it was probably inevitable that an uber-theory like "the Storm" would become an overnight sensation.

Part Pizzagate, part New World Order, and part hyper-partisan wishful thinking by defenders of Donald Trump, the Storm is a sprawling meta-conspiracy, with actors ranging from Hillary Clinton to model Chrissy Teigen, in which everything you know about the current investigations into Russian meddling in the 2016 election and potential collusion with the Trump campaign is upside down.[54]

Special Counsel Robert Mueller, in this alternative universe, is in fact preparing to indict hundreds of Democrats (including Clinton, Barack Obama, and financier George Soros) and Hollywood celebrities for their roles in a massive worldwide pedophilia ring operated by "globalists" who are conspiring to destroy Trump—and that the president himself is masterminding this "countercoup."

"What we have come up with is a possible coup," explained conspiracy theorist David Zublick in a late-November video, "not against Donald Trump, but by Donald Trump, working with Robert Mueller to bring down the Clintons, the Democrat Party, and the entire U.S. government involved in pedophilia and child sex trafficking."

In just a few short weeks in early 2018, the theory grew from a handful of posts on fringe Internet chat forums to become the overwhelming obsession of nearly every conspiracy theorist in the business, notably Alex Jones and his Infowars operation, as well as social media figures such as Liz Crokin. In addition to being a constant focus of discussion on Infowars, dozens of YouTube videos and thousands of Twitter posts exploring various facets of the conspiracy and presenting the usual dubious "evidence" to "prove" it have shown up on the Internet.

The origins of "the Storm" lie in Trump's cryptic remarks on October 6, saying that a gathering of military leaders represented "the calm before the storm." When asked what he meant, Trump responded: "You'll see."[55]

Three weeks later, as *New York Magazine*'s Paris Martineau reported, an anonymous poster on the Internet message board 4chan—one of the main organizing and recruitment forums for the alt-right—who claimed he had high-level "Q" national security clearance began publishing a series of cryptic messages that he claimed were "intel drops" intended to start informing the public through such channels about what was really happening inside the White House and what Trump really meant by his odd remarks.[56]

According to "QAnon," Trump's remark was a reference to the indictments handed down by Mueller in late October, ostensibly related to his investigation of the Trump campaign and its alleged collusion with Russian intelligence. Most news reports about those indictments, reported to number in the hundreds, presumed that they were related to criminal behavior around the campaign.

Not so, said QAnon, who claimed that Trump was never really under investigation. Instead, those indictments were all being directed at a massive conspiracy involving a global pedophilia ring operated by high-level Democrats and other "globalists" who were simultaneously part of a plot to overthrow Trump's presidency with a "deep state" coup.

This is the same pedophilia ring that was the focus of the Pizzagate conspiracy theory. However, in the new expanded version of the theory, the pedophilia ring had gone global, drawing in alleged participants from all around the nation and occurring in locations ranging from Hollywood to Europe. (One version of the pedophilia theory entertained by Jones claimed that the child victims secretly were being shipped to a colony on Mars.)[57]

QAnon and the conspiracy theorists who piled on at 4chan, 8chan, and on Twitter claimed that contrary to the running story in mainstream media, this pedophilia ring is the real focus of Mueller's investigation. The general conclusion, spread through the #qanon hashtag on social media, was that a wave of arrests—including Clinton, Obama, Podesta, Soros, Senator John McCain, and a number of leading Hollywood figures and Democrats was about to happen.

However, there was a credibility problem for QAnon early on, since he posted in early November a scenario in which hundreds of arrests and massive social turmoil were about to be unleashed within a matter of days. "Rest assured, the safety and well-being of every man, woman, and child of this country is being exhausted in full," he wrote. "However, the atmosphere within the country will unfortunately be divided as so many have fallen for the corrupt and evil narrative that has long been broadcast. We will be initiating the Emergency Broadcast System (EMS) during this time in an effort to provide a direct message (avoiding the fake news) to all citizens."

November came and went, of course, without any such event. But that didn't dampen the enthusiasm among QAnon's increasingly rabid horde of fans.

These apparently included a significant portion of radical right social media users, as indicated by the Southern Poverty Law Center's Hate Tracker, which monitors the spread of extremist ideologies and claims on Twitter. The #qanon hashtag began trending in late November and steadily grew during the ensuing weeks. By early January, it began regularly trending upward.[58]

"The Storm" reflects in many regards the need for right-wing conspiracists to constantly push the envelope of public discourse by proposing increasingly outrageous and arcane theories just to distinguish themselves in an ever-more-crowded field, especially on social media and YouTube. People who run such conspiracy mills, particularly Jones, have built their careers around attracting attention by pushing expansively unhinged and groundless claims.

However, the #qanon phenomenon in the context of 2018 and beyond also suggested that the spread of conspiracy theories was (and still is) being inflamed to the point of hypertrophy, largely through the growth of social media as a presence in people's daily lives. The surprising rapidity at which "the Storm" spread among shockingly gullible people is testament to the extent to which such claims gain real life and become widely believed.

The hashtag's rise on social media in late December 2017, probably not coincidentally, happened at about the time that Alex Jones adopted the QAnon theories and claimed them as his own: "A lot of what QAnon has said, I had already gotten separately from my White House sources, my Pentagon sources, my CIA sources," he told his audience on December 24.

He went on:

> We are seeing a slick countercoup to the globalists that they are calling a coup, because the criminals that have hijacked the country, and all their little minions that have bet on it, were wrong. They failed. . . .
>
> They're calling it a coup because it's justice. It's the crimes they've committed—the Uranium One, the pedophilia, the money launder-ing, all of it, and the executive order Trump signed to seize money connected to trafficking in people, women and children and slaves, and money connected to drug dealing, and all of the stuff . . . and they're all having to step down right now, and that's just the beginning.
>
> So "the Storm" is real. That's our storm of justice and resistance and standing up.[59]

Infowars correspondent Jerome Corsi—the longtime conspiracy maven respon-sible for many of the nonsensical claims about Obama's birth certificate as well as a host of other similarly flimsy theories—chimed in shortly with an "intelli-gence analysis" of QAnon's posts, from which he concluded that the anonymous poster was "legitimate," that is, someone genuinely working from within the White House with real knowledge of inside information.[60]

"The Storm is upon us," Corsi told an interviewer, continuing:

> 2018 will be the year of the counterattack that Donald Trump is go-ing to wage against the deep state. This is going to be a battle of enor-mous proportions which will determine whether or not the American republic as a constitutional republic sustains or does not. Depending upon Donald Trump's success or failure, we will have a coup d'état which will replace the Constitution with a globalist, socialist state.
>
> This is a battle of classic heroic proportions, which is going to be waged on the intelligence front and the average American person would be unaware of it had there not been an entity like QAnon who had come forward from a knowledgeable position to start dropping the clues, the breadcrumbs, as he says, that will lead people to the research they need to do and the understanding they need to achieve to see how our intelligence agencies, our justice system, the FBI have been corrupted and how dangerous this is. The republic is hanging by a thread and it's now going to be Donald Trump's unique oppor-tunity to save it and I don't think there is anybody better that I can

think of in the political landscape to be on the scene than Donald Trump.

Sprinkled in and subsumed under the rubric of "Storm" theories were a number of strangely associated theories, such as one positing that the Las Vegas shooter was actually an inside job carried out by Saudi-sponsored false flag terrorists or another claiming that the dossier compiled by a British intelligence agent on the Russian activity was a complete fabrication bought and paid for by Obama and Clinton. Within the 4chan and 8chan communities, a debate arose over whether children were being raped as part of a satanic conspiracy or a CIA blackmail scheme.

In many regards, however, the Trump countercoup component of the "Storm" was almost secondary to the overarching conspiracy theory that has been fueling much of the passion and animus accompanying its spread on social media—namely, the uber-Pizzagate belief that there is a massive conspiracy afoot in America to abduct, rape, and murder hundreds, perhaps thousands, of children to satiate the appetites of a satanic cabal operating at the highest levels of government.

Jones described the evil nature of this cabal to his audience in December:

> They literally created an army of people they can control who wanted to have sex with children and be evil, and who they could destroy at any time. And what's even sicker is the people above that aren't even into raping kids. They just want to kill kids. The lesser vampires just want to feed off their energy and rape them. These people want to kill them.

Then there was Liz Crokin, the onetime gossip columnist turned "investigative reporter" who writes for TownHall.com and has a large following on social media, in large part due to her long-running claims that pedophilia is rampant in America. She not only believes that QAnon is a legitimate inside information source, but that it actually is Trump himself, perhaps with the help of key aide Stephen Miller.[61]

She told an interviewer that she thought the president and his team had been doing "intel drops" at 4chan and 8chan and on social media as a way of red-pilling members of the public to soften the inevitable shock that will accompany the wave of arrests that's coming:

> Now, I believe Q is President Trump, working possibly with Stephen Miller, to drop this information behind the scenes to get a campaign going, to red-pill people as to what is going on with the Storm, and their takedown of the Deep State, which includes the Deep State

pedophile scene. I've been telling people for a very long time the stuff that goes on with these elitists, these occult elitists, who literally are raping, sacrificing children, drinking blood, like eating babies literally. It's too hard for an average person that has no idea that any of this is going on to take it in all at once.

So there's been a very orchestrated effort behind the scenes by President Trump and his administration to slowly wake up the public as to what, that (A), this goes on, that it's real, and (B), that they're taking down these people. When there are mass arrests, and there are names like Hillary Clinton that pop up, or thrown in prison for sex trafficking, there's not mass hysteria. People will realize, "Oh my gosh, maybe this is real," or like, this isn't just some kind of coup or whatever, this is real and this is really going on.[62]

Crokin was nothing if not indiscriminate in accusing people of participating in the pedophilia conspiracy, notably including well-known entertainment figures. In late December 2017, she tangled on Twitter with supermodel Chrissy Teigen and her husband, the Grammy-winning singer John Legend, claiming that pictures Teigen posted of her children indicated they were participants in the Pizzagate ring.

Teigen responded with a tweet indicating she was "disturbed" by Crokin's accusation. "Chrissy you run in circle with people who rape, torture & traffic kids. This is a fact, I expose sex trafficking for a living," responded Crokin.

Teigen replied angrily: "YOU POSTED MY DAUGHTER AND HAVE 50,000 PEOPLE ACCUSING ME OF BEING IN A PEDO RING. I don't care HOW you backtrack or WHAT you deleted. I have it ALL. I'm the last person you are f***ing with. You are DONE with me and my family. You are going to court."

Legend chimed in: "You need to take my family's name out of your mouth before you get sued."[63]

In the QAnon universe, the conspiracies kept building and building over time, especially as the person or people behind the Q persona posted at 8chan. So did the bizarre fanaticism of the theory's true believers.

A later iteration of the theories revolved around the mysterious jail suicide of billionaire Jeffrey Epstein, a friend of both Bill Clinton and Donald Trump (and many other celebrities and political figures) who was accused by multiple women of overseeing a massive sex-trafficking operation involving mostly underage girls, as well as personally assaulting a long list of these girls. Epstein, awaiting trial in New York, was found dead in his cell in July 2019, and the official verdict declared that he had hung himself.

Many people were skeptical of this conclusion (one poll found that less than a third of Americans believed Epstein killed himself),[64] but conspiracy theorists—particularly those convinced that Bill Clinton had a track record of murdering his political enemies and liabilities—went completely wild. This was especially the case for the QAnon theorists for whom the Clintons were central villains in their narrative; the possibility that Trump might have been responsible was not part of the discussion.

In short order, one of the most popular memes that first circulated in QAnon social media circles—the simple assertion, "Epstein Didn't Kill Himself"—spread quickly into the mainstream, where it was circulated through the likes of Fox News and Republican congressmen who shared it with the public.[65]

To no one's great surprise, the unhinging effect common to far-right conspiracy theories began manifesting itself in the real world. An out-of-work Marine veteran named Matthew P. Wright—armed with an AR-15 rifle, a handgun, multiple magazines of ammunition, and a flash-bang device—drove his homemade armored vehicle to the middle of the Mike O'Callaghan–Pat Tillman Memorial Bridge leading to the Hoover Dam one day in July 2018 and successfully blocked traffic for ninety minutes, complete with an armed standoff with law enforcement, at the end of which Wright was apprehended unharmed.[66]

It shortly emerged that the whole event had been inspired by Q. Locked up in Mojave County, Arizona, Wright composed a series of letters to President Trump and other elected officials that all signed off with the secret Q insiders motto, "Where We Go One We Go All." His letter to Trump referenced another Q belief—namely, the "Great Awakening," which was just another signifier for the "Storm" that Q believers still anxiously awaited.[67]

QAnon signs appeared on bumper stickers and on signs in people's yards. They would appear at Donald Trump's periodic rallies at various locales around the country, with followers wearing large "Q" signs and T-shirts adorned with variations on "#WWG1WGA."

Trump would even appear to acknowledge the QAnon believers from time to time—giving them the "thumbs-up" at his rallies, while Press Secretary Sarah Sanders denied any support. However, inside their own universe, QAnoners had become fully convinced that Trump in fact was secretly linked to Q, and he sent them all kinds of secret signals—gestures and phrases Trump would use, seemingly odd coincidences in his public appearances—as absolute proof that not only was Trump in on the plot-within-the-plot, but that indeed his invisible hand could be found in almost any and every news event, White House–related or not.

A well-known QAnon YouTuber named Michael Lionel Lebron one day posted a photo of himself in the Oval Office with President Trump and his wife, with just the script: "There are simply no words to explicate this profound honor." Lebron assured his followers that the president definitely knew about the QAnon conspiracy, though he later claimed that they didn't explicitly talk about it. No one could explain how or why he was in the Oval Office—which would have required clearance by senior staff—in the first place.[68]

Conspiracy theories not only crept into the Oval Office during Trump's tenure, at times they appeared to rule the place, long after birtherism withered into the nothingness from which it was born. And if the Jade Helm incident had demonstrated how conspiracy theories can affect and alter policies and official behavior, the Trump administration's conduct demonstrated what happens when the entire executive branch is in their thrall.

In August 2017, the magazine *Foreign Policy* published a memo by a man named Rich Higgins, who served on the staff of Trump's National Security Council. It was titled simply "POTUS and Political Warfare," and it opened with the assertion that the president was actually engaged in a conflict with nefarious cultural Marxists in a conspiracy.

> This is not politics as usual but rather political warfare at an unprecedented level that is openly engaged in the direct targeting of a seated president through manipulation of the news cycle. It must be recognized on its own terms so that immediate action can be taken. At its core, these campaigns run on multiple lines of effort, serve as the non-violent line of effort of a wider movement, and execute political warfare agendas that **reflect cultural Marxist outcomes.** The campaigns operate through narratives. Because the hard left is aligned with Islamist organizations at local (ANTI FA working with Muslim Brotherhood doing business as MSA and CAIR), national (ACLU and BLM working with CAIR and MPAC) and international levels (OIC working with OSCE and the UN), recognition should be given to the fact that they seamlessly interoperate at the narrative level as well. In candidate Trump, the opposition saw a threat to the "politically correct" enforcement narratives they've meticulously laid in over the past few decades. In President Trump, they see a latent threat to continue that effort to ruinous effect and their retaliatory response reflects this fear.[69]

It even had an explanation for the president's various personal scandals, including an audiotape in which he talked about grabbing women "by the pussy," as well as a payoff to a porn star who says they had sex while Trump's third wife Melania was pregnant:

> Responding to relentless personal assaults on his character, candidate Trump identified the players and the strategy: "The establishment

and their media enablers will control over this nation through means that are very well known. Anyone who challenges their control is deemed a sexist, a racist, a xenophobe, and morally deformed."— President Trump, Oct 2016

Culturally conditioned to limit responses to such attacks as yet another round in the on-going drone from diversity and multicultural malcontents, these broadsides are discounted as political correctness run amuck. However, political correctness is a weapon against reason and critical thinking. This weapon functions as the enforcement mechanism of **diversity narratives that seek to implement cultural Marxism**. Candidate Trump's rhetoric in the campaign not only cut through the Marxist narrative, he did so in ways that were viscerally comprehensible to a voting bloc that then made candidate Trump the president; making that bloc self-aware in the process. President Trump is either the candidate he ran as, or he is nothing. Recognizing in candidate Trump an existential threat to cultural Marxist memes that dominate the prevailing cultural narrative, those that benefit recognize the threat he poses and seek his destruction. For this cabal, Trump must be destroyed. Far from politics as usual, this is a political warfare effort that seeks the destruction of a sitting president. Since Trump took office, the situation has intensified to crisis level proportions. For those engaged in the effort, especially those from within the "deep state" or permanent government apparatus, this raises clear Title 18 (legal) concerns.

According to Higgins, those threatened by Trump include "'deep state' actors, globalists, bankers, Islamists, and establishment Republicans." Among the people whom he considered disloyal to Trump, he named National Security Adviser H. R. McMaster, his boss. Higgins was promptly given a pink slip.[70]

This, it shortly emerged, thoroughly infuriated Trump, who had gushed over the memo when it was given to him. A month later, he was "still furious" about the firing. The incident clearly indicated that the president, too, subscribed to the "cultural Marxism" conspiracy theory.[71]

Moreover, the paranoiac and conspiratorial view of its author was clearly pervasive throughout the Oval Office in nearly every policy initiative Trump pursued. Nowhere was that more true than with the raging debate over immigration.

From the start, accompanying the nativist rhetoric with which he had announced his candidacy in 2015 and continuing through both the campaign and his tenure as president, Trump's view of immigration was straight out of the Minutemen's paranoid playbook: the border's porousness was a threat to national security, because terrorists were secretly crossing into the United States there, and the immigrants were just a cover for them and they were destroying the culture anyway.

However, the Minutemen's grand plan to build a fence on the border (remember, that had been a scam, too) was not grand enough for Trump. No, his plan had to bigger. Better. He would build a wall! And indeed, "the Wall" became one of the centerpieces of Trump's campaign, the chant "Build the Wall!" ringing loudly at all his campaign rallies.

Once in office, not only did he pursue policies that emphasized the dehumanized view of immigrants inherent to conspiracy theories, which produced a family-separation policy that put large numbers of children in wire cages at detention centers, but eventually Trump publicly embraced conspiracy theories about the people coming to the American border.

So in October, with midterm elections just a few weeks away and the polls (accurately) looking grim for Republican chances of retaining the House of Representatives, Trump turned back to his tried-and-true formula that he believed won the election in 2016: fearmongering over immigration.[72]

And this time, it came with a conspiracy-theory twist.

On October 16, Trump tweeted out the alarm: "The United States has strongly informed the President of Honduras that if the large Caravan of people heading to the U.S. is not stopped and brought back to Honduras, no more money or aid will be given to Honduras, effective immediately!" It was just one of many the president posted that day on the subject and in the days following, as well.[73]

He had been spurred to action by a Fox News segment that had run that morning about a caravan of migrants, several hundred strong, from Central American nations who planned to seek asylum in the United States and were gradually making their way northward. Though nearly all of these refugees in fact were fleeing violence in their homelands and many likely would qualify for asylum in normal circumstances, Trump—with powerful assists from right-wing media, particularly Fox—persistently portrayed their gradual approach as an imminent existential threat to the United States.

The most hysterical pundit was Fox Business's Lou Dobbs, who trumpeted false information about the caravan nightly on his program for most of the month.[74] He hosted a guest named Chris Farrell, from a far-right Beltway organization called Judicial Watch, who solemnly informed Dobbs with great certainty that the caravan was being "orchestrated by the Soros-occupied State Department."

A guest on Laura Ingraham's Fox News show opined: "These individuals are not immigrants—these are people that are invading our country." Another chimed in that they sought "the destruction of American society and culture."[75] Even on CNN, the same rhetoric ruled: right-wing commentator Matt Schlapp got aggressive while interrogating host Alisyn Camerota: "Who's paying for the caravan? Alisyn, who's paying for the caravan?" Then he answered his own question: "Because of the liberal judges and other people that intercede, including George Soros, we have too much chaos at our southern border."[76]

At one point, Trump retweeted a video, first posted by Republican Representative Matt Gaetz of Florida, purportedly showing caravan participants receiving money that was being handed out in bundles. Gaetz speculated in his original post that the money might have come from George Soros. Trump asked: "Can you believe this, and what Democrats are allowing to be done to our Country?"[77]

A still taken from another Fox News video that seemed to show a Star of David sticker on the back of the cab of a truck hauling food for the caravan migrants also made the rounds quite a bit. It was particularly popular on the dark corners of social media, on white nationalist and neo-Nazi message boards where it was displayed widely as proof that the Jews were secretly behind the caravan. It was everywhere on Gab, which had become the social medium of choice for white nationalists and other bigots after being kicked off Twitter.[78]

One of the people who spread this photo was a forty-six-year-old white Pittsburgh-area man and heavy Gab user named Robert Bowers. At one time he had been a relatively normal employee at a local bakery, but he had drifted for years after leaving the job in 2002, taking up work as a long-haul trucker and finding odd jobs here and there. His neighbors at his apartment in Baldwin Borough said they hardly ever saw him.

His computer and social media records, though, showed that Bowers had developed an interest in the deeply bigoted Christian Identity movement, which preaches that white people are the true children of Israel, that today's Jews are actually demonic imitators descended from Satan, and that nonwhite people like blacks, Asians, and Latinos are soulless "mud people" whose humanity is of secondary value at best. He burnished these ideas with conspiracy theories and other far-right propaganda at message boards like 4chan, the *Daily Stormer*, and Stormfront.

On Gab, his anti-Semitic rants were visceral and angry. And as the month of October went on and the caravan dominated the news, his rhetoric grew threatening.

He reposted a message that Western civilization is "headed towards certain extinction within the next 200 years and we're not even aware of it." A Jewish relief organization called the Hebrew Immigrant Aid Society became the focus of Bower's ire: "You like to bring in hostile invaders to dwell among us?" he posted in a comment directed at HIAS.

Bowers also facetiously thanked HIAS for a post listing groups that had supported one of the organization's refugee benefits. "We appreciate the list of friends you have provided," he wrote.

On Saturday, October 27, he published a final post. "HIAS likes to bring invaders in that kill our people," he wrote. "I can't sit by and watch my people get slaughtered. Screw your optics. I'm going in."[79]

One of the Jewish congregations on that earlier HIAS fundraising list met at Pittsburgh's Tree of Life synagogue, located in the same Squirrel Hill borough that once was known around the world as *Mister Rogers' Neighborhood*. After filing his post, Bowers got in his car and drove the thirty minutes or so it took to get to Tree of Life.

He had a Colt AR-15 semiautomatic rifle and three pistols with him. He got out of his car and entered the synagogue. There were about seventy-five people inside beginning their morning Shabbat service. He opened fire with the AR-15 but, over the course of the next ten minutes or so, wound up using all four of his weapons.

The first people he killed were two elderly Jewish men who had turned to greet him; others were in their seats as he walked toward the front. The room cleared quickly, leaving only a scattered few targets, so he began shooting at people making last-second dashes out of the room.

Police arrived about ten minutes after he opened fire. Bowers then opened fire on the police, engaged them in a standoff for about thirty minutes, and surrendered.[80]

There were eleven dead, most of them elderly, and six people were injured, four requiring surgery. Bowers now awaits trial in Pittsburgh.

Over at 4chan, where a number of users on the /pol/ board remembered Bowers from his time spent there, the popular view was that the attacks were "accidentally red-pilling" people. Others denied the attack, claiming it was a false flag done by Jews to gain sympathy and that somehow Bowers had fallen prey to their machinations. They created a hashtag for him: #HeroRobertBowers.[81]

Chapter Six

THE RABBIT HOLE

It feels almost like a drug, the rush from learning and delving a new conspiracy theory. It's so powerful, so affirming, so empowering that of course you come back for more. Who wouldn't? That's why they call it red-pilling, right?

First, it's the secret knowledge. Only you and a select few have gleaned this information. The Powers That Be don't want it to be known. But it gives you special insight. You can see how things really work. You can see things at work that others can't.

Because you're smarter and cleverer than them. This is part of the ego boost: It's a rush seeing evidence of your superiority to others so clearly. The old word for the people who aren't as insightful or fortunate as you is sheeple, but nowadays the word is normies. Either way, they are objects of contempt.

Even before there was an Internet, the core appeal of conspiracism was the feeling of empowerment that came with it. But in the new age of social media, the "new conspiracism"—the kind without evidence, built on a combination of pure conjecture and a backlog of older conspiracy theories that act as a kind of body of knowledge separate from normal rules of evidence and factuality—that thrives and spreads in supposedly web-savvy environments is in many ways susceptible to manipulation thanks to its insistence on cynicism.

A lot of this has to do with what actually happens to us when we use social media. Brain scientists have found that certain kinds of stimulation on the Internet, particularly affirming and empowering responses people receive in their interactions, arouse certain pleasure response centers in the human brain, triggering the release of dopamine, a chemical messenger that travels along a reward pathway, making you feel good. That's why it becomes so addictive.

When you're on social media a lot and you're not getting those reward responses as frequently as you'd like, it all turns very negative. One German study found that one out of three people surveyed felt "lonely, frustrated or angry" after spending time on Facebook, often due to perceived inadequacies when comparing themselves to friends.[1] People often found themselves negatively comparing themselves to the happy lives they'd find their "friends" (most of whom, in fact, are actually strangers) sharing online.

This experience negatively affects people's self-esteem in often profound ways, making them feel low self-worth, particularly when it comes to their sense of agency in the world at large. In the great teeming world of social media, it's very easy to feel like a complete nobody. Unless, of course, you can find a way to make yourself a somebody.

People who fall into this pattern of thinking become susceptible to conspiracy theories precisely because they feel they have found a shortcut to empowerment that only the clever can seize. The theories are a way of reacting to uncertainty and powerlessness.

Samantha Kutner, a researcher who tracks the far-right Proud Boys street-brawling organization, says that most of the young men she's interviewed have described their "red-pilling" journey beginning with a kind of "cognitive closure" derived from "having seemingly random things explained in some grand overarching narrative."[2]

"I think there's an information addiction component to it as well," Kutner says. "You could think of it as being addicted to bad information that you don't see as bad."

The power of conspiracy theories, University of London psychology lecturer Rob Brotherton explains, is their ability to "connect the dots," to help people make sense of the seemingly random events in their lives by creating a pattern: "the cognitive equivalent of seeing meaning in randomness."[3]

"It's incredibly empowering to believe you have the true picture of reality and that everyone else is delusional," observes Nancy Rosenblum, a Harvard politics professor who has been cataloguing the costs of conspiracism in her recent work. "And if you look at conspiracists today, even the wackiest, like those writing about QAnon, they see themselves as the cognoscenti. They understand how the world really works, and they understand that the rest of us are brainwashed."[4]

However, this alienation is never ameliorated by the continuing descent down the rabbit hole; rather, the more isolated its inhabitants become, the more likely they are to become angry, perhaps violent.

The larger problem in all this is that the attitudes and assumptions that underlie conspiracism are common human traits—failings, perhaps, but also woven into the warp and weft of our cultures, particularly in the United States, where (as *Reason* editor and author Jesse Walker has helpfully explored) our Founding

Fathers were themselves prone to a paranoid streak about conspiratorial elites, some of it well-founded, some of it fantasy.[5]

"Cognitive and political psychologists will tell you the cognitive afflictions that result in the worst and most zealous kind of conspiracy theory really are common; we all share them," observes Rosenblum. "We like to think that agents are the causes of things, rather than accidents or unintended consequences being the cause. We like to think there's a proportionality between cause and effect, and that causes us to overreach for explanations."[6]

Brotherton explains that we know that "conspiracism is about more than mere evidence" in large part because the very fabric of the theories—namely, the seemingly random, disconnected events that are then woven into a pattern—is rarely, if ever, interpreted as the product of what we rationally already know about real conspiracies—namely, that they are by nature limited in scope, number of actors, length of time, and breadth of purpose. When a scenario falls outside those parameters, the likelihood of its being real is infinitesimal.[7]

Anyone committed to a rational exploration of an event—especially a highly public one, such as JFK's assassination or 9/11—would consider the possibility that unrelated conspiracies planned by independent groups with their own idiosyncratic motives and goals were involved. That never happens: "Instead, conspiracy theorists have a remarkable knack for weaving a multitude of seemingly unrelated events together, into a single rich tapestry," Brotherton observes.[8]

What makes conspiracy theories feel so empowering is that they bring order to chaos, make sense of events that don't. Facts and arguments built upon them are not just meaningless, they actually reinforce the conspiracist narrative, becoming proof that the conspiracy has reached monstrous levels for the believers. With "new conspiracism" particularly, the theories really are no longer based on facts—which is why their believers are immune to them.

Looking for and finding the patterns that have replaced facts in their epistemological universes really become the central preoccupations of people drawn into this alternative universe. This came up during a 2008 experiment by researchers Jennifer Whitson and Adam Galinsky[9] in which researchers asked participants to compose a short essay, after which they would complete a variety of tasks.

> Half of the participants wrote about a time they lacked control over their lives, while the others described a time when they were in control. This task was meant to induce a feeling of having or lacking control—and a lack of control is thought to be a troubling psychological state that people are motivated to resolve. In

follow-up tasks, the participants who had been manipulated to feel a lack of control were more likely to see patterns in noise, to make superstitious inferences about connections between events, and to perceive sinister conspiracies in ambiguous situations. Psychologists theorize that drawing connections and recognizing patterns in this way can help to restore a sense of control and certainty—to make sense of a world that, in that moment, seems difficult to predict or understand.[10]

This is why, for someone who operates in the workaday world outside the realm of conspiracy theories, coming into contact with a conspiracy theorist can be deeply unsettling, as though the whole ground of reality shifts like a weird field around them. Certainly trying to have logical conversations with them can leave people feeling discombobulated.

Philadelphia activist Gwen Snyder tracked the radicalization arc reflected in the Facebook timeline of a local man named Tom who began harassing and threatening her on Twitter. Snyder went through his Facebook "likes" chronologically and found that they told a story.

"Tom didn't start out as a guy who went around threatening to murder the loved ones of anyone who dared to criticize politicians for associating with white supremacists," she wrote. "He was an army vet who supported police. He watched the local Fox channel, sure, but he was as into the Beatles and hardwood floors just as much as he was into the cops. He even went out of his way to like his neighbor's African braiding salon."[11]

However, at some point, Tom changed, primarily when he discovered Fox News. Shortly after that, his timeline began sporting "likes" for the Conservative Tribune, for right-wing pundit Judge Jeanine Pirro, for right-wing news site NewsMax, and then for Donald Trump. Next came Breitbart News. "Soon, Tom is liking Steve Bannon's stuff, ICE, local anti-sanctuary politicians, white nationalist French candidate Marine Le Pen. And of course, Ben Shapiro."

What happened next was predictable: all these voices "bridged the gap," and in short order Tom was liking 4chan and 8chan and a number of alt-right websites, as well as a page dedicated to "Three Percenter" militiamen. He also linked up with local Republican politicians, including the mayoral candidate over whom Tom had threatened Snyder. And he posted on Twitter, defending the Proud Boys: "The Proud Boys aren't what you think. They're just some big dudes daring you Antifa snowflakes to swing a chain at them, or a pipe. Then, it's lights out."

Tom, now fully red-pilled, also became a full-on QAnon believer, posting tweets threatening Hillary Clinton for allegedly posting "coded assassination threats" against Trump.

Political scientist Joseph Uscinski explains that epistemology—the system of how we know things—works in an entirely different way for conspiracists:

It isn't just that conspiracy theorists have a different set of explanations, it is that their explanations call into question our knowledge-generating and knowledge-disseminating institutions. The establishment, in order to maintain control and function, must specify the parameters under which society is to operate; this includes stipulating the relevant facts and the methods of discovering those facts. Conspiracy theories undermine the establishment by providing alternative facts, realities, and ways of knowing. The bedrock factual matters people should be able to agree upon—such as facts about how society is organized—are often contested by conspiracy theorists.[12]

Normal reason and logic, in other words, don't work to persuade conspiracy theorists because they don't believe in them anymore; the shared reality that arises from those norms doesn't really exist for them. We all share the world, but conspiracists experience it in a very different way.

Buying into a conspiracy theory is a ticket into a realm, a reality unto itself, defined not by stodgy authorities issuing "official" stories to explain events unconvincingly but by clever "researchers" who seem to dig up nuggets of obscure information from all over that not only make the "official" story seem dubious but suggest an entirely different, and much more nefarious, narrative.

And the best part of this narrative is that it offers you hope—hope to become a hero yourself, to outsmart the evil plotters, to save your families and friends from their schemes. You only have to research it further and soon you will get to the bottom of everything.

Part of the addictive quality of conspiracy theories is finding yourself joining the "researchers"—spending time on search engines looking up tidbits of information that might help bolster your theory of interest. When you share it online, you wait and hope for approbation, lots of shares, and the rush that comes with that.

What you soon notice inside the rabbit hole is the way that your favorite theory, the one you spend your time researching, seems to connect with other conspiracy theories that come from completely different realms. How a theory about FEMA concentration camps connects weirdly with a completely different theory about Hillary's pedophilia ring, or how a long-forgotten tidbit about JFK proves Obama couldn't have been born in Hawaii. It's amazing what you find when you start digging through all the suppressed information.

One rabbit hole leads to another, downward into the maze, which becomes a realm unto itself. Your system of conspiracist beliefs begins growing, layer upon layer, like an onion. It becomes more complex and interconnected and filled with data from all kinds of sources, most of them dismissed by mainstream media, because of course they are. Who do you think runs the media?

The alternative universe of conspiracism may be ultimately the product of a mass of feverish imaginings by hundreds of different people, but it has rules.

- First, whoever is involved in the conspiracy is evil and their intentions nefarious. The people who are identified as leaders of the plot—such as George Soros or Hillary Clinton—are seen as not merely immoral but demonic. Opposing them is a noble, heroic act, performed by ordinary but morally superior citizens.
- Second, the people who publicize and research the conspiracy are innately the objects of persecution by the conspirators—and innately the heroes who will save the world from these evil plotters.
- Third, any "official" version or explanation of the story is necessarily false, while a wide variety of alternative, conspiracism-fueled versions may compete but are broadly deemed plausible. At the same time, the only facts deemed accurate and true are those that can be interpreted as proving or supporting a conspiracist explanation or adding to it. A nihilistic kind of selective skepticism arises in which any simple or clear explanation is disbelieved, while, conversely, any odd "fact" or alternative interpretation that supports a conspiracy narrative is seized upon with avid gullibility.
- Fourth, nothing is accidental. It's all intentional, and it all ties together. Indeed, a corollary aspect of this rule is that the conspirators themselves are phenomenally competent and mind-bogglingly clever in everything they do, not to mention overwhelmingly powerful, wealthy, and connected.
- Fifth, some theories may be ultimately rejected and discarded when they turn out to be unsustainable, such as claims that global climate change is a hoax, but that does not alter the larger conspiracist narrative to which the true believers rigorously adhere.
- Finally, any attempts to present contrary evidence is inherently proof that the conspiracy exists, and any such evidence is automatically presumed to be false or distorted. The people who embrace such facts are either active members of the conspiracy or hapless dupes.

These six rules are what psychologist Stephan Lewandowsky calls the parameters of "conspiracist ideation," the means by which conspiracy theorists create their own self-reinforcing universe. In this world, he writes, "nothing is as it seems, and all evidence points to hidden agendas or some other meaning that only the conspiracy theorist is aware of."[13]

Conspiracists are by nature untrusting of others, Lewandowsky says, which is why "contrary evidence is often interpreted as evidence for a conspiracy. This ideation relies on the notion that, the stronger the evidence against a conspiracy, the more the conspirators must want people to believe their version of events. This self-sealing reasoning necessarily widens the circle of presumed conspirators because the accumulation of contrary evidence merely identifies a growing number of people or institutions that are part of the conspiracy."[14]

University of Kent psychology lecturers Michael Wood and Karen M. Douglas explain: "If you want to know how seriously someone takes conspiracy theories, you should ask about how much they trust others, whether they are agreeable or open-minded, how much they think people are out to get them, and whether they routinely have unusual or paranormal experiences. Conspiracy theorizing may be driven in part by evidence, but is certainly driven by underlying psychological tendencies."[15]

"Whether conspiracy theories reflect what's really going on in the world or not, they tell us a lot about our secret selves," observes Rob Brotherton. "Conspiracy theories resonate with some of our brain's built-in biases and shortcuts, and tap into some of our deepest desires, fears, and assumptions about the world and the people in it. We have innately suspicious minds. We are all natural-born conspiracy theorists."[16]

The driver in all this, analysts consistently find, is people's sense of a lack of agency in the real world at large—a perfectly reasonable feeling, given the overwhelming numbers of humanity and the ease with which people become not just anonymous but disempowered economically and socially in modern mass society. On social media, this often translates into a syndrome long identified as a core reason people dive into these rabbit holes—namely, fear of missing out (FOMO), "a pervasive apprehension that others might be having rewarding experiences from which one is absent."[17]

The narratives that the conspiracy theories construct are all about explaining why their believers are being deprived of social status, in part by describing *who* is depriving them of it: that is, the narrative is ultimately designed to scapegoat people, either specific individuals who represent a larger target group or the target group itself. It does this by ultimately depicting those targets as both demonic and a source of pollution, people fit only for elimination.

"This is one of the paradoxical aspects of conspiracy theories—that they give people a sense of control by nominating these dark forces that are dominating their lives," says Lewandowsky. "So there is this sort of ironic blip in the entire psychology of it to begin with, which is that of regaining control by blaming it on dark forces that are uncontrollable. It's that sort of paradoxical thing. Then there's other literature showing that, for example, having an enemy is chicken soup for the soul, makes people feel better to have an enemy, bizarrely—under certain circumstances when they're feeling threatened."[18]

At its roots, it's about power: who has it and who doesn't.

"It should be no surprise that feelings of power are relevant to beliefs in conspiracy theories," explain Wood and Douglas. "On a very basic level, conspiracy theories are basically stories about power—the secret power of a particular group, and the new power of the people who have come to see through their deception. People who feel relatively powerless are more likely to agree with conspiracy theories, and general conspiracy mentality predicts prejudice against high-power but not low-power groups."[19]

In the end, as Brotherton puts it, "the prototypical conspiracy theory is an unanswered question; it assumes nothing is as it seems; it portrays the conspirators as preternaturally competent; and as unusually evil; it is founded on anomaly hunting; and it is ultimately irrefutable."[20]

Meanwhile, the prototypical person drawn to them is, typically, someone who feels keenly the kind of powerlessness common to modern life and is angry about it. As *Vox* writer Sean Illing puts it: "I think of conspiracy theorists as people who have rejected a world they don't fit into, and the theories themselves offer a way to make sense of it and invert the cause of the problem. In other words, if I'm unhappy or alienated, it's not my fault; it's these shadowy forces that are aligned against me. Plus, it gives the conspiracy theorist a sense of power—they understand what's really going on in a way no one else does."[21]

After a while, you start to notice that your friends and family and people you know in real life have decided not to join you down inside the maze. That's their loss, right? They're just normies. But soon it feels like your only friends in the world are the friends you meet in the conspiracy world.

At first, you're eager to share your newfound insight with your real-life friends. Then you stop when they start responding coldly and sometimes harshly. You get into arguments with family members.

Old friends unfriend you, both in real life and on the Internet. Relatives chastise you as stupid and gullible. Sometimes people you've known for decades attack you on Facebook for buying into conspiracist ideas. Social circles in which you used to run comfortably now feel awkward, and invitations are fewer.

You're confident that someday you'll be vindicated, that all the so-called friends and family who turned their backs on you will come crawling apologetically when the truth comes down. That becomes a kind of comfort even as your relationships with those people shrivel to polite hellos or perhaps even rancorous arguments.

It's OK, because the people in the conspiracy's community of true believers are there for you. They're your friends, and they reassure you that those schmucks who claimed they loved you really just wanted to control your mind and your life and you're better off without them.

You don't vote or participate in party politics anymore unless it has a conspiracist appeal. Democracy is a joke, you realize. All those dark, nefarious forces control too much, have rendered the entire political establishment a fraud and a waste. The sheeple, the people who think their votes and their efforts matter, spend their time on that stuff. You know better.

You don't watch the regular news anymore, certainly not the corporate-owned entities at "fake news" joints like CNN and MSNBC; at most, you'll watch some Fox News, though even that has become a bit too mainstream for your tastes. You're consuming lots of information, though, maybe more than you ever have—it's just from sources like Infowars, the Michael Savage show, various YouTube channels that specialize in conspiracy theories, message boards at places like 4chan, 8chan, and Reddit, or even video game chat rooms on platforms that come with the games.

It's very reassuring, and it still feels empowering, because you realize that you have become part of a much bigger community, a global community, one that contains a wealth of knowledge and insights and that layers more conspiracy theories to your own personal onion.

Then, even as the isolation in your real life sets in, you begin to have doubts—not about the theory, but about some of your fellow conspiracists. Always on the lookout for being taken advantage of, you start feeling that they are giving you reasons not to trust them. It creeps in.

One of the keys to Alex Jones's success as a conspiracy peddler is that he recognized early on that there was a community of like-minded conspiracy theorists built around his broadcasts, people who not only devoured gullibly his every utterance and hypothesis, but who would contribute "facts" and propose narratives that further contributed to the growing layers around his alternative universe of conspiracism. He did everything he could to encourage that community—not merely by helping it find platforms for contributing, but also by promoting their ideas on his airtime and sometimes crediting them.

This army became adept not merely at consuming Infowars programming avidly, buying Jones's health supplements and vitamins and tinctures—which, he assured them, would help overcome the effects of chemicals deliberately released by government operatives into the environment that have been proven to turn frogs gay and that will do the same to humans—but also descending like flying monkeys en masse upon anyone who dared criticize or attack Jones and his operation, harassing and sometimes threatening them: initially, during the first decade of the 2000s, through comments sections at websites and via emails and then, as social media came into play, via Twitter and Facebook and Instagram.

The Infowars crowd may be the most dominant and prominent exponents of conspiracism in America, but they are by no means the only entity participating in the larger alternative universe they are helping to create. Some conspiracy theorists, particularly those less prone to Jones's John Bircher–style politics, are almost entirely interested in health-related conspiracies—particularly those revolving around claims that vaccinations are secretly poisoning our children—whereas others are devoted to David Icke-esque theories about UFOs and aliens secretly in control of governments and the global economy. Conversely, many Infowars devotees want nothing to do with such obvious "kooks."

What they all share, however, is a general worldview that everything in the world is run by conspiracies, that no public event or outcome is what it appears to be, that the official explanation is never the truth, and that they are all up against dark, nefarious, and extraordinarily powerful forces. And around that, it's remarkably easy to form a shared community of the like-minded.

One study found, indeed, that a propensity for conspiracism was connected closely with a desire for belongingness—but almost exclusively among people with low self-esteem and low belief in their self-agency.[22] Among devotees of the QAnon conspiracy theories, it's a common sentiment that much if not all of the draw is the camaraderie of fellow conspiracists.

"There's a sense of fellowship in the QAnon community," explained researcher Travis View in an interview with the *Daily Beast*. "They imagine that they're all members of a small group of people who know about a coming glorious age in America. This fellowship isn't the same as actual familial relationships, but it's a workable substitute when relationships with family becomes frayed. So this creates a vicious cycle: they fall down the rabbit hole of QAnon, which hurts their real life relationships, and causes them to fall down the rabbit hole even further."[23]

"When people get involved in a movement, collectively, what they're saying is they want to be connected to each other," researcher Rachel Bernstein explained in a *Wired* interview. "They want to have exclusive access to secret information other people don't have, information they believe the powers that be are keeping from the masses, because it makes them feel protected and empowered. They're a step ahead of those in society who remain willfully blind. This creates feeling similar to a drug—it's its own high."[24]

The camaraderie feels like a kind of compensation for the rejection they experience among longtime real-world acquaintances, and this helps drive them further into the conspiracist community. The milieu can often turn out to be shallow and brittle in nature, given the paranoid and often contentious personalities attracted to this world. But in the short run, it keeps the followers huddled together.

One woman who remained a QAnon believer told reporter Kelly Weill: "I've done a complete 180. There are people in my family that don't understand as well. I've lost some friends, people I've known since high school that I'm Facebook friends with, for an example. They just blocked me, or decided I'm not their friend, or unfriended me. Who the heck came up with that definition of friend anyway? That's OK. It is what it is."[25]

As Wood and Douglas explain:

> [A] good deal of research points to a connection between beliefs in conspiracy theories and perceived "outsiderdom" or separation from mainstream society. This is especially evident when looking at work on the psychological concept of anomie. Anomie is a sense of social alienation or disconnection, a feeling that one's own values and beliefs are not represented in broader society. Feelings of anomie have been shown to correlate significantly with beliefs in conspiracy theories in diverse samples.[26]

"People in the QAnon community often talk about alienation from family and friends," View told the *Daily Beast*'s Kelly Weill. "Though they typically talk about how Q frayed their relationships on private Facebook groups. But they think these issues are temporary and primarily the fault of others. They often comfort themselves by imagining that there will be a moment of vindication sometime in the near future which will prove their beliefs right. They imagine that after this happens, not only will their relationships be restored, but people will turn to them as leaders who understand what's going on better than the rest of us."[27]

These communities seem quaint and harmless to outsiders who see the conspiracism as a kind of lark or a game. For the true believers, however, the conspiracies are matters of life and death. And so they take on a genuinely frightening aspect when they are turned into an army of avenging angels, seeking out the enemies of their conspiracist community leaders—the conniving "globalists," their media minions, or anyone who wanders into the path of their conspiracy theories, often accidentally and unwillingly.

The parents of the twenty children who were slain, along with seven adults, at Sandy Hook Elementary School in Newtown, Connecticut, on December 14, 2012, by a conspiracy theory–loving teenager named Adam Lanza, learned the power of Jones's followers in the weeks and months following the tragedy that devastated their lives. As horrific as that scenario is for any parent, Jones and his acolytes managed to make their personal nightmares unimaginably worse.

The day of the shooting, Jones floated the claim to his audience that the whole event was a false flag set up by the government in order to justify a federal crackdown on gun owners and particularly to target the semiautomatic rifles of the type that Lanza had used. For the next two years, Infowars continued to repeat this claim and build on it, amassing "evidence" involving such dubious data as supposedly altered timestamps for memorial websites to the victims.[28]

In September 2014, Jones escalated the claims, saying "no one died" at Sandy Hook and that the victims had all been "crisis actors." This claim was based on a typical Jones misinterpretation of a Connecticut state police crime report that had designated the Newtown case in a special category. That didn't matter, of course: his army of followers promptly set to work, finding usually blurry and always dubious portraits of the "child actors" who had played the children slain at Sandy Hook, in their universe at least.

Infowars fans had already been causing problems. In May 2014, a man named Andrew David Truelove stole a pair of memorial signs from two different playgrounds, dedicated respectively to victims Grace McDonnell and Chase Kowalski, then called both McDonnell's and Kowalski's parents, telling them he had stolen the signs because he believed their children's deaths were a "hoax." A few days later, Truelove called a writer for a liberal website and laughingly boasted that he had stolen the signs. Investigators were then able to quickly track him down, arrest him, and recover the signs from his home. Convicted of theft, he was sentenced to a year in prison.[29]

It got worse. Truelove was hardly the only person calling up the Sandy Hook parents and accusing them of participating in a false flag hoax, often in a threatening manner. A former Florida Atlantic University professor named James Tracy—who once taught a course on conspiracy theories—began proclaiming that the shootings hadn't occurred and started calling the parents and harassing them. Another Florida man, a retired school administrator named Wolfgang Halbig, became the "lead investigator" for those who were intent on proving Sandy Hook a hoax.[30]

Halbig went on Jones's Infowars show and proclaimed: "Children did not die, teachers did not die on December 14, 2012." Jones agreed wholly: "I mean, it's fake. . . . It's fake. . . . You've got parents acting. . . . It's just the fakest thing since the $3 bill."

The parents were inundated with phone calls and emails, and several were forced to take security measures after threats. One of them was Lenny Pozner, the father of six-year-old Noah Pozner, one of the victims. Pozner did not take the harassment lying down and began organizing support groups for the parents and their backers. In 2017, a Florida woman named Lucy Richards was convicted of sending death threats to Pozner.

Eventually, in August 2018, seven families took Alex Jones, Infowars, Wolfgang Halbig, and other conspiracy theorists to court for defamation and harassment. During the proceedings, Jones testified that he actually suffers from "a form of psychosis" caused by the media that makes him doubt everything.[31]

"I, myself, have almost had like a form of psychosis back in the past where I basically thought everything was staged, even though I've now learned a lot of times things aren't staged," he said. "So I think as a pundit, someone giving an opinion, that, you know, my opinions have been wrong, but they were never wrong consciously to hurt people."

He told the court that the source of his distrust of everything was the "trauma of the media and the corporations lying so much . . . kind of like a child whose parents lie to them over and over again."[32]

The Infowars program, however, never blinked and never stopped churning out the conspiracy theories.

After a while inside the conspiracy-theory community, you notice that your fellow true believers are kind of manic—or at least very aggressive and extremely assertive, especially when it comes to presenting or defending or discussing new evidence.

What you notice, in fact, is that there's competition inside the community, particularly among the researchers who are constantly stitching together the crumbs left by figures like Jones and, in the QAnon world, by Q. The competition often becomes a race to see who can come up with the most imaginative, the most in-your-face evidence or line of argument.

The suspicion among members of the community runs high, feelings often get hurt, and sniping goes on behind backs and to people's faces, and pretty soon things become complicated. In addition to being openly paranoid, a lot of the participants are also bellicose, quick to anger, massively egotistical with tender sensitivities, and, as time goes on, turn out to be rather unpleasant people to hang around. Trust issues turn formerly interesting forums into mutual sniping zones.

This is exacerbated by the unusual levels of financial hanky-panky that seem to haunt so many operations inside the conspiracy-theory universe. Scams abound (it turns out that Alex Jones's so-called health supplements operation essentially sells people items that they can find at a local store but at a huge markup), and everywhere you turn, conspiracists are hitting you up for donations or purchases of their products.

So, after a while, a lot of people find themselves shifting their communities around, depending on the interpersonal dynamics that evolve within the group—that, and the way people's ideologies begin evolving. Especially as they become increasingly exposed to the ideas underlying and animating these conspiracy theories.

Like, say, "cultural Marxism." There's so much seemingly scholarly and established evidence proving its existence, if you follow the trails on the Internet. It's yet another rabbit hole. Maybe it's the ultimate one.

Sometimes, the feuding breaks out on the surface, among the leading conspiracists: Noted "alt-lite" figures Jack Posobiec and Laura Loomer, in the summer of 2018, argued about who deserved credit for the conspiracy theory they both promoted that Stephen Paddock, the Las Vegas shooter, actually had secret ties to Islamic State. Loomer had in fact first promoted this absurdly baseless claim that members of Congress had been briefed on "ISIS ties" to the shooting.

"I just thought it was really shady how Jack calls himself my friend, but then he won't give me credit for my work," Loomer said.[33]

However, Loomer herself picked up the story from a group called Americans for Intelligence Reform, who claimed that an Australian man who also stayed at the Mandalay Bay resort that evening was somehow mysteriously connected to it all, and this man had not-altogether-clear connections to Islamic State. In the modern age of evidence-free conspiracy theories, this thin gruel was enough to fuel speculation for a week or so.

There have been other feuds, involving different dynamics: popular podcaster Joe Rogan and Alex Jones quarreled over the Sandy Hook conspiracy theories, which Rogan found embarrassing. Roger Stone, the onetime Donald Trump aide, and conspiracy-meister Jerome Corsi, who at one time were bosom allies, broke into a vicious feud over their respective roles in the investigation into Russian interference in the 2016 election led by Robert Mueller, in which they both were witnesses.[34]

However, most of the real internecine warring within the world of conspiracy theories takes place on the Internet among the various would-be participants, researchers, and self-proclaimed "investigators" and "citizen journalists." It also occurs vividly among the conspiracy-fueled street-fighting organizations like the Proud Boys and their various cousins.

One of the more prolific such groups, in terms of organizing street protests that are designed to devolve into mass brawls and riots, is Patriot Prayer, an outfit based in Vancouver, Washington, across the Columbia River from Portland, Oregon, a city whose small but established population of anarchists and antifascists is the target of the events. Although Patriot Prayer founder Joey Gibson—himself a mixed-race Japanese American—occasionally denounced white supremacists, his events regularly attracted significant numbers of skinheads, white nationalists, and neo-Nazis, in addition to the Patriot/militia bikers that formed the group's original core.[35]

This created tensions within the group, many of whose members were just fine with the presence of bigots, whereas others loudly denounced them. Moreover, the Oregon chapter of the Proud Boys were among Patriot Prayer's sturdiest supporters and, in fact, formed its largest and most violent street-fighting faction. Gibson's right-hand man, a hulking Samoan named Tusitala "Tiny" Toese, was certainly the most prominent of these Proud Boys, as well as one of its most prolific brawlers, resulting in numerous arrests and, eventually, a police investigation.

During the winter of 2018–2019, however, Patriot Prayer and the Proud Boys started feuding, likely because the inclement Northwest weather dampened enthusiasm for the street events. It devolved into a cesspit of internal squabbling, accompanied by fever-pitched talk of committing violence, some of it directed at one another.

This cluster of far-right activists, mostly based in the exurban and suburban areas around Vancouver, had been ratcheting up the violence inherent in their rhetoric for the previous year and a half, beginning with a rally that drew a massive counterprotest shortly after an alt-right figure who had attended Patriot Prayer events stabbed two men to death on a Portland commuter train.[36] That was followed by Gibson-organized events that turned into massive brawls in Olympia and Seattle, Washington, and in San Francisco and Berkeley, California.[37]

They also favored violent conspiracist rhetoric. Gibson regularly wore an Infowars shirt to his events. Gibson and Tiny Toese both sported "Pinochet Did Nothing Wrong" shirts sold by the Proud Boys, featuring graphics showing people being pitched out of helicopters, at events the summer of 2018. And both talked increasingly about the need to "step things up" on the Facebook videos they liked to post. Even before a June 30, 2018, event that turned into a riot, Patriot Prayer had been vowing to "cleanse" the streets of Portland.[38]

In the meantime, Toese went on a far-right podcast and explained that he didn't really have any problems with white supremacists. "I don't give a fuck if real racists come to the rallies, real alt-right," he said. "We've been trying to beat these people up for a long time; it ain't gonna work. The only thing that we can do to solve this whole fucking problem with Nazis and all this shit is to have a civil conversation. And both sides understanding what the other side wants."[39]

It's not clear what precipitated Toese's falling-out with Patriot Prayer, but it appeared to revolve around Haley Adams, a young blonde who had been an increasingly visible presence at the organization's events during the previous year. Social media conversations suggested that Adams may have been planning to "dox" some of the Proud Boy participants, which led Toese, who had become increasingly loyal to the Proud Boys over the same period, to denounce Adams. According to one account, Adams had actually been denounced by Proud Boys "elders."

In response, Adams's most fervent defenders in Patriot Prayer took to social media to make the split with Proud Boys clear and unequivocal. "Haley Adams has my full approval to say whatever she wants to say," a man named Russell

Schultz said in his video. "If the Proud Boys want to attack her, that just tells me they are getting triggered and beat by a little girl."

Calling the Proud Boys "beta," Schultz went on to promise he would "kill" any Proud Boys who wanted to fight him over the dispute. "This shit cannot happen," he said. "You are a psycho; you need to get out of the fucking movement. If you're afraid of being doxxed, get out of the fucking movement; you don't need to be here; you're a cancer. You have a problem with me, want to come at me, I'm gonna fucking waste you. You have no chance against me. I may even come looking for you one day."[40]

Now you no longer know who to trust. Your fellow "independent thinkers" have proven to be untrustworthy. You feel more alone than ever.

Turning back to your family and friends is out of the question. They've already betrayed you. You can envision the gloating looks on their faces if you try turning back to them. That's not an option.

So you just go it alone. A lot of people quit their jobs and get work where they don't have to be in touch with normies because they can't stand trying to fake their utter contempt for these people. It's not that hard to do in the Internet age; you can work out of your home.

Other people move to remote, rural places where their contact with other people is even further minimized. They don't mind. They are going to be laughing when the shit hits the fan and the end of the world comes and everyone else is unprepared.

You won't be, even if you have to go it completely alone. A lone wolf, that's what you are.

It probably is no surprise that a community built around paranoia and suspicion and a highly fluid standard regarding what comprises factual reality would eventually devolve into squabbling, threats, and even violence. That certainly is what has happened, time and time again, within the world of conspiracy theories. And yet the theories themselves continue to exert a powerful gravitational pull that keeps most of the people who tumble down the rabbit hole well within their orbit.

It's almost inevitable that people who remain within the conspiracist alternative universe for any extended period will eventually feel almost completely isolated because of the kinds of personalities the universe attracts: insecure, possessing low self-esteem about their place in the world, yet bellicose, angry, aggressive, and often egotistical. People within this universe form fast, intense friendships that often burn out quickly, leaving a trail of hard feelings, small betrayals, and personal antagonisms that remain buried in their psyches.

Eventually, the isolation becomes complete. The end point of the conspiracist narrative is a person who is cut off from everyone in the world—his family, his old friends, his coworkers, even his next-door neighbors—because they all are either suspected active members of the conspiracy or are hapless, gullible pawns. He has no political power because he does not vote and does not participate in any part of the process. He even is cut off from the rest of the culture because he no longer consumes any media except material that helps support the conspiracy narrative.

"All this conspiracism erodes trust not just in public institutions but in our fellow citizens," observes Nancy Rosenblum. "We're obliterating trust in each other and in the political competition, and that's a direct attack on the foundations of democracy. Liberal democracy requires a minimum amount of mutual trust among citizens, and conspiracism destroys it."[41]

It is at these endpoints—when the conspiracist is utterly convinced he is alone in the world—that the real danger of violence becomes manifest, particularly if the true believer becomes convinced, for one reason or another, that he *must* act in order to save mankind or his family or his race or whomever he perceives as being threatened.

"The relationship between conspiracy theories and violent action is complicated, and researchers are only beginning to examine its complexity," writes University of Miami political scientist Joseph Uscinski. "Perhaps those who commit violence would do so regardless of their conspiracy beliefs. Maybe conspiracy theories are only one of many motivations for violence. Researchers don't yet know.

"But the latest findings suggest that those most likely to believe in conspiracy theories are also (1) more likely to support violence against the government, (2) more likely to oppose gun control measures, and (3) more likely to agree that it's acceptable to engage in conspiracies themselves to achieve goals. It's not hard to see how the approval of violence, lax gun laws, and secret plotting could form a toxic combination driving some to fight fire with fire."[42]

Not all conspiracy theorists, of course, wind up engaging in a mass shooting. The vast majority, in fact, simply remain within that realm and often wind up amassing a huge alternative universe comprised of entire libraries of arcane "facts," ruminations, conjectures, and naked lies.

However, their presence as a factor in nearly every single major mass shooting and domestic terrorist event of the past thirty years makes it irrevocably clear that they play a critical role in the unhinging of people who go down that path: the dehumanization of other people, the sense of surreality that everyday life acquires, and, most of all, the ongoing and ultimately complete disconnectedness of the conspiracist from everyday life and ordinary human contact—all these combine for a lethal combination that destroys the lives of the people it infects and then destroys the lives of the thousands of innocents whose misfortune places them within their sphere. They are quite literally killing us all.

Chapter 7

CHAOS BY DESIGN

What's on the menu? When it comes to everyone's social media diet, there's one constant you can count on: misinformation.

It's built into the system. Sociologist Zeynep Tufekci explained it succinctly in her TED talk:[1]

> So in 2016, I attended rallies of then-candidate Donald Trump to study as a scholar the movement supporting him. I study social movements, so I was studying it, too. And then I wanted to write something about one of his rallies, so I watched it a few times on YouTube. YouTube started recommending to me and autoplaying to me white supremacist videos in increasing order of extremism. If I watched one, it served up one even more extreme and autoplayed that one, too. If you watch Hillary Clinton or Bernie Sanders content, YouTube recommends and autoplays conspiracy left, and it goes downhill from there.
>
> Well, you might be thinking, this is politics, but it's not. This isn't about politics. This is just the algorithm figuring out human behavior. I once watched a video about vegetarianism on YouTube and YouTube recommended and autoplayed a video about being vegan. It's like you're never hardcore enough for YouTube.
>
> So what's going on? Now, YouTube's algorithm is proprietary, but here's what I think is going on. The algorithm has figured out that if you can entice people into thinking that you can show them something more hardcore, they're more likely to stay on the site watching video after video going down that rabbit hole while Google serves them ads. Now, with nobody minding the ethics of the store, these sites can profile people who are Jew haters, who think that Jews are parasites and who have such explicit anti-Semitic content, and let you target them with ads.

They can also mobilize algorithms to find for you look-alike audiences, people who do not have such explicit anti-Semitic content on their profile but who the algorithm detects may be susceptible to such messages, and lets you target them with ads, too. Now, this may sound like an implausible example, but this is real. ProPublica investigated this and found that you can indeed do this on Facebook, and Facebook helpfully offered up suggestions on how to broaden that audience. BuzzFeed tried it for Google, and very quickly they found, yep, you can do it on Google, too. And it wasn't even expensive. The ProPublica reporter spent about $30 to target this category.[2]

As Internet companies like YouTube and Facebook have struggled with the deluge of far-right extremism, racial bigotry, and conspiracy theories that have filled their platforms, it's becoming increasingly clear that there's one very simple and yet insurmountable reason they haven't been able to get it under control: their revenue streams are built around attracting such content.[3]

YouTube executives, as a Bloomberg News piece exposed in early 2019, have remained lackadaisical about the problem over the years that it has accumulated. "Scores of people inside YouTube and Google, its owner, raised concerns about the mass of false, incendiary and toxic content that the world's largest video site surfaced and spread," Peter Bergen reported. "Each time they got the same basic response: Don't rock the boat."[4]

Getting these platforms to clamp down on speech that helps fuel racial violence—notably including conspiracy-theorist content that scapegoats targeted minorities—is made more difficult both by the traffic-boosting incentives in place to permit it to continue, as well as by the ease with which targeted offenders can escape their wrath and continue to post content.

The conspiratorial mindset is threaded throughout the social fabric of YouTube. It's part of the warp and weft of its production economy. "YouTube offers infinite opportunities to create a closed ecosystem, an opaque algorithm, and the chance for a very small number of people to make a very large amount of money," observes Alexis Madrigal, deputy editor of the *Atlantic*. "While these conditions of production—which incentivize content creation at a very low cost to YouTube—exist on other modern social platforms, YouTube's particular constellation of them is special. It's why conspiracy videos get purchase on the site, and why they will be very hard to uproot."[5]

No one is more emblematic of that problem than conspiracy-meister Alex Jones of Infowars, who was officially banned from YouTube and Facebook in August 2018. Even though Jones had a long and horrific track record with his videos, the lawsuit filed by the parents of Sandy Hook victims plagued by Infowars followers made clear the potential liability that every platform that hosted his work faced.[6]

Jones has not disappeared easily, however. His Infowars content has been reposted by a number of mirror sites that eventually have been removed—one as recently as just after the attacks in Christchurch. In spite of this, Media Matters notes: "Channels that violate YouTube's rules by exclusively sharing Infowars content are easily found on YouTube, but the video platform doesn't appear to be devoting many resources to enforcing its own rules."[7]

Indeed, YouTube very nearly installed a remuneration system for its video creators in 2017 that would have made Jones the site's highest-paid contributor and only changed course after its platform was linked to various acts of violence.

The top priority at YouTube is "engagement": getting people to come to the site and remain there, accumulated in data as views, time spent viewing, and interactions. Moderating extremist content is often devalued if it interferes with the company's main goals. The key for gauging engagement is a metric the algorithm designers call "watch time"—that is, the amount of time you spend consuming media on the site.

Becca Lewis, a researcher with the technology research nonprofit Data & Society, warns that this fixation on watch time can be either banal or dangerous. "In terms of YouTube's business model and attempts to keep users engaged on their content, it makes sense what we're seeing the algorithms do," Lewis said. "That algorithmic behavior is great if you're looking for makeup artists and you watch one person's content and want a bunch of other people's advice on how to do your eye shadow. But it becomes a lot more problematic when you're talking about political and extremist content."[8]

The company announced early in 2019 that it intended to crack down on the conspiracism. However, part of its problem is that YouTube in fact created a huge market for these crackpot and often harmful theories by unleashing an unprecedented boom in conspiracism. That same market is where it now makes its living.

The formula for success that emerged over time at YouTube is simple: "Outrage equals attention." Brittan Heller, a fellow at Harvard University's Carr Center, observed that it's also ripe for exploitation by political extremists and hucksters. "They don't know how the algorithm works," she said. "But they do know that the more outrageous the content is, the more views."[9]

And the more views, the more money these platforms—not just YouTube, but Google and Facebook and Twitter and Instagram—roll in. Hate and division become the fuel for profit in this system.

Information scientist Safiya Umoja Noble observes that "the neoliberal political and economic environment has profited tremendously from misinformation and mischaracterization of communities, with a range of consequences for the most disenfranchised and marginalized among us." She has particularly zeroed in on the way that search engines have bolstered white nationalist and similarly extremist ideas through their "algorithms of oppression": "Search results, in the context of commercial advertising companies, lay the groundwork . . . for implicit bias: bias that is buttressed by advertising profits."[10]

Algorithms not only are designed to reinforce racial stereotypes and narratives, they actually help encourage people to be radicalized by extremist political ideologies—particularly white nationalism.

It may be the most notorious Google search in history: "black on white crime." That was the search that sent Dylann Roof down the path that led him to murder nine black parishioners inside a Charleston, South Carolina, church one evening in June 2015.

He described this path in a post on the white supremacist website he had created.

> The event that truly awakened me was the Trayvon Martin case. I kept hearing and seeing his name, and eventually I decided to look him up. I read the Wikipedia article and right away I was unable to understand what the big deal was. It was obvious that Zimmerman was in the right. But more importantly this prompted me to type in the words "black on White crime" into Google, and I have never been the same since that day. The first website I came to was the Council of Conservative Citizens. There were pages upon pages of these brutal black on White murders. I was in disbelief. At this moment I realized that something was very wrong. How could the news be blowing up the Trayvon Martin case while hundreds of these black on White murders got ignored?
>
> From this point I researched deeper and found out what was happening in Europe. I saw that the same things were happening in England and France, and in all the other Western European countries. Again I found myself in disbelief. As an American we are taught to accept living in the melting pot, and black and other minorities have just as much right to be here as we do, since we are all immigrants. But Europe is the homeland of White people, and in many ways the situation is even worse there. From here I found out about the Jewish problem and other issues facing our race, and I can say today that I am completely racially aware.[11]

Roof actually has provided a kind of map of radicalization online. As information scientist Michael Caulfield explains, this whole process is actually produced by a kind of self-contained data spiral that's based to a large extent on "curation"—that is, the way we collect web materials into our own spaces and annotate them.[12] That curation creates a data feedback for the algorithm that then directly affects what you see. Curations, he warns, can warp reality because of the resulting feedback loop: they "don't protect us from opposing views, but often bring us to more radical views."

Caulfield observes that "black on white crime" is a data void—that is, it's not a term used by social scientists or reputable news organizations, "which is why the white nationalist site Council of Conservative Citizens came up in those results. That site has since gone away, but what it was was a running catalog of cases where black men had murdered (usually) white women. In other words, it's yet another curation, even more radical and toxic than the one that got you there. And then the process begins again."

Noble explains that the framing a person brings to his or her Internet experience shapes what kinds of results they see on a search engine, or a video recommendation, or a social media news feed. "In the case of Dylann Roof's alleged Google searches," she writes, "his very framing of the problems of race relations in the U.S. through an inquiry such as 'black on white crime' reveals how search results belie any ability to intercede in the framing of a question itself. In this case, answers from conservative organizations and cloaked websites that present news from a right-wing, anti-Black, and anti-Jewish perspective are nothing more than propaganda to foment racial hatred."[13]

The key to this process of radicalization is its incremental nature: people undergoing it don't recognize what is happening to them, since each step feels normal initially. This is in fact precisely by design by the organizations and ideologues who are trying to recruit people into their conspiracy theories, which are ultimately about belief systems and political movements.

A onetime "red-pilled" conspiracy theorist named Matt described how he became trapped in a curated spiral like this for Kelly Weill of the *Daily Beast*. It began when he innocently watched a video of Bill Maher and Ben Affleck discussing Islam, and at its completion, the algorithm recommended several much more extreme videos attacking Islam, including some produced by Infowars conspiracy theorist Paul Joseph Watson. One video led to the next and the next.[14]

"Delve into [Watson's] channel and start finding his anti-immigration stuff which often in turn leads people to become more sympathetic to ethnonationalist politics," Matt said. "This sort of indirectly sent me down a path to moving way more to the right politically as it led me to discover other people with similar far-right views."

Now twenty, Matt has since exited the ideology and built an anonymous Internet presence where he argues with his ex-brethren on the right.

"I think YouTube certainly played a role in my shift to the right because through the recommendations I got," he said, "it led me to discover other content that was very much right of center, and this only got progressively worse over time, leading me to discover more sinister content."

"The thing to remember about this algorithmic–human grooming hybrid is that the gradualness of it—the step-by-step nature of it—is a feature for the groomers, not a bug," says Caulfield. "I imagine if the first page Roof had encountered on the CCC page had sported a Nazi flag and a big banner saying 'Kill All Jews,' he'd have hit the back button, and maybe the world might be different. (Maybe.) But the curation/search spiral brings you to that point step by step. In the center of the spiral you probably still have enough good sense to not read stuff by Nazis, at least knowingly. By the time you get to the edges, not so much."[15]

Peter Neumann, of the United Kingdom's Centre for the Study of Radicalisation, identifies six steps on the ladder of extremist belief. "The first two of these processes deal with the consequences of being exposed to extremist content," he writes. "No single item of extremist propaganda is guaranteed to transform people into terrorists. Rather, in most cases, online radicalization results from individuals being immersed in extremist content for extended periods of time, the amplified effects of graphic images and video, and the resulting emotional desensitization."[16]

Beheading videos, photos of corpses, suicides, and mass murders, all these things are part of these first two steps in the immersion process. Neumann calls this *mortality salience*—material intended to create an overpowering sense of one's own vulnerability to death, as well as to heighten the viewer's moral outrage.

The next two steps are also key to the process—namely, immersion in extremist forums, where deviant and extremist views are normalized, and online disinhibition, wherein people lose their normal inhibitions about violence because of their relative anonymity online. "Some of the participants get so worked up that they declare themselves ready to be terrorists," notes psychologist Marc Sageman. "Since this process takes place at home, often in the parental home, it facilitates the emergence of homegrown radicalization, worldwide."[17]

The final stages occur when online role-playing occurs—the kind in which new recruits more or less practice their ideology in gaming situations, often in the context of modern video games. The participants project themselves into their gaming avatars, giving themselves traits that they usually do not possess in real life. After a while, this divide becomes noticeable and drives further radicalization: "[A]fter recognizing the gap between their avatar's mobilization and their own physical mobilization, many online participants begin taking steps to reconcile the gap," observe researchers Jaret Brachmann and Alex Levine.[18] This is when they take the last step: using the Internet to connect directly to terrorist infrastructures that then begin to mobilize them.

Caulfield believes one of the keys to preventing this kind of radicalization lies in establishing "digital literacy" programs wherein young people new to the

Internet can learn how to confront, cope with, and overcome the challenges they will be forced to navigate there. And it all begins with the curation process, how we accumulate the materials for our personal spaces.

"So, the idea here is that you might start in a relatively benign space with some kind of ideological meaning, and then someone uses this term 'black on white crime,'" Caulfield says. "It's probably a stretch to call the Google search results a curation, but you can think of it along the same lines. You put in a term, and Google is going to show you the most relevant, not necessarily the best, but the most relevant results for that term. And now you have a set of things that are in front of you. Now, on each of those pages, because you picked 'black on white crime,' if you click into that page that has 'black on white crime,' there are going to be other phrases on there."[19]

Even people with normal levels of skepticism can find themselves drawn inside. "So you go, and you do the Google search, and you're like, 'You know what? I can't trust this page. I'm going to be a good info-literacy person, and what I'm going to do is, I'm going to just check that these crimes really happened.' OK, so what do you do? You pull these crimes and what you find is that these crimes *did* happen, and the pages they're going to are more white supremacists talking about how these are actually black on white hate crimes. And now they're mentioning more things, and they're mentioning more terms, and they're mentioning changes in law that now make it easier for black people to kill white people.

"So you're like 'Oh, well, I've got to Google this change in the law.' But who's talking about this thing that's broadly made up, or it's a heavy misinterpretation of something? Well, again it's white. . . . So you keep going deeper and deeper, and every time you're pulling out something to investigate on that page, it's pulling you into another site, and that other site of course is covering a bunch of other events and terms and so forth. And you end up going deeper and deeper into it."[20]

Caulfield argues that educators need to help their students develop better informational literacy, including learning how to recognize when they are being recruited into a radical belief system or cult or are being manipulated for either financial or political motivations.

"My contention is that the students are practicing info-literacy as they've learned it," he says. "And as a matter of fact, this approach to researching online is what they have learned from a fairly early age in terms of how to approach sources and information on the web.

"I think a lot of academics and teachers would say, 'but that's not what we're teaching,'" he adds. "Let's just put that whole argument aside because it doesn't matter. Whatever we're teaching, these are the lessons they take away from it. So they are practicing info-literacy as learned, and through either chance or through engineering or through fate, whatever it is, these techniques plug really well into radicalization."[21]

—————

Sometimes the people who fall down the rabbit holes and are recruited into communities organized around conspiracy theories would have ended up in a similar situation regardless. But people are also being actively recruited for a combination of political, ideological, and financial/economic motivations. And they are being actively deceived.

"We are all targets of disinformation, meant to erode our trust in democracy and divide us," warns University of Washington information scientist Kate Starbird.[22]

She came to this stark conclusion while conducting a study at the University of Washington involving the evolution of the discussion about the Black Lives Matter movement on social media—and found herself walking into the unexpected realization, supported both by data and a raft of real-world evidence, that the whole discussion was being manipulated, and not for the better. The more the team examined the evidence, the clearer it became that this manipulation was intended to fuel internal social strife among the American public.[23]

The study quickly morphed into a scientific examination of disinformation—that is, information that's intended to confuse and distort, whether accurate or not—which exists on all sides of the political spectrum.[24] One of their key studies focused on Twitter to see how bad information immediately follows major crisis-type events such as mass shootings and how those rumors "muddy the waters" around the event, even for people who were physically present, and in particular how such rumors can permanently alter the public's perception of the event itself and its causes.

Consider exhibit A: the nearly instantaneous claims by Alex Jones and other conspiracy theorists that the Las Vegas mass shooting of October 1, 2017, was a false flag event and the ensuing swirl of confusion around it, which eventually permanently obscured the public's understanding that the man who perpetrated it was unhinged and at least partially motivated by far-right conspiracy theories about guns. Police investigators avoided the evidence that this had been the case as well.

The chief reason we perceive stories, whether real or not, as "true" depends in large part on our unconscious cognitive biases, Starbird says—that is, when our preexisting beliefs are confirmed along the way. We've seen how these biases can be targeted by technology companies. Well-equipped political organizations can manipulate disinformation in much the same way.

"If it makes you feel outraged against the other side, probably someone is manipulating you," she warns.[25]

The main wellspring of the disinformation Starbird dealt with in her study was Russia and its "troll farms" that introduced industrial-strength data pollution into the American discourse via social media during the 2016 election campaign and afterward. However, she says that the disinformation can be, and often is, run by anyone sophisticated enough to understand its essential principles. These include white nationalists, a number of conspiracy-oriented campaigns involving vaccines and other health-related conspiracies, and in recent years, QAnon.

The strategy, she says, is not just consistent, but frighteningly sophisticated and nuanced. "One of these goals is to 'sow division,' to put pressure on the fault lines in our society," she explained in her findings. "A divided society that turns against itself, that cannot come together and find common ground, is one that is easily manipulated. . . . Russian agents did not create political division in the United States, but they were working to encourage it."[26]

These outside organizational entities make full use of a preexisting media ecosystem featuring "news" outlets that claim to be "fair" and "independent," but which are in fact only propaganda organizations, nearly all of them right-wing. As Starbird explained in one of her studies:

> This alternative media ecosystem has challenged the traditional authority of journalists, both directly and indirectly. . . . Its development has been accompanied by a decreased reliance on and an increased distrust of mainstream media, with the latter partially motivated by a perception of widespread ethical violations and corruption within mainstream media. . . . Indeed, many view these alternative news sites as more authentic and truthful than mainstream media, and these effects are compounding—as research has found that exposure to online media correlates with distrust of mainstream media.[27]

False information renders democratic discourse, which relies on factual accuracy, impossible, and as Starbird notes, "with the loss of commonly-held standards regarding information mediation and the absence of easily decipherable credibility cues, this ecosystem has become vulnerable to the spread of misinformation and propaganda."[28]

Because it's actually a fairly closed, self-contained, and narrow ecosystem, it becomes a real echo chamber, with stories being repeated among the various "independent" news sites, even if they seem not to show up on the major networks (Fox being the most common exception). After a while, the repetition acts as a kind of confirmation for the stories—if people keep seeing different versions of the same headlines, they'll start thinking the information has been confirmed by a "variety" of sources.

"The tactics of disinformation can be used by anyone," Starbird says. "The Internet seems to facilitate access towards targets of different kinds, and we are definitely seeing disinformation from multiple sets of actors, including from the U.S., including foreign actors and domestic actors as well. There's a certain flavor of Russian disinformation that is perhaps different from some others, but the tactics are known and they are easily learned and portable."[29]

Unwinding the relationship between authoritarian governments like Russia—which has been promoting far-right political movements around the world, particularly in Europe—and white nationalists trying to "red-pill" vulnerable young people is complicated. "There are some movements, particularly these far-right movements, whose disinformation aligns neatly with Russian disinformation as well," Starbird observes.

"It's a chicken-and-egg problem. The current manifestation of the far right or alt-right or whatever we want to call it, the information systems and some of the mechanisms for information flow all seem to have Russian disinformation integrated into them. It's hard to know what's cause and what's effect, but they seem to be intertwined. In a similar way, we can see far left ecosystems around things like Syria and Venezuela are integrated with Russian disinformation as well. . . . We don't know how causal that is versus opportunistic."[30]

Among the most radical—and simultaneously, the most active—movements organizing and recruiting online, particularly on social media, are the white nationalists and misogynists who comprise the alt-right. Their homes are websites like the overtly neo-Nazi *Daily Stormer* site and a handful of other similar places, whence they spread out to a multitude of other forums to find potentially vulnerable recruits, most of them young.

The radical right itself has little compunction about identifying its target demographic for red-pilling. Andrew Anglin, publisher and founder of the *Stormer*, wrote: "My site is mainly designed to target children."[31] At the annual white nationalist American Renaissance conference in Tennessee in April 2018, longtime supremacists bragged about their demographic support: "American Renaissance attendees are now younger and more evenly divided among the sexes than in the past," one speaker noted before gushing over the white nationalist college campus group Identity Evropa.[32]

When authorities, both in the United States and abroad, have talked about online radicalization in the recent past, most of us have tended to think of it in terms of radical Islamists from groups such as Islamic State, who have been known to leverage the technology to their advantage, particularly social media. A study by terrorism expert J. M. Berger published in 2016 found that white nationalists were far outstripping their Islamist counterparts, however: "On Twitter, ISIS's preferred social platform, American white nationalist movements have seen their followers grow by more than 600 percent since 2012. Today, they outperform ISIS in nearly every social metric, from follower counts to tweets per day."[33]

"Online radicalization seems to be speeding up, with young men, particularly white men, diving into extremist ideologies quicker and quicker," Berger said, adding that "the result seems to be more violence, as these examples indicate. It is a serious problem and we don't seem to have any real solutions for it. These cases also show that an era of violence brought on by the internet is indeed upon us, with no end in sight."

The radicalization process itself often begins with seemingly benign activity, such as spending hours in chat rooms or playing computer games, and these activities provide a kind of cover for the process as it accelerates. Eventually, two things happen: The fresh recruits become eager to take their ideology to the streets, to make it manifest in real life and not merely online. At the same time, the ideology itself often becomes much more radical, often swiftly, ending in an embrace of explicit fascism and white supremacy.

That is how Patriot Front came into being: best known for its members plastering overtly racist and xenophobic fliers around campuses and various locales around the nation, it nonetheless recruits and organizes almost entirely online.[34]

The origins of Patriot Front lie in neo-Nazi organizing that began in 2015 at the message board IronMarch.org, itself an outgrowth of the community of dedicated fascists who commented at online forums such as 4chan and Stormfront and allegedly founded by Russian nationalist Alexander Slavros. IronMarch in turn spun off the activist group Atomwaffen (German for "atomic bomb") Division, whose members engaged in various far-right actions in both 2018 and 2019.[35] Atomwaffen activists favored plastering flyers advertising their organization, and their reach included the University of Washington campus in Seattle.[36]

Although Atomwaffen Division was explicit in its embrace of German-style Nazism, other fascists at IronMarch began discussing ways to broaden their reach in order to compete with alt-right and identitarian groups such as Identity Evropa for young recruits. Out of these discussions they created a new group in 2015, first named Reaction America, then renamed in 2016 as American Vanguard. When one of that group's leaders was exposed for offering up information to an antifascist group and IronMarch users and administrators began "doxxing" American Vanguard members, the group broke away from IronMarch. In early 2017, the organization once again rebranded as Vanguard America. After an Atomwaffen Division member in Florida shot and killed two other members in May 2017, telling authorities the group was planning to blow up a nuclear plant, a number of Atomwaffen participants joined ranks with Vanguard America.[37]

The leader of Vanguard America (VA), a Marine Corps veteran from New Mexico named Dillon Irizarry (but better known by his nom de plume Dillon

Hopper), began organizing rallies at which members openly carried firearms. On its website, VA claimed that America was built on the foundation of white Europeans and demanded the nation recapture the glory of the Aryan nation, free of the influence of the international Jews.[38]

Vanguard America had a significant presence in Charlottesville, Virginia, for the August 11–12, 2017, "Unite the Right" rally, as several of its members joined in the Friday-night torch-bearing march onto the University of Virginia campus. The next day, a phalanx of VA marchers chanting "Blood and soil!" marched toward the protest at a city park and then were recorded acting as a shield wall meant to protect the park and its monument to Robert E. Lee, whose feared imminent removal by city fathers was, symbolically at least, the nominal focus of the protest.

Among those VA marchers was James Alex Fields, the twenty-year-old Ohio man who, later that afternoon, drove his Dodge Challenger into a crowd of counterprotesters and maimed twenty people, killing one, thirty-two-year-old Heather Heyer. VA later issued a statement claiming that Fields was not actually a member of the organization.[39]

Another marcher that Saturday in Charlottesville—indeed, photographed only two marchers away from Fields—was Thomas Rousseau, who not only was a VA member but had taken a prominent leadership role in the group online. Based in Texas, Rousseau noted in chats that VA's statement "never said that [Fields] did anything wrong." Soon he and other participants were recommending yet another name change.[40]

On August 30, Rousseau announced, in a major split with Irizarry/Hopper, that "we are rebranding and reorganizing as a new entity," henceforth to be known as "Patriots Front" (the "s" was dropped in short order). "The new name was carefully chosen, as it serves several purposes. It can help inspire sympathy among those more inclined to fence-sitting, and can easily be used to justify our worldview."

The mention of "fence sitting" was a reference to the ongoing discussion within the online neo-Nazi community about engaging and recruiting young men sympathetic to their underlying cause but not yet fully radicalized. There had been similar discussions about drawing in "patriots" from the far-right militia movement, who have traditionally insisted on drawing a line on participating in outright white supremacist activity.

Rousseau also made it clear that the plan was to translate online discussion into real-world actions, concrete activism: "You will be expected to work, and work hard to meet the bar rising," he wrote. "Inactivity will get you expelled, unwillingness to work and contribute in any capacity will as well."[41]

As Patriot Front's organizing has played out in real life, that "work" has primarily comprised making their presence felt at rallies and protests, spreading the word with freeway banners, and plastering flyers in public locations, where they are often summarily removed.

That ethos is how Patriot Front organizing generally has played out on the ground. The group first made its presence felt in Houston in September 2017, when about a dozen members appeared outside a book fair and demanded a fight with antifascist organizers who reportedly were inside giving a talk. (Rousseau later led a similar protest outside an Austin bookstore.)

Other members around the country began taking their activism public by erecting banners promoting the Patriot Front website on freeway overpasses, frequently for just short periods and removed before authorities arrived to remove them. In Seattle's Fremont neighborhood, a group of masked neo-Nazis briefly unfurled a swastika-laden banner advertising IronMarch.org; two months later, in suburban Bellevue, a similar group put up a banner advertising bloodandsoil.org on an Interstate 90 overpass, where it was shortly removed by Department of Transportation workers. In October, someone erected a Patriot Front "Resurrection through Insurrection" banner on a freeway near Los Angeles, California. And in November, Patriot Front activists put up a banner in San Antonio, Texas, on the Texas–San Antonio campus.

The most widespread manifestation of Patriot Front's organizing efforts, however, has been the appearance of its flyers in public spaces around the country. Their stark black-and-white posters—featuring a variety of slogans, including "We Have a Right to Exist," "Fascism: The Next Step for America," "Will Your Speech Be Hate Speech?" as well as screeds urging "patriots" to "reconquer your birthright," while others exhort "all white Americans" to "report any and all illegal aliens"—have been either taped or glued to lampposts, telephone poles, windows, doors, bulletin boards, and anywhere else they can be seen by the public. They have especially targeted college campuses.

However, Patriot Front is notable for its utterly undisguised and unrepentant fascism. It's also utterly lacking in the often juvenile transgressive humor and use of pop culture and irony that are core to much of the appeal of the alt-right online. Instead, its dead-serious advocacy of white supremacist ideology is intended to appeal to a more militant mindset, an important byproduct of its origins in the IronMarch.org community. As the manifesto on its website explains in depth:

> An African may have lived, worked, and even been classed as a citizen in America for centuries, yet he is not American. He is, as he likely prefers to be labelled, an African in America. The same rule applies to others who are not of the founding stock of our people, or do not share the common unconscious that permeates throughout our greater civilization, and the European diaspora. The American identity was something uniquely forged in the struggle that our ancestors

waged to survive in this new continent. America is truly unique in this pan-European identity which forms the roots of our nationhood. To be an American is to realize this identity and take up the national struggle upon one's shoulders. Not simply by birth is one granted this title, but by the degree to which he works and fulfills the potential of his birth. No man is complete simply to live, but to do more than that, to strive to create a path onward for his people, and to connect with the heritage he is undeniably a part of. That is what completes a man. Only then is he truly deserving of the title and a place among his people.

To date, Patriot Front appears mainly to be comprised of small clusters of dedicated neo-Nazis intent on spreading their fascist gospel to other right-wing extremists, especially "fence-sitting" alt-righters potentially attracted to violent street action. It is noteworthy mainly because of the ease and rapidity with which it has spread to nearly every corner of the country, and the open appeals to young white males, who are the focus of their recruitment.[42]

Atomwaffen Division, however, became another matter altogether. It came to national prominence after the arrests in summer of 2017, when one of its members murdered his two roommates, who also belonged to the overtly neo-Nazis training organization, and a third, who wasn't present when the killings occurred, was shortly caught with a carful of homemade explosives, arrested, and convicted. A few months later, another Atomwaffen member murdered a gay Jewish student from California.

A *ProPublica* exposé of Atomwaffen Division published in February 2018 revealed that its members had been undergoing arms training in the woods, while plotting to target key members of the public for assassination and ultimately a "race war." They also discussed domestic terrorism, including poisoning city water supplies, bombing natural gas lines, and destroying electric infrastructure.

"We're only going to inspire more 'copycat crimes' in the name of AWD. All we have to do is spread our image and our propaganda," one of its leaders exhorted his cohorts.[43]

Getting red-pilled actually means a lot of different things to the people who claim it, though it generally refers to embracing any of a number of conspiracy theories and absorbing the conspiracist worldview—which can often morph into something even more radical very quickly.

A large collection of group chats among explicitly fascist ideologues and organizers was analyzed by the open-source journalism site Bellingcat, which examined the process by which recruits became increasingly radicalized and absorbed into the belief system.[44]

It found that most agree that the key is acknowledgment of the Jewish question, or JQ; that is, whether or not Jewish people are at the center of a vast global conspiracy, the end goal of which is usually "white genocide." The participants in the chats described red-pilling as a gradual process, but the end point seemed to be almost uniformly alt-right white nationalism.

"Individual people can be red-pilled on certain issues and not others," the report noted. "Stefan Molyneux, a popular author and far-right YouTube personality, is seen as being red-pilled on race and 'the future of the west' even though he is not considered as a fascist. Prominent YouTuber PewDiePie is also often considered red-pilled. It is accepted that media personalities need to hide their outright fascist beliefs, or 'power level,' in order to have a chance at red-pilling the general population."[45]

Recruitment techniques, in fact, tend to dominate the discussions, and disagreements often erupt over which are the most effective, though everyone concurred that people who harbor an animus toward "social justice warriors" (known more often by their acronym, SJWs) and "political correctness" are prime targets. They also agree that Donald Trump is seen as the source of red-pilling for many Americans.

Males comprised the vast majority of these fascist activists—some, in fact, doubted that women can be red-pilled at all. When women did appear on the scene, they made their marks by being even more extreme than the typical conspiracy theorist.

Most of them, though not all, were being radicalized online: the report found thirty-nine of the seventy-five fascists whose chats it studied credit the Internet as their red-pilling source, with YouTube the website most frequently referenced. However, the report notes that "when indoctrination begins offline new converts inevitably go online to deepen their beliefs."[46]

A user named barD described his red-pilling process:

> Get redpilled on Feminism after reading some crazy SJW posts about MLP [My Little Pony] being racist and sexist and anti-lesbian, get redpilled on islam after getting intruiged by some islamisists taking in a youtube comments section. Get redpilled on GG [Gamergate] from sargon.[47]

The spiral that barD described continued ratcheting up, ranging from comment-section disputes to consuming videos from far-right YouTube personalities to participating in the comments at "the_donald" subreddit and 4chan's infamous white nationalist–dominated /pol/ board, eventually concluding at fascist Discord servers.

Radicalized recruits are fond of claiming that they actually never used to be racist at all but that an argument with an "SJW" online made them so angry they turned to white nationalist ideology. They insist that racist remarks they make are meant only "ironically," rather like the OK sign. Bellingcat found a user named FucknOathMate who, when asked if he was "only doing it ironically at first," replied, "Well sort of"—then added that, before he was red-pilled, he knew Jewish people were "weird" and "ran everything," but he hadn't yet become a Holocaust denier or a fascist as he was now.[48]

Conspiracy theories, particularly those peddled by Alex Jones, Paul Joseph Watson, and their multimedia Infowars operation, also played a key role in the "red-pilling" process for many of the people Bellingcat identified as dedicated fascists.

"Conspiracy theories appear to be one of the more well-trodden roads into fascist nationalism," it reported. A key example was provided by a Discord user using the nom de plume Harleen Kekzel, who claimed to have identified at the age of sixteen as a "polyamorous genderqueer masculine leaning pansexual" and that Alex Jones started her on the journey to becoming "red-pilled"—or rather that she "was conspiracy pilled" along with her husband.[49]

However, for all his usefulness, Jones and Infowars actually are viewed with considerable skepticism by many serious fascists who dismiss them as "controlled opposition." Jones, who denounced David Duke after having him on his program, is generally viewed as too compromised and too milquetoast for serious National Socialists—as are other right-wing pundits with a conspiracist bent, such as Michael Savage and David Horowitz, both of whom are Jewish.

The most striking and powerful pathway to radicalization for these young fascists, however, was YouTube.

"Fascists who become red-pilled through YouTube often start with comparatively less extreme right-wing personalities, like Ben Shapiro or Milo Yiannopolous," Bellingcat reported. "One user explained that he was a 'moderate republican' before 'Steven Crowder, Paul Joseph Watson, Milo Yiannopolous, Black Pidgeon Speaks,' and other far-right YouTubers slowly red-pilled him. Over time he 'moved further and further right until [he] could no longer stand them. That's why [he likes] those groups even still, because if we just had the Fascists, we'd never convert anyone.'"[50]

The serious fascists, however, view the alt-right as having something of an image problem, particularly in how it appropriates mainstream cartoon and humor imagery, like Pepe the Frog, who is widely recognized as the alt-right's chief mascot. "Fascist activists view the alt-right as silly, but also as a crucial recruiting ground," noted Bellingcat.[51]

And it doesn't get much sillier—or stranger and ultimately disturbingly toxic—than the Church of Kek.

You may have seen the name bandied about on social media, especially in political circles where alt-right activists and avid Donald Trump supporters lurk. Usually it is brandished as a kind of epithet, seemingly to ward off the effects of liberal arguments, and it often is conveyed in memes that use the image of the alt-right mascot, Pepe the Frog: "Kek!"[52]

Kek, in the alt-right's telling, is the "deity" of the semi-ironic "religion" the white nationalist movement has created for itself online—partly for amusement, as a way to troll liberals and self-righteous conservatives both, and partly to make a kind of political point. He is a god of chaos and darkness, with the head of a frog, and the source of the alt-right's memetic "magic," to whom white nationalists and Donald Trump alike owe their success, according to their own explanations.

In many ways, Kek is the apotheosis of the bizarre alternative reality of the alt-right: at once absurdly juvenile, transgressive, and racist, Kek also reflects a deeper, pseudo-intellectual purpose that appeals to young ideologues who fancy themselves deep thinkers. It dwells in that murky area they often occupy, between satire, irony, mockery, and serious ideology; Kek can be both a big joke on liberals and a reflection of the alt-right's own self-image as serious agents of chaos in modern society.

Most of all, Kek has become a kind of tribal marker of the alt-right: its meaning obscure and unavailable to "normies," referencing Kek is most often a way of signaling to fellow conversants online that the writer embraces the principles of chaos and destruction that are central to alt-right thinking. Many of them like to think of it as a harmless 4chan meme—though in the end, there really is nothing harmless about it.

The name, usage, and ultimately the ideas around it originated in gaming culture, particularly on chat boards devoted to the World of Warcraft online computer games, according to Know Your Meme.[53] In those games, participants can chat only with members of their own faction in the "war" (either Alliance or Horde fighters), while opposing players' chats are rendered in a cryptic form based on Korean; thus, the common chat phrase "LOL" (laugh out loud) was read by opposing players as "KEK." The phrase caught on as a variation on "LOL" in game chat rooms, as well as at open forums dedicated to gaming, animation, and popular culture, places such as 4chan and Reddit—also dens of the alt-right, where the Pepe the Frog meme (originally an apolitical cartoon frog created by a liberal named Matt Furie) also has its origins and similarly was hijacked as a symbol of white nationalism.

At some point, someone at 4chan happened to seize on a coincidence: there was, in fact, an Egyptian god named Kek. An androgynous god who could take either male or female form, Kek originally was depicted in female form as possessing the head of a frog or a cat and when male, a serpent, though during the Greco-Roman period, the male form was depicted as a frog-headed man.

More importantly, Kek was portrayed as a bringer of chaos and darkness, which happened to fit perfectly with the alt-right's self-image of being primarily devoted to destroying the existing world order.

In the fertile imaginations at play on 4chan's image boards and other alt-right gathering spaces, this coincidence took on a life of its own, leading to wide-ranging speculation that Pepe—who, by then, had not only become closely associated with the alt-right, but also with the candidacy of Donald Trump—was actually the living embodiment of Kek. And so the Cult of Kek was born.

Constructed to reflect alt-right politics, the online acolytes of the "religion" in short order constructed a whole panoply of artifacts of the satirical church, including a detailed theology, discussions about creating "meme magick," books and audiotapes, and even a common prayer:

> Our Kek who art in memetics
> Hallowed by thy memes
> Thy Trumpdom come
> Thy will be done
> In real life as it is on /pol/
> Give us this day our daily dubs
> And forgive us of our baiting
> As we forgive those who bait against us
> And lead us not into cuckoldry
> But deliver us from shills
> For thine is the memetic kingdom, and the shitposting, and the winning, for ever and ever.
> Praise KEK[54]

Kek "adherents" created a cultural mythology around the idea, describing an ancient kingdom called "Kekistan" that was eventually overwhelmed by "Normistan" and "Cuckistan." They created not only a logo representing Kek—four Ks surrounding an E—but promptly deployed it in a green and black banner, which they call the "national flag of Kekistan."

The banner's design, in fact, perfectly mimics a German Nazi war flag, with the Kek logo replacing the swastika and the green replacing the infamous German red. Alt-righters are particularly fond of the way that the banner trolls liberals who recognize its origins. It was all a goof. But it also wasn't.

Alt-right marchers at public events planned to create violent scenes with leftist, antifacist counterprotesters and have appeared carrying Kekistan banners. Others have worn patches adorned with the Kek logo.

Besides its entertainment value, the "religion" is mainly useful to the alt-right as a trolling device for making fun of liberals and "political correctness." A 2017 alt-right rally in support of adviser Stephen Bannon in front of the White

House, posted on YouTube by alt-right maven Cassandra Fairbanks, featured a Kekistan banner and a man announcing to the crowd a "free Kekistan" campaign.

One of the leaders of the group offered a satirical speech: "The Kekistani people are here; they stand with the oppressed minorities, the oppressed people of Kekistan. They will be heard; they will be set free. Reparations for Kekistan now! Reparations for Kekistan right now!"[55]

"We have lived under normie oppression for too long!" chimed in a cohort.

"The oppression will end!" declared the speaker.

The main point of the whole exercise was to mock "political correctness," an alt-right shibboleth, and it was deeply reflective of the ironic, often deadpan style of online trolling in general and alt-right "troll storms" especially. Certainly, if any "normies" were to make the mistake of taking the "religion" seriously and suggesting that its "deity" was something they actually worshipped, they would receive the usual mocking treatment reserved for anyone foolish enough to take their words at face value.

Yet at the same time, lurking behind all the clownery is an idea that alt-righters actually seem to take seriously: namely, that by spreading their often cryptic memes far and wide on social media and every other corner of the Internet, they are infecting the popular discourse with their ideas. For the alt-right, those core ideas all revolve around white males, the patriarchy, nationalism, and race, especially the underlying belief that white males and masculinity are under siege—from feminists, from liberals, from racial, ethnic, and sexual/gender minorities.

In such alt-right haunts as Andrew Anglin's neo-Nazi website the *Daily Stormer*, references to the Kek "religion" have become commonplace, and, besides electing Trump, Kek as the "god of chaos" has been credited at the site with killing more than thirty people in a fire at an Oakland artists' collective. A very early *Stormer* disquisition on Kek by "Atlantic Centurion," published in August 2015, explores the many dimensions of the Kek phenomenon in extensive theological detail, connecting their belief system to Buddhism and other religions.

> It is the Kek the Bodhisattva who can teach our people these truths, if we are willing to listen and to commit ourselves to the generation of meme magick through karmic morality and through the mantra of memes. By refusing to cuck and by rejecting the foul mindsets of our invaders and terrorizers, we will move the nation away from its suffering under the pains of hostile occupation, and closer and closer to its final rebirth. If instead, our people cuck and adopt the foul mindsets, they will generate not Aryan karma but further mosaic samsara.
> The trve power of skillful memes is to meme the karmic nation into reality, the process of meme magick. By spreading and repeating

the meme mantra, it is possible to generate the karma needed for the rebirth of the nation.[56]

Anglin himself frequently references Kek, making clear that he too subscribes to the underlying meme-spreading strategy that the "religion" represents. Describing a black artist's piece showing a crucified frog—which appeared to Anglin to be a kind of blasphemy of the Kek deity—he declared that "there's some cosmic-tier stuff going on out there." Another post, published in March, was headlined: "Meme Magic: White House Boy Summoned Spirit of Kek to Protect His Prophet Donald Trump."

Anglin devoted the post to explaining a teenager's use of an alt-right hand signal while meeting Trump, concluding that "the only possibility here is that this is an example of Carl Jung's synchronicity—seemingly acausal factors culminating to create an event based on its meaning. But it is not really acausal—it merely appears that way to the nonbeliever. It is our spiritual energies, channeled through the internet, that caused this event to manifest," he wrote. "It is meme magic."[57]

Kekistan, according to Bellingcat, is a frequent topic of discussion on the fascist Discord servers whose chats they examined. "Opinions vary from calling it a 'forced meme' to expressing serious devotion to the idea. Kekistan flags and other regalia are often seen at Patriot Prayer rallies and other far-right protests. Some fascists lament that many people who fly the flag don't understand the Nazi origins of its design. But many know exactly what they are signaling when they put one on a flagpole, or their helmet."[58]

Whether they really believe any of this or not, the thrust of the entire enterprise is to mock everything "politically correct" so loudly and obtusely—and divertingly—that legitimate issues about the vicious core of white male nationalism they embrace never need to be confronted directly. The alt-right's "meme war" is ultimately another name for far-right propaganda, polished and rewired for twenty-first-century consumers. The ironic pose that Kek represents and accompanying claims that the racism they promote is innocently meant to provoke in the end are a façade fronting a very old and very ugly enterprise: hatemongering of the xenophobic and misogynistic kind.

And the current running through all of this is also very ancient, very human, and very worrisome: authoritarianism.

Chapter 8

EVERYBODY GET IN LINE

Imagine what a state can do with the immense amount of data it has on its citizens. China is already using face detection technology to identify and arrest people. And here's the tragedy: we're building this infrastructure of surveillance authoritarianism merely to get people to click on ads. And this won't be Orwell's authoritarianism. This isn't *1984*. Now, if authoritarianism is using overt fear to terrorize us, we'll all be scared, but we'll know it, we'll hate it and we'll resist it.

But if the people in power are using these algorithms to quietly watch us, to judge us and to nudge us, to predict and identify the troublemakers and the rebels, to deploy persuasion architectures at scale and to manipulate individuals one by one using their personal, individual weaknesses and vulnerabilities, and if they're doing it at scale through our private screens so that we don't even know what our fellow citizens and neighbors are seeing, that authoritarianism will envelop us like a spider's web and we may not even know we're in it.—Zeynep Tufekci[1]

Now, when most of us hear the term or think about authoritarianism, we usually do so in the context of the leaders throughout history who have headed up authoritarian regimes—everyone from Napoleon to Hitler and Stalin to any number of petty banana republic dictators. But that's not what actually makes authoritarianism work, or at least it's not the whole story.

No authoritarian regime has ever existed without a substantial percentage of the population it rules actively supporting and preferring it. They all have large armies of followers who sustain them in power. So to understand authoritarianism, it's essential first to understand the distinctive personality types that are attracted to it and support it.

Grappling with the human dimensions of this phenomenon has occupied a number of psychologists, sociologists, and psychiatrists since World War II. At times it has been analyzed as totalitarianism or totalism; in more recent years, *authoritarianism* has become the preferred term in part because it has a broader sweep.[2] Some of the more recent work by psychologist Robert Altemeyer of the University of Ontario and American political scientists Marc Hetherington and Jonathan Weiler has been especially useful.[3] As their studies have explored, most people have some level of authoritarian tendencies, but these are often leveled out by such factors as personal empathy and critical thinking skills, which tend to lead to a less black-and-white view of the world.

Nor is authoritarianism relegated just to the right side of the political aisle. There are also left-wing authoritarians, as any survivor of Stalinist Russia can attest. Theirs is a variation wherein the desired utopian rule becomes the objective.

Current Fox overblown propaganda about the dread specter of "antifa" notwithstanding, these authoritarian tendencies on the left nevertheless have been *comparatively* muted in twenty-first-century American society, at least among mainstream liberals. Average Democrats generally fall well into the zone of personality types that are resistant to authoritarianism, even if they underestimate it.

I say "comparatively" mainly because we are currently awash in a flood tide of right-wing authoritarianism that has fully reached mainstream conservatism and overwhelmed it—the presidency of Donald Trump being only the most obvious and powerful manifestation of it. However, this authoritarianism began infecting the Republican Party long before Trump ascended to the party's nomination; it will maintain its toxic gravitational pull on the nation's politics long after he departs the scene. And the main factor enabling this authoritarian toxicity all along has been conspiracism.

Are right-wing authoritarians born or made? Probably a combination of both, though it's clear that people's authoritarian tendencies increase the more fearful they are. Identifying a threat and forming a focus on it are essential to shaping these personalities. Some are wired this way from birth. Early theories on authoritarian personalities, now largely discredited, argued for a Freudian model in which harsh rearing environments and personal traumas produced people inclined to insist on a world in which strong authorities produce order and peace.

Most analysis today finds that it usually depends on circumstances. Because it is innate to human personalities, it can remain latent during periods when people do not perceive a threat and increase when they do. Authoritarianism significantly rose in the United States after 9/11. Periods of intense social change also can produce authoritarian backlash, as such changes are often perceived by some personalities as a kind of threat. This is why civil rights advances, such as Black Lives Matter, have so often been perceived as an attack on whites. It's why white nationalists argue that multiculturalism is a genocidal assault on the white race.[4]

Right-wing authoritarian (RWA) personalities are built around three behavioral and attitudinal clusters, which are closely related groups of human psychology that essentially shape our worldviews.

- Authoritarian submission. This is the eager adherence to edicts, rulings, and opinions of the authorities and leaders who are deemed legitimate, built around the belief that a civil, ordered, and secure society requires such submission.
- Authoritarian aggression. This is the physical, verbal, and social aggression displayed toward anyone or any trend that runs counter to those authorities or, in the case of leadership, is deemed illegitimate.
- Conventionalism. The adamant embrace of what is perceived as the social norm and the "real" national identity and the belief that oneself reflects that "real" identity.[5]

These three clusters interact in myriad ways and produce a long list of identifiable traits. Altemeyer in particular has identified about a dozen such traits.

- Such people are highly ethnocentric, inclined to see the world as their in-group versus everyone else.
- They are highly fearful of a dangerous world.
- They are highly self-righteous.
- They are aggressive.
- They are highly prejudiced against racial and ethnic majorities, non-heterosexuals, and women in general.
- Their beliefs are a mass of contradictions dependent on compartmentalized thinking.
- They reason poorly, and they are prone to projection.
- They are highly dogmatic.
- They are dependent on social reinforcement of their beliefs.
- Because they severely limit their exposure to different people and ideas, they vastly overestimate the extent to which other people agree with them.
- They are prone to conspiracist thinking and a gullibility about "alternative facts."[6]

Authoritarianism as a worldview always creates a certain kind of cognitive dissonance, a feeling of unreality, because it runs smack into the complex nature of the modern world. The authoritarian worldview attempts to impose its simplified, black-and-white explanation of reality onto a factual reality that contradicts and undermines it at every turn.

People with authoritarian personalities willingly slip into the alternative universe created by their distorted, if not deranged, epistemology because it helps soothe this dissonance, allowing its occupants to glide over inconvenient facts because they participate in a larger "truth." This bubble, as a creation of right-wing authoritarians, has always played a key role: a refuge for people who reject factual reality, a place where they can convene and reassure one another in the facticity of their fabricated version of how the world works.

So conspiracism is especially appealing to people with these personality traits—the people who tell pollsters they "don't recognize their country anymore" and are discomfited and bewildered by the brown faces and strange languages that have been filling up their cultural landscapes in places where they never used to be.

One study found that conspiracy theories seem to be more compelling to "those with low self-worth, especially with regard to their sense of agency in the world at large." They often long for a 1950s-style America with lawns and cul-de-sacs and are angry that the world no longer works that way. Whereas the mainstream media simply present the world as it is, conspiracy theories offer narratives that explain to them why the country is no longer what they wish it to be, why it has that alien shape. And so in their minds, the theories—because they never believe just one conspiracy theory but rather an interconnected web of them—represent a deeper truth about their world while repeatedly reinforcing their long-held prejudices and enable them to ignore the real, factual (and often uncomfortable) nature of the changes the world is undergoing.[7]

Simply put, the assembled narrative provides a clear, self-reinforcing answer to the source of their personal disempowerment. It also has the advantage of telling believers that they are the solo, go-it-alone action heroes in the movies of their own lives.

The deep irony in all this, as we have seen, is that the larger psychological and even political effect of conspiracy theories is that they are profoundly disempowering in and of themselves. Conspiracists disconnect from the rest of the world, whom they either hold in paranoid suspicion or contempt. The narrative arc of the conspiracy universe begins with the adrenaline rush of empowerment and ends with isolation, anger, and potentially even violence.

There can even be outright cognitive effects, sort of a hardened variation of the old Upton Sinclair adage: "It is difficult to get a man to understand something, when the entire worldview around which his emotional life revolves depends on his not understanding it."[8] People who are "red-pilled" see themselves as utterly disattached from their communities, fighting a desperate battle with only the help of their fellow conspiracists against truly dark and evil forces. It's this heroic self-conception that really holds people inside these worlds, but in the real world it rarely, if ever, works out well.

Alex Jones continually refers to his targets as "demonic." It's not just a bleak world, it's one in which people can become overwhelmed with feelings of helplessness and anger in the face of existential evil. So out of this universe proceeds a steady trickle of people who have decided it is time to act—usually out of a desperation fueled by rage over their sense of deep disempowerment, all of it a product of a belief in conspiracy theories.

The violence committed by these domestic terrorists serves the purposes of authoritarians in profound ways, because it ratchets up the levels of fear in society generally, and resorting to the false security of authoritarianism is a common psychological response.

This is where the role played by authoritarian leaders is key. Because rather than ease people's fears, as a normative democratic leader would do, authoritarians immediately reach for the panic button. Keeping the populace in a fearful state is a cornerstone of their rule. Just ask Donald Trump.

———

While the rest of the world mourned the fifty lives lost in the March 15, 2019, attacks on two mosques in Christchurch, New Zealand, the far right and its trolls were celebrating. From Breitbart News to Infowars to the sewers of 4chan, 8chan, and the *Daily Stormer*, extremists were unequivocal in reveling in the massacre.[9]

"This is a good start," wrote one commenter at Breitbart, beneath a headlined story detailing the mass murders. "That man is a goddam hero," wrote another, as E. J. Gibney documented on Twitter. "[A] real feel good story!" added yet another.

Someone writing as "White Pride" chimed in: "payback is a bitch! Gun control and bans are futile!!! He is giving them another taste of their own medicine by fighting fire with fire! An eye for an eye, Tit for Tat, quid pro quo!!!"

"Armed Infidel" chimed in: "The rag heads could easily avoid this by not infesting the rest of the world with their presence." Another commenter added: "I've thought about it and decided. . . . I don't care. It's not as though there was any humans involved."

Stewart Rhodes, leader of the neo-militia organization Oath Keepers, went on Alex Jones's Infowars program and told listeners that the terrorist's motives were legitimate:

> When a guy who's worried about or concerned about mass immigration of Muslims into Europe goes crazy and kills people, then they're

gonna blame all the rest of us who have the same concern. That's how it's gonna be used. And this is why we have to just fight back and say, "You know what, that doesn't erase the fact that this is a problem. This is what drove this guy over the edge."

Conspiracy theorist Matt Bracken also went on Jones's show and appeared to urge others to follow in the terrorist's footsteps. "The globalists want to keep the borders open and keep flooding America and the West with unassimilable Third-Worlders for as long as they can before there's a rupture," Bracken told Jones. "What the guy . . . did in New Zealand was try to speed it up so that the cataclysm happens sooner rather than later."

Other white nationalists whined that the attacks made them look bad. "Can you imagine always being blamed for things that you have absolutely no control over? Can you imagine always being asked to apologize for these things?" noted anti-Semite Mike Peinovich wrote on Twitter. "Can you imagine being hated whether or not you do apologize? This is what being a White person in America today feels like."

The man who perpetrated the massacre left behind a manifesto crediting Donald Trump as among his inspirations: "Trump is a symbol of renewed white identity and common purpose." Trump sent out a defensive tweet: "The Fake News Media is working overtime to blame me for the horrible attack in New Zealand. They will have to work very hard to prove that one. So Ridiculous!"[10]

In a press gaggle later, Trump opined that he didn't see white nationalism as a problem: "I don't really. I think it's a small group of people that have very, very serious problems. It's certainly a terrible thing."[11]

Authoritarian leaders have a personality type quite distinct from their followers. It is called social dominance orientation (SDO), which is essentially a form of narcissism on steroids.[12]

SDOs are far more interested in the personal acquisition of power than are RWAs, who by nature are more inclined to march on someone else's behalf. They also have different reasoning capacities and are far more calculating and manipulative.[13]

What they have in common, more than anything else, is a shared dismissive view of equality as an important social value. They both believe that inequality is the natural state of the world and that any attempts to tamper with it are doomed to fail and screw everything up. Like Jordan Peterson, the "intellectual dark web" psychologist associated with far-right "traditionalists," described this in a new foreword for Solzhenitsyn's *Gulag Archipelago*:

Inequality is the iron rule, even among animals, with their intense competition for quality living space and reproductive opportunity— even among plants, and cities—even among the stellar lights that dot the cosmos themselves, where a minority of privileged and oppressive heavenly bodies contain the mass of thousands, millions or even billions of average, dispossessed planets. Inequality is the deepest of problems, built into the structure of reality itself, and will not be solved by the presumptuous, ideology-inspired retooling of the rare free, stable and productive democracies of the world.[14]

This simultaneous contempt for attempts to overcome inequality and for the democratic institutions intended to give ordinary people the political power to do so is a thread that runs throughout authoritarian discourse, among both the angry foot soldiers and their narcissistic leaders. They both believe that there is a natural hierarchy of the gifted and the less so.[15] It's just that SDOs tend to see themselves among the former, while RWAs are more likely to view themselves among the latter but harbor ambitions to rise to that other station, along the lines of the aphorism attributed to Steinbeck: "Socialism never took root in America because the poor see themselves not as an exploited proletariat but as temporarily embarrassed millionaires."[16]

Given its innate preference for autocratic rule, authoritarianism is also toxic for any kind of democratic society. The alt-right's express hostility to democracy and its institutions makes its rise as a political phenomenon a concern not just in the United States, but around the world—especially as conspiracism begets more and more violence.

We also run the very real risk of an era of scripted violence: the phenomenon that occurs when a major cultural figure uses his position and the media to call for violence against a targeted minority group and his fanatical followers carry it out.

———————

For Cesar Sayoc, becoming a follower of Donald Trump was "like my newfound drug." He saw himself as a warrior "on the front lines of war between right and left." He believed leftists had tried to kill him by tampering with his van's electrical wiring and blamed it on "liberal left leaders" who "encourage attacks and violence."[17]

In retaliation, he sent pipe bombs to sixteen different recipients in October 2018, all of them targets of Trump's incendiary rhetoric. Among them: former president Barack Obama, Hillary and Bill Clinton, George Soros, actor Robert De Niro, CNN, and the *Washington Post*.

The #MAGAbomber, as Sayoc, fifty-six, became known, was instantly identified upon his arrest with his Trump sticker–festooned van. Social media posts quickly revealed him as a steroid-abusing bodybuilder from the Miami area who wore the red ball caps, traveled to Trump rallies, and was a rabid fan of the president. In April 2019, he pleaded guilty to an array of domestic terrorism charges.[18]

The bombing scare (the devices were incapable of harming anyone) quickly vanished down the public memory hole. But the episode remains a stark reminder that America has entered a new age of scripted violence—also known as stochastic terrorism, a scenario in which "a leader need not directly exhort violence to create a constituency that hears a call to take action against the named enemy"—in which the president himself is writing the scripts for others to follow and enact violence.[19]

A letter that Sayoc wrote to the judge in his case, released after he entered his guilty plea, underscored the extent to which the right-wing authoritarian cult around the president is likely to act out violently. In it, Sayoc described attending a Trump rally in Chicago in which he was attacked by leftist counter-protesters, whose presence he blamed on Mayor Rahm Emanuel. Yet the string of targets—all of them verbally targeted by Trump—made the source of his inspiration unmistakable.[20]

There really has been little question, in fact, that Trump's hatemongering fueled not just the #MAGAbomber rampage, but a number of other acts of terroristic violence: the synagogue massacre by white nationalist Robert Bowers in Pittsburgh; the mosque attacks in Christchurch, New Zealand; and a stymied domestic terrorism plot in Illinois. Similarly, the sudden sharp increase in hate crimes of the past three years is increasingly tied to Trump's rhetoric, especially since a large portion of the crimes are now accompanied by references to Trump. This was notably the case in places where Trump held rallies, which saw a 226 percent increase in hate crimes.[21]

Trump has a history of encouraging violence explicitly—as when he told rally audiences that he'd like to punch protesters, just before members of the audiences sometimes did—as well as implicitly by rationalizing the behavior as excusable. When two Boston men in 2015 brutally beat and urinated on a Latino man and then credited Trump as inspiration, he made excuses for them: "I will say that people who are following me are very passionate. They love this country and they want this country to be great again. They are passionate. I will say that, and everybody here has reported it."[22]

How does scripted violence work? Analyst Chip Berlet explains:

> The potential for violence in a society increases when the mass media carries rhetorical vilification by high profile and respected figures who scapegoat a named "Other." This dangerous "constitutive rhetoric" can build an actual constituency of persons feeling threatened or displaced. Or to put it another way, when rhetorical fecal matter hits

the spinning verbal blades of a bigoted demagogue's exhortations, bad stuff happens.

The resulting violence can incite a mob, a mass movement, a war, or an individual actor. Individual actors who engage in violence can emerge in three ways. They can be assigned the task of violence by an existing organizational leadership; they can be members or participants in an existing organization, yet decide to act on their own; or they can be unconnected to an existing organization and act on their own. According to the US government definition, a "Lone Wolf" is a person who engages in political violence and is not known by law enforcement agencies to have any current or previous ties to an organization under surveillance as potential lawbreakers. The person committing the violence may expect or even welcome martyrdom, or may plan for a successful escape to carry on being a political soldier in a hoped-for insurgency. Either way, the hope is that "a little spark can cause a prairie fire." Revolution is seldom the result, but violence and death remains as a legacy.[23]

This plays a key role in how violence created by a tide of young men radicalized online by far-right ideologues and conspiracy theories is spread. Having a figure like Trump both normalizing their extremism and encouraging violence in support of it means that it is being spread throughout American society.

The way this finds expression is with men like Cesar Sayoc, who see themselves as "warriors" in a larger fight against evil itself, which in their view is embodied by liberals and leftists. This is why so many right-wing Trump supporters speak so eagerly of launching a "civil war" against urban liberals.[24]

Trump himself indulges in this "warrior" mentality. A 2017 *New York Times* piece explained Trump's worldview somewhat nonchalantly in an article exploring why the president attacked NFL players:

> In private, the president and his top aides freely admit that he is engaged in a culture war on behalf of his white, working-class base, a New York billionaire waging war against "politically correct" coastal elites on behalf of his supporters in the South and in the Midwest. He believes the war was foisted upon him by former President Barack Obama and other Democrats—and he is determined to win, current and former aides said.[25]

Trump thus continually justified the violence inflicted by his supporters, suggesting that the victims have it coming. Infamously, after Heather Heyer was killed and multiple people injured by neo-Nazi James Fields in the August 11–12, 2017, "Unite the Right" protests, Trump insisted that there were "some very fine people" among the polo-shirted men marching with their tiki torches.[26]

The bigger problem is that Trump himself doesn't need to identify the targets, since there is a long history of domestic terrorists motivated by ideology, rather than the authoritarian defense of a political leader. Sometimes the two are mixed.

———

We'll never know for certain whether accused domestic-terrorist-in-the-making Christopher Hasson ever would have acted on the desire to spark a racial civil war for white supremacy by committing the assassinations and mass killing for which he had so thoroughly prepared and about which he endlessly fantasized. We do know, however, exactly what might have been the spark to send the forty-nine-year-old coastguardsman from Baltimore on a killing rampage, though: the impeachment of President Trump.[27]

Buried in Hasson's deleted emails, along with correspondence to neo-Nazi leaders and ruminations on his admiration for Norwegian mass killer Anders Breivik, were his working notes for events around which he was planning actions, notably: "what if trump illegally impeached" and "civil war if trump impeached."[28]

It's not difficult to find where Hasson might have obtained the belief that civil war would erupt if President Trump were to face impeachment: after 2017, the possibility of the outbreak of a civil war became a frequent talking point and source of speculation among right-wing pundits. The same week Hasson's arrest was announced, longtime Republican operative Joseph diGenova went on Laura Ingraham's Fox News show and warned:

> We are in a civil war in this country. There's two standards of justice, one for Democrats, one for Republicans. The press is all Democrat, all liberal, all progressive, all left—they hate Republicans, they hate Trump. So the suggestion that there's ever going to be civil discourse in this country for the foreseeable future in this country is over. It's not going to be. It's going to be total war. And as I say to my friends, I do two things—I vote and I buy guns.[29]

This seemingly hysterical pronouncement, in fact, is fast becoming a commonplace among right-wing pundits. It has been circulating on the right for a long while and is now being whipped up to new heights—notably, into the mainstream of conservative movement discourse.[30]

After Trump's election, the radical right's focus turned to his rabid defense, vowing to protect him from any kind of attempt to impeach or otherwise remove him from office with force of arms. Moreover, this meant characterizing organized antifascism—relabeled "antifa" to make it seem less than benign—as an insidious, evil force that was the face of a Communist plot to remove

Trump—and of course, right from Trump's inauguration, small groups of anti-Trump protesters became the embodiment of this paranoid fear.[31] Leading the paranoia parade, as always, was Alex Jones, who leveraged his considerable history of promoting the idea of civil war into a remarkable yearlong run pushing the idea after Trump was elected and who is still doing so today.[32] So was Michael Savage, who warned in the summer of 2017 that impeachment would mean civil war.

Jones became especially frantic in the fall of 2017, first warning after the Las Vegas massacre that Democrats were going to begin mowing down Republicans soon, then hyping a nonsensical claim that, just like at Inauguration Day, evil antifa/Communist/satanic Mars colony pedophilia forces were plotting a nationwide strike that would paralyze the country and create the opportunity for a coup on November 4, 2017. As with all of his previous completely bizarre failed predictions, Jones never acknowledged that such a coup attempt never even came close to manifesting itself in the real world.[33]

Maybe, all along, the whole thing was just projection.

What did Michael Cohen mean by this?

> Given my experience working for Mr. Trump, I fear that if he loses the election in 2020 that there will never be a peaceful transition of power, and this is why I agreed to appear before you today.[34]

The pre-prison testimony by Donald Trump's longtime personal attorney in February 2019 before the House Oversight Committee—which described the president as being like a mob boss, speaking in cryptic code that communicates an ongoing thuglike criminal intent—was shocking at times and deeply disturbing most of all. But reflecting that Trump might try to cling to office even after defeat at the polls was like looking into the abyss.

It's one thing for someone outside of Trump's circle, particularly anyone who's opposed Trump, to say such a thing. However, we're talking about the man who was Donald Trump's legal fixer for ten years. A man who once said he'd take a bullet for Trump. But a man who now believes the person to whom he gave his loyalty is in fact a "racist, a con man, and a cheat."

Cohen's closing note, before he shuffled off to prison for lying to the FBI during the investigation into Russian interference in the 2016 election—which felt something like a cryptic warning—came as he put the finishing touches on describing the president he knows as a conniving charlatan who gets his way the same way any mob boss does: by demanding undying fealty from his underlings, by being an absolute authoritarian.

Cohen provided a little more context by noting that he had long been party to Trump's wrongdoings but that he could no longer bear "silence and complicity in the face of the daily destruction of our basic norms and civility to one another" as a consequence. Among the most longstanding of those norms, of course, has been the peaceful handover of power by American politicians when they lose elections.

Yet Trump himself raised the specter of an American president who refused to leave office even before winning election in 2016 when he adamantly refused to say whether or not he would concede the election to Hillary Clinton if he were to lose, telling a debate audience coyly, "I'll tell you at the time. . . . I'll keep you in suspense, okay?"[35] He set the stage to never concede the election if he chose not to. "This whole election is being rigged," Trump would tell his roaring crowds. "The whole thing is one big fix. One big ugly lie. It's one big fix."[36]

At a press conference held to announce whether he would concede, Trump told reporters:

> I would like to promise and pledge to all of my voters and supporters, and to all of the people of the United States, that I will totally accept the results of this great and historic presidential election . . . if I win.[37]

The outcome negated any need to test Trump's willingness to ignore precedent, of course.

Politico's Jack Shafer reviewed Trump's options and concluded that the reality is that he doesn't have many when it comes to clinging to power in the face of an election loss, although postponing the election always remains one of them—and breaking precedent seems less like an obstacle with this president than it does an incentive.[38] Yet as the *Washington Post*'s Aaron Blake observed, Trump's odds of success in any event would be extremely low.[39]

However, Trump himself has rarely been dissuaded by low odds, if his history as a politician is anything to judge by. Moreover, there is one possibility that neither Shafer nor Blake pays much attention to but which happens to be the scenario a classic populist authoritarian might deploy: an appeal to a popular uprising to prevent his removal. In other words, green-lighting the civil war his followers have begun discussing with fevered rhetoric.

The problem is that this scenario becomes more likely as Trump himself becomes increasingly authoritarian when his power is challenged. And the army of authoritarian followers has made it explicit in multiple online rants and Twitter threats that they dream of a day when they can take up arms on behalf of the president. This is a running current through the QAnon movement.

Conspiracism creates a toxic mindset, a worldview in which the world is actually being run by secretive, powerful schemers intent on suppressing the believers, against whose immense power an ordinary individual is almost entirely powerless. Even their neighbors are suspect. The people who are "red-pilled" have been primed not just to hate their liberal neighbors, but to prepare to eliminate them. And they have a leader who appears inclined not only to let them, but to encourage, perhaps even empower, them.

This is the real-life manifestation of Altemeyer's "lethal union" of right-wing authoritarian followers with a social dominance–oriented authoritarian leader: that moment, as Altemeyer says, when "the two can then become locked in a cyclonic death spiral that can take a whole nation down with them."

In the end, the question everyone should ask themselves is: what happens if I take this red pill?

It promises being awakened to "the way things really are," like in *The Matrix*. Except . . . *The Matrix* is fiction. And so is any "red-pilled" version of reality comprised of the thin gruel of conspiracy theories and conjecture: fictions, when examined with any rigor, created by a cluster of self-described "antiglobalists" whose concocted universe becomes a conduit for white nationalist extremism.

People who sell the "red pill"—usually desperate for fellows in the increasingly isolated worlds they inhabit—want you to believe that you are freeing yourself from a worldview created by a nefarious cabal of Jewish scholars or perhaps moneygrubbing bankers, something along the traditional lines.

What they're not telling you is that when you take it, you are submitting yourself wholly to a universe created by a weird agglomeration of paranoid personalities and white nationalist bigots. They don't tell you that, once you swallow the pill and are inside the universe, there really isn't any dissent regarding what is real or not. And what is real is what the leading voices of the theories—Alex Jones, or Q, or the alpha dogs of the online communities where conspiracies and "evidence" are produced and regurgitated endlessly—tell everyone it is. It's a reality constructed and ordered by people claiming that reality is constructed and ordered by someone else: an endless hall of mirrors.

And if you've taken it, it's worth wondering what you've done to yourself. Eventually your example—depending on how far along the narrative arc you are—will stand as a warning to anyone considering swallowing the red pill.

Sure, at first it was empowering and exciting. It was more than an adrenaline rush—it became positively addictive, especially a participatory conspiracy theory like QAnon. But as time wore on, the seamy side of this world—the scams, the easy and loose relation with facts, the willingness to backstab—began to wear thin.

Pretty soon, you're isolated. Your family won't talk with you, and your old friendships have mostly died away. You're alienated from your colleagues, and you don't know whom to trust. Even your neighbors are suspects. The only friends you have are people inside the "red-pilled" world, and as time wears on, there are increasing problems with them, too. If you go to a traditional or even evangelical church, you eventually find that you can no longer trust them, either.

You no longer vote; you no longer participate in the political process at all, because you've come to believe democracy is a joke. So you also have zero political power. After a while the isolation and frustration and anger become intense.

That's what red-pilling actually does: it promises freedom, and it eventually binds you in cords that creep around you in your sleep.

So let's consider a blue pill: an antidote to this bizarre epistemological pill promising to awaken you but that actually puts you to sleep. A pill that would honestly awaken people to an embrace of traditional reality and normative versions of factuality and reason.

What would that look like?

Chapter 9

A PILL FOR HEALING

When we consider further the social and psychological roots of the collective urge to kill the world, we are likely to see more of ourselves in it and to begin to think of such groups as something of a dark underside or "cultural underground" of our own society. We are also likely to discover that whatever renders our society more decent and more inclusive in its benefits is likely to undermine the totalistic impulse to destroy everything. But since that impulse will not disappear, we had better continue to bring our imaginations to bear on confronting and exploring it, on finding the means to resist its lure and oppose its destructive projects.

—Robert Jay Lifton, *Destroying the World to Save It*[1]

BuzzFeed reporter Joseph Bernstein befriended Lane Davis well before he stabbed his father to death on Samish Island—"Seattle4Truth" was one of his key sources for an exposé of Milo Yiannopoulos that Bernstein published in 2016, along with several other "researchers" who specialized in Gamergate and Pizzagate conspiracy theorists.

He was shocked by the murder and traveled to the remote, generally soggy little western Washington town to compose an insightful piece about its aftermath. Like me—I attended several of Lane's hearings, which culminated in him copping a guilty plea that put him behind bars for the next seventeen years—Bernstein found Davis's family unwilling to talk to the press. Considering how much they lost, no one can really blame them.[2]

He also kept exploring the important subtext of Lane Davis's story: namely, how conspiracism and extremist ideas can unhinge people to such a remarkable extent that they will kill other people, even their own parents—and, more important, whether there is anything we can do about it, both collectively as a society and individually as ordinary people.

The very difficult truth, as Bernstein found, is that many hundreds of thousands of people absorb and participate in conspiracy theories without ever becoming so unhinged that they act out violently and commit mass murder. Indeed, although an extraordinarily high percentage of mass killers hold conspiracist worldviews, which play a significant role in the disconnectedness and isolation that fuels these actors, in reality they comprise only a small percentage of the total number of people who participate in this alternative universe.[3]

That tells us there is no singular, one-size-fits-all, easy-to-swallow answer, no "blue pill" that could prevent Lane Davis from stabbing his father or Stephen Paddock from opening fire on a country music festival. And there's no easy way of predicting or mapping exactly what beliefs or ideas eventually will result in tragedy.

"The truth is, as researchers of violent extremism like James and Horgan will tell you, the vast majority of people who use Gab and Stormfront will never commit a violent crime," he wrote. "That's not to absolve online communities of the beliefs of their members. It's not to say digital spaces can't play a major role in ushering people toward violence. As the lasting influence of Anwar al-Awlaki and Dylann Roof show, they can. It's not even to say such spaces have a right to exist on private hosting services. They don't—at least not as far as the First Amendment is concerned. But there isn't an easy answer when it comes to finding the small number of people who will commit extremist violence."[4]

Bernstein's retrospective explained:

> Researchers have long known that the common risk factors for violent extremism have no real predictive power. A February 2018 literature review prepared for the Department of Homeland Security by the research giant RTI International found that "it is unrealistic to expect that the presence of any risk factor—or even the combination of several risk factors—can or will predict 'with any accuracy' whether an individual will engage in violent extremism." Indeed, the risk factors are all backwards-looking. Applying them to the general population makes that obvious.
>
> Take a few of the big ones: a feeling of moral outrage, identification with an in-group perceived to be under threat, and underemployment. That describes a lot of violent extremists. It also describes a lot of journalists. Even if you add more specific risk factors, like mental health issues, having a criminal history, and a recent triggering event like a death or a divorce, well, that could still describe a lot of people who will never even consider violence. It's impossible to come up with a checklist of risks and pop out a violent extremist.[5]

It would be a mistake for any program intended to prevent the downward spiral into violence to try basing its prescription on a psychological map, mainly because the human variables involved are so large. "The permutation of risk factors raises an uncomfortable possibility: that the route to violence is so complex and unique that there is no meaningful way to map it," says Bernstein. "As much as we want to talk about structural forces like socioeconomics and racism in determining who becomes violent and who doesn't, an impossibly huge number of individual variations appear to play a significant role as well."[6]

One of the insidious aspects of conspiracism is that it has a built-in immunity to what might be a normative means of drawing people out of that belief system—namely, a rational and reasoned application of factual evidence and logic. Anyone who tries to persuade someone who's been "red-pilled" with such methods quickly finds themselves dismissed as either a willing dupe or an active coconspirator. Like most right-wing authoritarians, their compartmentalized thinking enables them to believe two completely contradictory things at once and to ignore factual evidence when presented as "tainted."

The narratives that bind people to conspiracy theories are often large-scope mythologies that make them feel heroic as well as part of something bigger. These are normal drives in human beings but have been twisted by the disinformation to which they've been exposed. These mythologies are also highly personalized and often gut-level in nature. This is why there are no immediate, large-scale solutions to the problem, fixable through mass media or other appeals.

So there really is no "blue pill," as it were, no universally applicable remedy that would cure people of their conspiracy-bred delusions. The only way to actually draw people out of the conspiracist universe and back into the sometimes murky light of the real world is on a one-to-one basis, one at a time, very slowly, and with an emphasis on empathy—as well as an understanding that even the best efforts in these areas often fail.

It's a slow, often painful, and only sometimes rewarding process. But for people determined to not simply cope with this phenomenon in their lives, but to confront and overcome it, there's not really any other option.

———————

What *is* nearly universal about conspiracy theorists and the "red-pilled" ideologues who are sucked into the darkest corners of authoritarian ideologies by them is that their personal lives are nearly *always* in shambles. They alienate family members, old friends, new friends, neighbors, business and work associates, customers, you name it—they churn through relationships like raccoons through a trash pile, picking up and discarding with startling ease.[7]

For family and old friends, this ongoing churn and otherworldly alienation is extremely disorienting and frequently heartbreaking. But as it happens, these are the people with the greatest likelihood of changing the trajectory of a red-pilled person and perhaps drawing them back into the normative world and the warmth of healthy human relationships.

It's a very difficult proposition, however, and carries many risks. The first is that many such attempts actually drive the red-pilled true believers even deeper into their rabbit holes. You may think you're doing the right thing by plopping facts in front of them, but it's more likely to worsen things. Multiple studies have demonstrated that the most common response to this approach is for the conspiracy theorists to see your facts as further proof of the conspiracy—as well as clear evidence of your gullibility, at least, if not your active complicity in the plot.

Radicalization expert Peter Neumann acknowledges that there are innate limitations to this approach. "There is a big debate around to what extent counter-messaging is possible and to what extent that can ever work," he says. "I think in most cases, when you're talking about extremists rather than conspiracy theories, in most cases it was a face-to-face interaction that pulled people out, and I don't think it's easy to convince people on the Internet that they are wrong about these things.

"And if you do it badly, it may actually have the opposite effect. This is what psychologists call *reactance*, which is the idea that if you confront someone who is very entrenched in their views and you're trying to convince them of the opposite, you're actually provoking resistance, and with the result that that person becomes even more entrenched in their views."

Secondarily, your relationship with the person will further fray and destabilize along the way. If they are prone to anger—and most conspiracy theorists seem to be—you well could bear the brunt of it and all that entails.

Neumann warns: "Of course, one of the first things that is important to understand is that not everyone can be deradicalized. So, if you have someone that is very deep in those conspiracies, is very convinced about them, and feels very happy and comfortable with that identity, it's very hard to pull them out. It's like if you have someone who's a hardened neo-Nazi and who is moving within that milieu who is perhaps also having, let's say, a family relationship or relationships within that group of people, it's very hard to pull him or her out.

"Deradicalization can work, in two situations. The first arises when people are still exploring and before their extremist identities are being settled, so if you get them at an early enough stage while they're still having a degree of openness about the different questions that they are exploring, you can still engage them. And the other situation where deradicalization can work is at the very end of the process when people start having doubts, start becoming disillusioned, or for other reasons really are looking for a change.

"I used to be a smoker myself. It's like quitting smoking. . . . [P]eople will tell you that it's not possible to quit smoking unless you really want it, unless you are convinced that you want to change your lifestyle. And I think the same is true with extremists or people who are very deep in these weird theories. Unless they themselves have questions that you can leverage and unless they themselves are having doubts that you can work with, it's basically not possible."[8]

So the first question any person trying to tackle the problem should ask themselves is, will it be worth it? Be honest with yourself and about the other person, because that will be crucial.

However, if you decide to proceed and try to help someone who has become enmeshed in conspiracy theories and the extremist ideologies that accompany them, I've assembled a number of steps for doing so, compiled from the best advice available from experts—psychologists, sociologists, researchers, and activists with real-life experience drawing people out of the rabbit holes and back into the bright light of normative reality.

The key, again, in all this is the human variables: every person is different, every path down into the rabbit holes is personal, every force keeping the red-pilled trapped inside their alternative universe varies from case to case. And always keep in mind that success is difficult and rare. Every choice you make depends on the circumstances, personality, and beliefs of the person involved.

Whether this one-at-a-time, interpersonal, and typically slow approach ever gains enough momentum to solve the problem on a large scale is anyone's guess. "Everyone is looking for the silver bullet, and it doesn't exist," says Neumann. "It's something that requires education. It's something that will not happen within the next couple of months, but maybe the next couple of decades if people really get behind it, but it's a really hard, long-term project."

At the same time, most of us see no other options—we just know we must try.

So I engaged some of the best minds on this subject in extended conversation and asked them: if you could devise a toolkit that ordinary people could use to bring their friends and loved ones out of the dark world of conspiracy theories and back into the sunlight of reality, what would it look like?

After listening to their advice, I compiled an incremental, step-by-step set of conceptual approaches to the problem—tools, as it were—that ordinary people can use. There are fifteen of them.

Fifteen Steps

1. First, an ounce of prevention is worth a pound of cure: the most effective way of overcoming the effects of "red-pilling" is immunizing people beforehand.

Psychologist Stephan Lewandowsky recommends working incrementally with people who have had little exposure to conspiracy theories: "Now we do know that what tends to work is to inoculate people against conspiracy theories by exposing people to the theory ahead of time and saying, well you know, if you ever come across this, be aware of the fact that it's complete nonsense. And that can be done; a colleague of mine, Karen Douglas, has done that with anti-vaccination conspiracy theories.

"She finds that if you expose people to a small dose, just like a vaccine, of the conspiracy theory up front, then it finds less traction when people are actually exposed to it. So you can educate, sort of protect people against conspiracy theories, but of course the crucial is you got to get to them first, because if you try to do it after they've already been exposed to it then it's far less effective. So you have to get people educated about the existence of theories ahead of time.

"And it has to be proactive. Now of course, there's a risk in that as well. Some people might never encounter conspiracy theory and if you had never mentioned it, they would have never gone on the Internet to look it up. So you may have in fact protected some people, but inadvertently tip others into the rabbit hole.

"Nothing is perfect and that is an obvious risk: that if you're exposing people to something to protect them against it, then that may backfire conceivably. Now the other thing is that what colleagues and I have done repeatedly is to look at the reasoning flaws that are part of conspiracy theories—one of them being the pure chance of it, and the other one being the unrealized implications of some of those claims."[9]

Information scientist Michael Caulfield believes that the most effective form of immunization comes from teaching young people better methods of consuming digital information. That's especially the case, he says, in the new age of conspiracism, when everything connects like an elaborate Tinkertoy set. It adds a level of complexity that most people are unprepared to deal with.

"The newer thing is the absolute connection between all of these conspiracies," Caulfield says. "The truth is, almost everybody believes in one conspiracy. Almost everybody. This is true going back a long time. You can go back to the '70s, '80s, or whatever. You'll find that people believe in one conspiracy or another.

"I think what is happening increasingly now is that people get into the one conspiracy that everybody is going to get into anyway. They're going to choose a conspiracy and be into it. But the conspiracy communities are very connected—the viral mechanics across these communities are very connected—and then the bad actors in this space are very aware of how to pull people in from relatively harmless conspiracies, deeper into other conspiracies.

"I saw this horrifying YouTube video that was basically an anti-Semitic, Jews-control-the-world video, but of course none of it said that explicitly. It was an animated thing with a voiceover, and you've seen these sorts of things. But a big piece of it was, 'Oh, society is trying to medicate you, and there's a big conspiracy to try to keep you medicated, or from seeing the truth,' and so forth.

"I just thought about how compelling this would be for someone who had been on Ritalin all their life, or something like that. Looking at this saying, 'Yeah, what's that all about?' and having some actual fear and concern that, what if there is a pharmaceutical conspiracy to keep us all medicated?

"Of course the piece of it that was really smart, in this horrific way, about what this person was doing, was as you looked at the imagery, if you were literate in this, you saw, oh what they're looking up to is actually this Jewish-controlled, banker-funded conspiracy to keep everybody down. But of course that doesn't pop out to the person first watching the video. What pops out is, 'Oh, this is validation for what I feel.' So they're very smart in how they go into these things."

Caulfield believes that an understanding of context is essential for effective digital literacy. "I do really believe that if on day one you're looking at that video, and you realize, 'Hey, wow, this is a video put out by a group of literal neo-Nazis,' I think you would back off of it.

"But through this process of grooming, whether it's algorithmic grooming, which just sort of happens via YouTube's algorithms or whether it's grooming by bad actors explicitly, this process relies on you not fully understanding your destination until you're in it.

"My belief is that the process works because you don't understand what the destination is of this stuff, before you're already so deep into it that you're living in a different epistemology."[10]

Most people outside the epistemic bubble, however, don't see that there's a destination. All most people see is that you're having a conversation with someone in a chat room or a forum for conversation, which becomes a mechanism for recruitment that can be used across all kinds of digital platforms. Video gamers, for instance, will go into a video chat room, hanging out with other players; pretty soon someone starts bitching about how "social justice warriors" want to ruin their first-person shooter games. That it's a feminist conspiracy and so on. Then someone pipes up: "Well, you know why they're doing that, right? It's all about cultural Marxism." And soon the whole chat room is getting filled in on the nefarious work of those Jews in the Frankfurt School and down the rabbit hole they go.

Caulfield explains that this is heightened by how we teach kids to research information on the Web, exemplified by the bizarre radicalization spiral of biased curation that helped Dylann Roof dive off the deep end. "You've got this loaded search-term problem, right? So when you see this cycle, . . . someone says, 'Oh, it's all about cultural Marxism,' and then you go and read the stuff: you plug 'cultural Marxism' into the search engine. But because of the curation loop, you're not going to get a relatively academic treatment of how the Frankfurt School changed the application of Marxist thought to contemporary cultural issues.

"You're going to get all this stuff, which is going to have more terms, and each thing you read is going to have more terms and more examples. They'll pull out one example of this that's particularly advantageous to what they're arguing, and you google that example. And of course who is talking about that example?

"Is it NBC News? No, because the example usually is this one-off event where some unknown feminist said something to someone. It's a nothing thing. The only place it's a something thing is in this misogynistic world where you're actually dealing with a white supremacist community. So you get pulled deeper and deeper into it, step by step by this."

This, he says, is the model we teach young people for researching information on the Internet, built on older models in which publication of information was more carefully vetted, which are inadequate for an age in which deliberate disinformation is not merely common but often pervasive, depending on the platform.

"It's a model of reacting and going deeper," Caulfield says. "Interestingly, it's a model that involves a lot of reading. It involves a lot of deep reading of all these texts, and my qualms with the media literacy and info-literacy we give students is that what we teach students to do is to deeply read texts and look at the internal logic of them and to think about the arguments."

This is a bad thing when it comes to white nationalist propaganda and disinformation. "This is not what you actually want them to do with this stuff," he explains. "What you want them to do with this stuff is: 'Please dear God, stop reading until you know where this came from, what its agenda is, and how it fits into broader expert, or reporting, or any broader consensus, right?

"So we teach students to dive in and read deeply and think deeply about these things—but this is just really bad advice."

Caulfield has constructed a model with the acronym SIFT: stop, investigate, find, trace. It emphasizes teaching young would-be researchers to contextualize their information before they absorb it. Once they're at a website, stop and look at what else that site does, how reliable its information appears to be, who runs it, and what, if any, agenda it has. And then keep expanding the context.

"The first move in SIFT is stop. Stop reading, just don't do anything. Stop. Before you go deeper into this stuff, before you read it, before you react, before you get angry, before you start going into search term after search term, and these sorts of things: stop.

"*I* is investigate the source. *F* is find better coverage. *T* is trace claims, quotes, and images to the original context and see if they're being misportrayed.

"The idea is, if we can get people to, in a sense, read less and react less, we can maybe break that cycle, which gains such a momentum. And you just see it. I saw it with a family member of my own. Not deep into the white supremacist territory, thankfully, but into some other things that were extremist, the Seth Rich sort of stuff.

"It happens too quickly, but it happens because these people are actually being voracious readers and voracious 'researchers,' but they're not actually orienting themselves to the discourse that they've landed themselves in."

2. Immunization, of course, is not always possible. Most of the time conspiracism shows up at our dinner tables unannounced. Prepare to be blindsided, so arm yourselves with knowledge.

Stephen Lewandowsky was drawn into the world of conspiracism and disinformation when he composed a scientific paper examining theories denying that global climate change is a reality. "What we did in the paper that we wrote about was to explore the implications of that claim," he says. "What that actually means and what would have had to be true for that claim to be true. When you look at that, then you find that the claim just falls over in a heap because the moment you start thinking about what the implications are, it just becomes ridiculous."

He found that an early application of scientific rigor was helpful, but it only helped when people promoting denialist climate theories had to face consequences within their scientific peer communities for their own frequent lack of rigor. "One thing that might be helpful is to expose people to the consequences of their own faults and it becomes obvious very often to anyone who is capable of standard cognition that the claim just makes no sense because the implications don't materialize," he says.

"Then the other thing we know about conspiracy theories is that they tend to come together in clusters so people tend to believe more than one conspiracy. If you believe one, then chances are you'll believe more than one. It's not just an isolated thing.

"People tend to believe in multiple conspiracies and that also identifies them as being a particular type of person, because it's not just that they have information about Pizzagate that no one else has, but that they actually have a personality or cognitive style that makes them susceptible to believing a lot of weird things. So, first of all, that's an important thing to tell others who you might protect against conspiracy theories by just noticing that, hang on, people who believe one conspiracy also believe in another. Do you really want to believe in all that stuff?"

That, however, assumes they haven't already become ensnared.

"Reaching the people who have gone down the rabbit hole is extremely difficult because one of the problems now is that on the Internet they will find support in their views that seems strong," Lewandowsky says. "This is one of the really pernicious aspects of the Internet as completely underappreciated in my view: the social signals you get on the Internet are completely miscalibrated. I can believe anything I want no matter how absurd. I'll find a thousand people on Facebook who share my views, whatever they may be. I can say the Earth is flat or Obama is a lizard person, and somebody will share that view.

"At the moment people have a community, they become entrenched in those views. And that is what makes it more difficult to break than it used to be, because at least thirty years ago, people knew they were cranks because no one else believed anything that they said, but that's no longer true. Now people have the Internet and they get back up from a thousand others. Which is a trivially small number given how many people are on Facebook, but it's sufficient to create an illusion of support.

"At the moment you find a community, that's it. You're stuck in the rabbit hole and you're no longer feeling isolated because there are these other people egging you on."

Lewandowsky cautions that "you're talking about a certain type of person who falls into that rabbit hole"—namely, authoritarian personalities. "That is triggered by their personal circumstances and their feeling of alienation from society, and there's some evidence to suggest that," he says. For example, the people who believe everything Donald Trump says are of a certain type, right? Not everybody falls for Trump, quite the contrary.

"So the difficulty is that a lot of the fertile ground for this nonsense—for Trump and conspiracy theories and everything else—is political in nature. And it's the politics of the last twenty or thirty years that have just disempowered a lot of people, or they feel that they have lost out, regardless whether that feeling is real or not.

"All of this is unfolding against a political structure that is extremely difficult to change, and finding the antidote is almost impossible without changing the politics or changing society at large."

3. Your relationship with the person is what will guide them out of the rabbit hole.

The most powerfully toxic effect of conspiracism is that it isolates people—cuts them off from the rest of society, encourages them to walk away from it, from democratic institutions, from their own political franchise. Friends and coworkers peel away gradually as they grow uncomfortable with the conspiracist's growing obsession. Family members become alienated as the red-pilled begin insisting that they convert to their belief system, usually claiming they're doing so for everyone's protection.

Eventually their only social contact is with other true believers. That becomes their community—and after a while, they can't even trust those, right? In a very powerful way, when people dive down the conspiracist rabbit holes, they lose touch with their own humanity.

So any kind of sincere attempt at empathetic or—more importantly—nonjudgmental exchange of personal contact with a conspiracy theorist is likely to have some reasonable chance of success, because they often are starved for a sympathetic ear. However, during these initial stages, they'll remain highly suspicious, typically paranoid, and on the lookout for any sign of disrespect or judgment that they are crazy or stupid—all things they have heard many times before.

Dishonesty in these situations is always disastrous, but so is too much transparency. The ideal approach is a clinical one: think of yourself as someone conducting an interview in a professional manner, one in which the questions have already been laid out and the nature of your query is constrained by them.

Sociologist Samantha Kutner, who has researched both the organizing principles of far-right Proud Boys as well as methods of deradicalization, says she often thinks of Kenneth Burke's rhetorical concept of identification when approaching these situations—that is, in order for any kind of persuasion to take place, one or both parties involved must "identify" with the other. So when starting out—whether with an established relationship or with a new one—it's essential to find common ground over which you can bond, at least a little.

"I like seeing how something resonates with an individual," Kutner says, most particularly, "whether when you see someone else's plight, whether you empathize with them and want to support them." She says that, as with any human exchange, it's essential to play it by ear, roll with the punches, and maintain your own integrity in the relationship. It's even possible to gently mock them, she says.

"There has to be a gentle kind of pro-social way to respond to these people that's like, 'Hey, you're wrong. But we still care about you,'" Kutner says. "The tone is hard to replicate, but the times that I've been able to do it, it's been successful. I'm sure there are other people that are into the pro-social trolling where, yes, you're mocking them, but you're not doing it in a way that's showing that you dehumanize them. It's just nudging them in a certain direction or hoping they see something."

C. V. Vitolo, a professor of debate at University of Wisconsin–Madison and one of the activists involved in direct contact with deradicalization work, explains that "recognizing that radicalization is a process and not a state of being and that it is worthwhile to intervene at any point in that process" are fundamental to any kind of success.

"And so just because you are not good at dealing with full-blown 14/88 Nazis doesn't mean that you don't have a role to play in stopping radicalization. Don't sell yourself short or think your interventions are small if you're intervening at the beginning or the middle of the radicalization process."

The next fundamental, in Vitolo's view, is the human connection. "Relationships are the key," she says. "There are people who, it took me two, sometimes even three years to get through to, who started very strong in one direction and had to work piece by piece from outright to civic nationalists to libertarian, and eventually becoming a little bit more properly left leaning, in my opinion. And that's something that's not possible if someone doesn't have some kind of trust-based relationship with you.

"That process of repetition is so important. Relationships don't just afford you trust, they also afford you the ability to say things over and over and over to people. And repetition has a big impact. If you only hear someone make an argument once, no matter how good it is, it's not necessarily going to sit with you. That's not how our brains work. We don't take a piece of information and process it through every single thing we know, you know?"

4. Therefore, the key to all of your actions is empathy—not blind, unquestioning empathy, but the mindful kind, attuned to the faults of the other person and maintaining normal moral boundaries, while also being willing to simply listen.

If your goal is to help another person emerge from the conspiracist cocoon through the gravitational pull of your relationship, then large doses of empathy and forbearance will be required on your part. This is always much easier said than done, especially because red-pilled people are so often angry, contentious, suspicious, and generally cantankerous.

Samantha Kutner says that avoiding a really confrontational approach is key. She describes her sessions as "more of a respectful listening. Being willing to listen to them." She says she studied psychologist Carl Rogers's "nondirective approaches" to interviewing subjects, which helped her tremendously.

Maintaining this empathetic approach, however, should never mean sacrificing the boundaries of fundamental human behavior—violence and threats are always intolerable, whether directed at you or anyone else. And you should never sacrifice those boundaries for the sake of maintaining the relationship.

As journalist Noah Berlatsky has observed, empathy as a simple principle is a two-edged sword that can make the world better, but it can be used to make things worse. "The problems with empathy bias are compounded by the fact that it's possible to weaponize empathy to create support for ugly political programs, and even for violence," he writes. "Trump leverages our empathy bias by presenting himself as the spokesperson for good, normal, white people against untrustworthy, dangerous, racial others. When he talks about immigrants, for example, Trump constantly aligns himself with those he claims are victims of immigrants. He focuses on the people who will supposedly suffer when immigrants take jobs or commit crimes."[11]

Paul Bloom, a psychology professor at Yale University, argues for a different model of empathetic behavior he calls "rational compassion," which mitigates and redirects the claims of empathy. Trump's calls for empathy for victims of crimes committed by undocumented immigrants, he suggests, should elicit a search for data. "You don't have to be a cold-blooded utilitarian," Bloom says, "but people should appreciate that facts matter. If Trump says or implies that an extraordinary number of illegal immigrants are murderers and rapists, before you start putting yourself in people's shoes and feeling their pain, you should ask, is it true?"

C. V. Vitolo says she has grappled with how different people's grasps of the world can really be. She emphasizes "just the importance of holding another person's epistemology and of understanding a lot of this as epistemological problems, where it's not just that they don't understand the data or they don't understand what the science says.

"Sometimes it's not a question of, 'Could you, in theory, separate people into races biologically?' Sure, you can separate people into any number of things biologically if you wanted to. You could do it twenty different ways. You can do whatever you want. But it's essential to understand: why sort people this way in the first place, right? They often invert the scientific process. What is driving the mode of scientific inquiry that you're participating in?"

5. After you listen, ask the right questions.

All of this underscores, perhaps, the difficulty of attempting to deradicalize someone when it's being done by an ordinary person without training in these techniques, and it reminds us that making this attempt probably means learning new interpersonal skills that may not always be successful. Maintaining a calm professionalism in the face of a raging conspiracy theorist is not for the meek at heart.

Kutner recommends using Carl Rogers's listening strategies to defuse tense situations.[12] These involve two key steps: first, seeking to understand the other person's ideas, then "reflecting back to them what it is you think that they're saying."

"There's a lot of, 'This is what I think you're saying. Is that accurate?'" she explains. "And then going back and forth and having them identify."

As the conversation proceeds, she says it's essential to respond with your questions to what they're saying, as well as to help them to elucidate rationally what they otherwise simply have a strong feeling about. Having an actual back-and-forth exchange, and not purely a clinical one, works best.

Vitolo says it's essential that those who undertake this process comprehend that they're confronting an "evil that is worth dedicating a ton of time and resources to pushing back against," but also that they "do not believe that the people attached to those ideologies are also just not worth our time or are irredeemable in any way. Persuasion hinges on your ability to be likable.

"And it's not really likability, because usually it's not anything that would pass as civility in normie culture. But it is about adopting the kind of social cues of that audience and saying things and making arguments in ways that you know are reaching out to them on really human levels and holding their perspectives and taking them seriously, taking their pain seriously, taking their own causes of liberation, even if they may seem trivial in comparison, seriously. It's hard to find people who have that balance of empathy and also are resilient enough to not fall for it."

> 6. Don't fall down the rabbit hole yourself while attempting to help someone else out of it.

One of the first things that those who are attempting to draw someone out of the red-pill rabbit hole have to do is immunize themselves from the attractions of conspiracism. So at every step in your process of listening to and discussing a red-pilled person's beliefs, it's essential to keep in mind the distinction made in chapter 1 between conspiracies and conspiracy theories—namely, the three primary limitations of real conspiracies (duration, numbers of actors, scope, and breadth) and the known attributes of conspiracy theories (the long period of time over which they occurs, their large numbers of participants, and the global reach of the plots).

Stephan Lewandowsky says he's frequently criticized by people asking how he can dismiss the theories when in fact there have been real conspiracies. His answer: "If you look at true conspiracies that we now acknowledge have hap-pened—like the Volkswagen diesel scandal [in which the carmaker was caught falsifying emissions data on its cars], which is classic conspiracy, right? That was uncovered by very conventional means. That wasn't cranks who invented this and then found it confirmed. No, these were professionals that noticed some weird stuff and they investigated that. And the same is true for Iran Contra, true for Watergate, COINTELPRO."

As he observes, there's never been a real conspiracy uncovered by a con-spiracy theorist.

"The important thing . . . is [that] the cognition of the people who uncov-ered these true conspiracies is usually totally straightforward," he adds. "I mean, they're not cranks—they are investigative journalists or they're whistleblowers or they're academics or journalists. They're completely mainstream people whose job it is to go after the evidence. And in contrast to that, the people who believe that NASA faked the moon landing, if you look at how they considered the evi-dence, you can just identify all these cognitive flaws. So true conspiracies exist, yes—but if you think like a crank, you'll never find a true conspiracy."

A shorthand version of this, he acknowledges, is that much of the conspiracy theories he sees are readily discarded when the people pitching them have exten-sive records of promulgating misinformation, falsehoods, and nonsense: "Often, I'm very skeptical simply because the people involved make no sense."

Those are the most essential and simple guides. It's also wise never to be-come cavalier about conspiracy theories and treat them as mere mental games, diversions, or entertainments.

"In many ways there is nothing harmless about conspiracy theories," ob-serves Lewandowsky. "I think it used to be the case that people cavalierly just dismiss them as being a fringe phenomenon, and they were some weird people out there who believe that Elvis was still alive in North Korea. People were amused by it and would go, 'Aha, yeah, isn't that funny?'

"And perhaps that was appropriate at the time before the Internet came along and gave them a mushrooming platform and before they were recognized. I think what we're experiencing now is that conspiracy theory has been increas-ingly conducive to political extremism, and of course in a sense that is nothing new, because the history of anti-Semitism is basically just one big weaponized conspiracy theory. So in that sense, there is nothing new under the sun; it is simply that we now have broader dissemination of this. It's much, much easier to spread this stuff, and I don't think they're harmless."

Kate Starbird warns that the newer conspiratorial appeals are increasingly sophisticated and capable of ensnaring even well-educated people. "I can see the rhetoric of critical thinking is used constantly within the conspiracy theory ecosystems that we study," she says. "They've manipulated the tools of critical thinking, and they use it to take apart reality, and in ways that are not healthy for society.

"So how do we give people the tools not to take everything apart, but to learn how to build back some sense of what we can trust, and not to be skeptical of everything, but to figure out what we should assign credibility to? In terms of the next generation of digital literacy, or just information literacy, I think that's going to be really important for us, to figure out how to trust things."

Lewandowsky observes that for conspiracists, "the targets are almost arbitrary. It's just a matter of finding somebody you can hate. Doesn't matter if they're gay or Jewish or Muslim or whatever, it's just fulfilling the same function, which is to give people somebody to hate, because they're being disenfranchised or disgruntled with their own lives and then somebody comes along and tells them that it's all the fault of the Jews or Muslims or whatever and then, aha! All of a sudden they no longer have to take responsibility for their own actions or they can blame somebody for whatever misery they are experiencing and then some people will just go boom."

> 7. As you ask questions, search mainly for the conspiracist's deeper motives.

When you're asking all these questions, you're doing more than just getting them to explain themselves in a way that perhaps you can understand, even if it seems absurd and unlikely. What you're really after is their underlying reasons for believing these conspiracy theories to be true. Because those reasons are the key to changing the course of their trajectory.

Although throwing facts at them in rebuttal is not merely pointless, but counterproductive, getting them to explain their thinking coherently and honestly has its own effect.

"It's virtually impossible to convince them, certainly with facts, but it becomes possible when they start having doubts about their own theory or when they have been disillusioned for other reasons," says Lewandowsky.

"And that's the important thing, that it's not . . . always about the conspiracy theory. No, the conspiracy theory is the symptom, in many cases, of other problems that these people are having in their own life."

A lot of times the search leads from one buried motive to another, deeper and farther down the path that brought them to this point in the first place. This is especially the case when it comes to complicated hatreds like misogyny, which usually is entangled with the person's emotional development and health or lack thereof. But even with simpler, more visceral and less explicable hatreds such as racial or ethnic bigotry, a more complex and often deeply personal experience or trauma may form its real core.

"Someone said to me—again, someone who has a lot of practical experience in working with neo-Nazis—she said she's never met a happy racist," says Lewandowsky. "All these people who turn toward these ideologies, toward these hateful ideologies, are often people who've made a lot of wrong choices and they're not very happy with their lives, and the embracing of that ideology is the consequence, it's not the cause of their problems. So, it's also about trying to identify what are the problems or underlying things that may have led them to embrace that."

C. V. Vitolo believes it's essential to "make it intelligible to them that there's another world out there where you get the things that you want. The ethnostate—it's not an end in and of itself. It's a means to your feelings of security, your feelings of safety, your feelings of, honestly, futurity. . . . I can certainly tell you that there's a process involved that you can be an active participant in which your needs will be taken seriously. And I think making sure they know that the uncertainty you feel is the uncertainty everyone feels. And you don't have to control it all to know that you'll be given a fair shake."

> 8. Recognize that these underlying motivations and needs have other ways of being met—so find them.

The very personal needs and motives that fuel most conspiracists' attraction to them are not easily generalized—sometimes they arise from individual traumas, sometimes from idiosyncratic upbringings, or their own personal wiring, and they are often related to the nuances of the widely varying material realities of their daily lives.

However, there are threads that also run through conspiracism and the authoritarian personalities drawn to them that often surface with deeper questioning. A common theme that comes out is the heroic ideal: many if not most red-pilled conspiracists see themselves as part of a heroic effort to save whatever is the focus of that person's motives: their families, their communities, their region, their nation, their entire race ("my people" is how they usually express the latter), sometimes all of the above.

This heroic self-conception is common among right-wing extremists in part because they often have personal stories that are not so heroic, and announcing their heroism is a means of overcoming that past. It also becomes a useful rationalization for a wide range of behaviors, from believing palpable nonsense to committing hate crimes.

Indeed, it's something they share with hate crime perpetrators. A number of psychological studies of such criminals has found that nearly every one of them believed they were committing a "message" crime on behalf of their community and in its defense, believing the mere presence of the target minority posed a threat of some kind to it. Hate criminals and domestic terrorists both cast themselves in a heroic light. It's central to their self-rationalization for their acts.

Lewandowsky recalls the case of Timothy McVeigh's accomplice in the 1995 Oklahoma City bombing, Terry Nichols. "He used to be a guy in his mid-thirties who had not accomplished anything: he had not been able to maintain a relationship, he had broken off his education, he wasn't able to maintain any jobs. By any standards, he was a bit of a loser, and he realized it. He was very frustrated and becoming depressed about his situation," he recounts.

"And then at some point, he gets in touch with members in Michigan of the Aryan Nations, and they basically changed him. He starts hanging out with them, they embrace him, but they also give him a new philosophy, which says to him, 'None of this is actually your fault, it is the government's fault.' And suddenly he feels very empowered and he basically said, 'Wow, I've actually been a victim. None of this has been my fault. It's been the government's fault. There's this vast conspiracy operating against people like me. And now I'm no longer a loser; in fact, I'm becoming a freedom fighter, I'm embracing this cause.' And adopting this ideology was incredibly powerful for someone like him to make sense of his personal troubles, but also to find something that he could embrace and work for, for the first time in his life."

"Look at the various reasons that people are engaged in conspiracy ideation and conspiratorial cultures," Michael Caulfield explains. "One of the big ones, of course, is it's really easy to earn intellectual respect in these communities, right? I mean, compared to everywhere else, where it's actually quite expensive to earn intellectual respect.

"If you go into the flat Earth conspiracy, you can be Stephen Hawking in five months, the Stephen Hawking of that community. So getting intellectual respect in those communities is actually quite cheap. You suddenly don't have to deal with the fact that 'Oh, I have these opinions, but there are people smarter than me that have other opinions, so maybe my opinions aren't the center of the discourse universe.'"

Caulfield was struck by a mother's tale of deradicalization in the *Washingtonian* that described a woman's struggle when her thirteen-year-old son joined the alt-right. Angry and resentful over a false accusation of sexual harassment, he had gravitated into online circles (particularly at Reddit) that discussed the plot against young white men and, eventually, "cultural Marxism." He tried attending a Proud Boys rally.

Eventually, meeting some of his online alt-right heroes turned out to be disillusioning, and he peeled away from the scene. Some weeks later, he told his mother what was going through his head.

"I'd always had my doubts," he said. "I knew liking them was wrong. But I wanted to like them because everyone else hated them."

She asked him whether *he* liked them.

"I liked them because they were adults and they thought I was an adult. I was one of them," he answered. "I was participating in a conversation. They took me seriously. No one ever took me seriously—not you, not my teachers, no one. If I expressed an opinion, you thought I was just a dumbass kid trying to find my voice. I already had my voice."[13]

Caulfield recognized this scenario: "It's almost traditional grooming in the sense that the big thing they had with the son is that the community, he felt, took him seriously. And he felt that his other communities, including his parents, didn't. And even though that's about a thirteen-year-old, I think it's also very similar to why a lot of adults gravitate to these communities.

"It's not all just racism and threats and so forth. A lot of it is they have a desire for some kind of stature, and they're not going to make that stature by saying something that everyone else is saying. And they're not going to get that stature in a community that consists of millions of people versus a smaller community where they can be a quicker superstar."

The motivating dynamics of conspiracy theorists all vary widely, but these core motivations tend to arise out of commonly held beliefs and views that have been distorted and misshapen by the false information and sociopathic worldview innate to conspiracism. There are, of course, many other ways to feel heroic and appreciated than to join extremist organizations, and getting people to change course may require being imaginative about finding other ways of making them feel valued.

The narratives that are the grist of these buried mythologies are usually gut level in nature: we buy into the myth of heroism on a visceral level. But those who do find themselves caught in an endless dynamic in which generating, identifying, defeating, and then eliminating the enemy—which is the essence of the heroic narrative—becomes their sole preoccupation. As we have seen, this can have toxic and tragic consequences.

9. Avoid challenging the person's core underlying beliefs that motivate his or her embrace of conspiracy—at least initially.

A number of studies of the deradicalization process found that any attempt to pull a person out of a rabbit hole immediately turned sideways if the interlocutor challenged any of the core cherished beliefs of the conspiracist's worldview.

Sometimes these beliefs reside in the range of normative society—such as, say, the belief that abortion is murder—and become malignant only when a range of toxic conspiracy theories is adopted to support them. At other times, however, these beliefs originate wholly within the realm of conspiracists' alternative universe, such as the belief that Hillary Clinton presides over a global child slavery and pedophilia ring.

And throughout most of the process of persuading people to draw back out of their rabbit holes, they clutch these core belief "jewels" tightly and jealously. Facts that challenge those beliefs, in particular, are not helpful at this point. Because for the true believers, reality becomes the precipice.

"It's who you are," says Kutner. "This really fragile sense of self you've constructed in the movement, it falls apart when it's challenged like that. And then you're back to feeling lost and alone and, 'My girlfriend left me,' and 'Who the fuck am I?' Most people don't want to deal with that."

When she encounters these moments, Kutner says she sees it as an opportunity to explore those core motives: "For me, I think it's more, 'What are your thoughts on this?'"

Often she can advance the conversation by tossing out published material from other sources: "Just articles that have a different perspective," she says. "'I was reading this and I haven't had a chance to talk to many people who've had your experience. What do you think about this?' And kind of playing up to their ego, like they're qualified to speak on the topic. Especially if they're guys, because ego plays a central role in so much of this."

The world is dominated—though not solely populated—by men. And so many of the deradicalization efforts have a strong pheromonal scent.

"They're very aggressively performing masculinity," Kutner says. "I think some of them have severe depression that comes with the package.

"With that is that lack of agency," she adds, referencing one of the key traits of people drawn to conspiracism. "I talked to a Proud Boy, and I said, 'Is it kind of like putting on a new suit and seeing if it fits? And if you wear it long enough, you may not feel as depressed as you were?'

"We agreed that was a big thing—that masking depression through becoming overly violent or aggressively posturing was a really big deal. I think that men have a hard time approaching what some healthy level of masculinity looks like because no one really knows, so they go to everything that's been hardwired into society. They take it to the most extreme route because it's like, 'If I feel like a weakling, then if I'm an alpha male maybe that will compensate for my deficiencies.'"

10. Keep it real and make it genuinely about helping your friend or loved one. If the person you are attempting to rescue suspects ulterior motives, you will be sunk.

Samantha Kutner says she works hard to make her interchanges with radicalized Proud Boys "empowering" but in a healthy direction.

"It would come from a source of empowerment with them," she says, adding that groups like the Proud Boys recruit with the same idea in mind: "I think they're initially sold on this pitch: 'You get a chance to be blah, blah in this organization.'"

She offers them a different, similarly empowering narrative: "I think that selling them on, 'You're an expert in yourself,' and encouraging self-reflexivity is key," she says.

It's essential, Michael Caulfield says, to gradually move the conversations into friendlier territory without playing into the process that led them to con-spiracist beliefs in the first place. Making your relationship with them distinct from that part of their lives is also helpful—and when drawing them back to the real world, begin asking their advice on matters and questions that lie wholly outside that realm.

"I think in the process of that, when it's spotted, and when people both understand how to not play into the whole process, I think we can have some effect," Caulfield says. "And the way that we have that effect is just a simple conceptual question I would have them ask: 'I'm not sure this is what you think it is, but here's something that you might be interested in.'"

Caulfield says he avoids asking: "Oh, is this trustworthy or not?" "I actually don't think that that's the thing, because when you get into these things, it's trustworthy because it supports your thing."

He says it's good to challenge them on a rational level on non-core issues, and best to challenge them on core issues when they show signs of deepening radicalization: "When someone starts to drift this way, they'll post something, maybe their initial post about QAnon," he says, "or just a little further along," he will attempt to steer them away, "saying, 'Okay, my source is better than your source, and your source sucks.'"

"I think you could say, 'Hey, I'm not sure if you realize this, but that's actually a known white supremacist site'—but then really quickly validate their concern, find a piece of their concern that you can validate, and say: 'However, your post did get me interested in some of these issues, and I found this article from *The Atlantic* that makes some related points.'"

"And that gives that person an out, and they are more likely to withdraw and say, 'Okay, some of my feelings and tension about this is not completely invalidated, but yeah, it looks like I've messed up here. And I didn't mean to tweet out a white supremacist source."

Still, it's important in the process to leave room for their beliefs, even as you're getting them to think and behave more rationally.

"I do think that the universes there become just so encased," he says, "the way that it is sort of a bubble—not a bubble like it protects us from things, but like in science fiction: a bubble universe, a little universe that is internally consistent but exists outside of Earth Prime. They live in a bubble universe, everything is internally consistent in there, and you can't pull out the Seth Rich conspiracy without it unraveling into a million different issues."

The sheer mass of this universe can be daunting for anyone dealing with it. "That's just harder because their belief system has become so plugged into these things and so densely interconnected," Caulfield says. "There's such a density to conspiratorial belief. Even more than just belief. You would think the world is the most densely linked thing, but conspiratorial belief is just everything links to everything.

"It's like a game of Jenga at that point. What can you actually pull out that's not going to threaten this person's central identity at this point? That's the much more difficult thing."

> 11. Take the time to establish real-world activities with the other person that have nothing to do with politics or conspiracies. Do things, don't just talk.

The human experience itself of being on the Internet and its limitations as a form of human interaction both have a great deal to do with the spread of conspiracism well beyond merely giving the theories a platform and a means to circulate widely. Much of it—particularly the ugly trolling behavior and ultimately the extremist ideologies and violent radicalism that emerge in the worst corners—reflects the disembodied nature of that experience and the easy dehumanization that comes along with it.

"Disembodiment and dematerialization are generally assumed to be intrinsic consequences of digital media because of the implicit immateriality of digital information and because the user's interaction with the media is estranged, or alienated, from instinctual corporeal authenticity," observed one study, which then explained that these were mostly misconceptions.[14]

However, the otherworldly aspect of being online is part of why it's easy to dehumanize other people there: in our online exchanges, it's just bits on a screen—there's no body nearby, no vocal intonation, no eye contact or expression, no hand gestures, all normal parts of full human communication. It's easy to troll someone else. There's even a thrill involved.

This environment also enables conspiracism to run unchecked. The cottage industry that produces most of the world's conspiracy theories competes constantly to "push the envelope" of outrage and hysteria, which are the meat and potatoes of their existence. This means that even vile racial bigotry comes into play—along with the whole raft of white nationalist and other forms of extremism.

Personal relationships have difficulty swimming in this environment. So it's a great idea to spend shared time away from it. When undertaking the task of deradicalizing someone, it's ideal to meet up at least occasionally for in-real-life activities: coffee, lunch, beers, golf, tennis, movies, pizza, whatever. Putting a real face and person to all these bits on the screen alters the dynamic substantially.

If you're doing this with someone entirely online, this is much more complicated but still possible. It mostly means agreeing to do things away from the computer monitors, out in the real world, and then sharing those things with the other person. You can go see movies, read books, watch TV shows, whatever works.

Samantha Kutner likes to have a "literary component" to her exchanges with far-right extremists. Sometimes this involves reading the same book and discussing it. Sometimes it involves both sides keeping a journal and then discussing them afterward.

"I've journaled since I was eleven, and I think that that has allowed me to constantly be willing to evaluate my perspective and really know myself in that way," Kutner says. "I think that encouraging self-reflexivity and having them read, where you're just exposed to a multitude of different themes, is essential to this."

Sometimes the reading would simply entail "articles or summaries of articles that talk about hate residuals," she says. "It's how your brain is wired in a certain way after being in these organizations. Your neurons repeatedly fire together, wire together. That's the statement that they say. You may be wanting to leave the group, but you may still be in that mindset where your program or your pattern of thinking has been shaped in this way that it's going to take a really long time to unlearn these things."

She focuses on helping them understand "it's normal to experience what they're experiencing, and they're not alone in it, reducing shame and stigma, so that it's not a process where you have to go it alone, and you can become an expert in yourself. You can heal from your experience and whatever it is that can take you out of it."

12. As the bond builds, opportunities will arise in which to undermine some of their conspiracism with factuality—though again, this has to be done gradually and sensitively.

Time is the ally of anyone working to draw conspiracists out of their rabbit holes, because the more contact they have with someone whom they previously thought of as a hapless pawn or a corporate sellout, a potential plotter or some other stereotype used to dismiss doubters, has turned out to be someone who values them and what they think. Eventually, this may lead them to rethink these perceptions, though not always.

Samantha Kutner was an egghead academic when most of her subjects met her. Initially they were hostile and skeptical but, over time, came to see her as a friend. What worked? "I think prolonged contact with them and showing them that I'm not an angry feminist, antifa, SJW individual, and I'm listening to them," she answers. "I don't think these men were listened to like that in their lives. I think that was a really powerful thing.

"I wasn't passive. If they were wrong in something, I'd say, 'Here's how I understand it, but here's how most people see this.' I was always trying to get them to kind of reconcile the two different things. I think for those two Proud Boys, that was really important because they were confronting all of these discrepancies between what they thought the group was and what the group actually is. They were doing it in a kind of safe environment where they know that I'm not going to dox them, and I'm not out to get them, and they could confide in me. I think that helped a lot with those two members that left."

What never works, as Michael Caulfield advises, is shaming them—though he believes public shaming of high-profile figures or participants in violent behavior can be very effective in changing people's behavior. "But for your friends and family, what's the alternative?" he asks rhetorically. "You have their relationship with them, and it's the only bargaining chip you have, it's the only thing that you've got. And if you make them make a choice between that and you, I'm just not sure what that does for the relationship."

A rhetorical strategy that can be effective at this stage is to find narratives that neutralize and potentially can replace the older narratives around which they have constructed their worldview—particularly the visceral, gut-level narratives that are so appealing to them. Drawing someone enmeshed, for instance, in QAnon conspiracy theories away from those beliefs is always helped by nudging reminders, delivered nonthreateningly, that the billionaire president really did not have the best interests of ordinary people in mind.

"We have a lot of data showing that if you want people to give up on misinformation, you have to provide them with an alternative that explains the noise," says Stephan Lewandowsky. "'Why is it that you shouldn't believe climate deniers?' 'Well, they're funded by Exxon,' is what they're going to say. That is a thing that is clearly doable and works for some people.

"At most, people do not want to fall victim to a con man so if you can convince them that they have been taken advantage of or victimized, then that might turn them against the con man. However, in practice, that doesn't always work because people, once they become vested in something, are reluctant to admit that they've been fooled. They don't want to be fooled. So you have to somehow provide that alternative narrative without emphasizing the fact that they've been fooled themselves. It should be more like, 'Look at all these people out there who are exploiting vulnerable people with their nonsense—surely you wouldn't fall for that type of stuff.' Or, 'This guy is victimizing you, I want to help you get out of this hole that he's pulled you into.'"

> 13. Over time, your relationship with the other person will become important enough to them that they will become more open to your perspective and more willing to reconsider theirs.

Peter Neumann has seen how difficult it can be to deradicalize someone. "We know this from a lot of European far-right extremists—you have to get them out in a way that, first of all, understands that if you've been involved in a particular extremist milieu or in conspiracy—like if you've been a 9/11 truther for the past ten years—a lot of your social relationships, both online and offline, will be based on that theory. Maybe you even got married to someone because you met him or her in the context of these ideas. So this is about deconstructing social relationships as much as it is about convincing them that they were wrong.

"And then, of course, . . . if you've dedicated ten years of your life towards promoting these ideas, you become very invested, and it's hard for anyone—nevermind an extremist, it's hard for anyone—to admit that they basically wasted ten years of their life on something that is completely untrue. So, in providing them with a new framework, you also have to make sure that, as absurd as that sounds, you respect what they've done and that they don't feel like their entire life has been completely wasted.

"So, you have to allow them to embrace something new without necessarily making them feel bad or without basically telling them that they are complete losers who've been hooked to a lie, and you have to channel that into something else. That's why quite a few extremists who deradicalize then become very vigorous advocates of deradicalizing other extremists, because this is a new project that they can channel their energies into and where their own involvement and extremism is actually something that's valuable because they understand it, so they can say, 'Well, I've not wasted these five years. They're actually useful for me, because I now understand how these people work.'"

> 14. Keep multiplying. Once they begin emerging from the rabbit hole, help them to reconnect with their personal world—restoring old relationships that have been ruptured—as well as to expand their world by getting new experiences that may undermine some of their bigoted or paranoid beliefs.

Samantha Kutner has found that helping her interlocutors actually come face to face with some of the people they have demonized in their conspiracist's imagination has a powerful effect.

"I would really focus on having them come into contact with the groups and the people that they've demonized in a controlled, safe setting," she says. "And having them see that the idea of whoever it is, whether it's a Jewish person or a black person or a Hispanic person, the idea that they've been sold about these groups of people is not true; these stereotypes are lies.

"I think the contact hypothesis would be a really good approach to the reflective, literary component. There would be self-work. There would be outreach for people who were former extremists, and then there would be people who don't fit that mold that they've been conditioned to believe. It would involve speaking to them and just saying, 'Look, this is my life.' Spend a few hours with me, and this is what I do." People, after all, tend to shed their horns and pitchforks after a cup of coffee with them.

> 15. Help them to heal. That must be the abiding principle behind every one of these steps.

The baseline of this kind of undertaking is fixing something that has been broken. Conspiracy theories break people. They break relationships, families, communities, nations. They can be overcome only by human healing and compassion backed by moral and ethical clarity, the antithesis of the sociopathic world they engender.

The success of the process may hinge on the extent to which you and the person you're helping can interact in the real world. That's Peter Neumann's advice, at least.

"They say of course the Internet offers opportunities to find people that perhaps you wouldn't interact with normally, but I think the aim should then be to have an off-ramp where you pull it back into face-to-face conversation," he says. "I mean, a conversation can start on the Internet, and if someone is willing to engage with you, that's great, but I think ultimately the solution needs to be face-to-face.

"And that's why a lot of people are currently talking about this combination, on and off, looking for people online, trying to figure out who is potentially open to engaging, who has doubts and questions, but the endgame is always to engage with them face-to-face and to have facility that basically allows them to get real help and solve the problem that they have."

The work of saving the world from a descent into the madness of conspiracism need not, of course, fall entirely on the shoulders of the friends and family members of the people who fall into its snares. They may turn out to be the most effective tool, but government, business, and society at large have critical roles to play as well.

Peter Neumann's International Centre for the Study of Radicalisation at King's College, London, studied the problem of American online radicalization in depth as early as 2013 and published a comprehensive overview of how authorities can tackle it.

The first step: reducing the supply of extremist content. But that comes with a major caveat.

"First comes the recognition that—for constitutional, political, and practical reasons—it is impossible to remove all violent extremist material from the Internet and that most efforts aimed at reducing the supply of violent extremist content on the Internet are costly and counterproductive," it explains at the outset.[15]

Next: reducing the demand. These measures would work, "for example, by discrediting, countering, and confronting extremist narratives or by educating young people to question the messages they see online."

Finally: exploiting the Internet. Making practical use of online content and interactions for the purpose of gathering information, gaining intelligence, and pursuing investigations is essential for preventing violence and terrorism.

Neumann and his team explain that the steps involved in reducing the supply of the content are limited, particularly in the United States because of its constitutional free speech protections, in which censorship is extremely circumscribed. In European nations, nationwide filters and legal restrictions may affect the spread of extremist material in nations where laws exist prohibiting it, but that won't affect American consumers to any appreciable extent. Indeed, "most of the traditional means for reducing the supply of violent extremist content would be entirely ineffective or of very limited use in the U.S. context," the study explains.

The most viable option in the United States would involve commercial takedowns of extremist material from the platforms where they fester, such as YouTube, Facebook, and Twitter. Those companies have, since early 2019, begun making serious efforts at removing extremist content from their platforms, though with mixed results.

"One practical option could be for government agencies to create and, where appropriate, strengthen informal partnerships with Internet companies whose platforms have been used by violent extremists," the study suggests. "The objective would be to assist their takedown teams—through training, monthly updates, and briefings—in understanding national security threats as well as trends and patterns in terrorist propaganda and communication. As a result, online platforms such as Facebook and Google would become more conscious of emerging threats, key individuals, and organizations and could align their takedown efforts with national security priorities."

Reducing demand for extremist and terrorist material online is a much more complicated proposition. Neumann's study focuses on "activating the marketplace of ideas"—that is, conducting outreach in the very spaces where the radicalism is growing. It notes that chief among the drawbacks to engaging people online is the decided "enthusiasm gap": "Instead of having extremist views drowned out by opposing views, the Internet has amplified extremists' voices." The strategy is also hampered by significant gaps in the pluralism of ideas, as well as major gaps in skill level.

More promising, it suggests, would be measures aimed at "creating awareness" in a way that was effective and "building capacity in order to assure that alternative voices are heard." Countermessaging—which would expose people to messages that are specifically designed to counter the appeal of extremism—can also work, but it too has limitations when coming from officials or authorities. For such campaigns to really work, they have to be fueled and propagated at the grassroots level by ordinary people.

The study also discusses ways that the Internet can be an effective tool for gathering intelligence on political extremists, because so many of them organize online. It can also be used by investigators in collecting evidence of crimes afterward.

However, the centerpiece of the study was its finding that promoting digital-media literacy was the "most long-term—yet potentially most important—means of reducing the demand for online extremism."

"In recent years, educators and policymakers have recognized the unique risks and challenges posed by the Internet," the study notes. "Most efforts have focused on protecting children from predators and pedophiles, with the result that—in practically every school—kids are now being taught to avoid giving out personal details and to be suspicious of people in chat rooms. Little, however, has been done to educate young people about violent extremist and terrorist propaganda."

Neumann says that families and friends still hold the keys for preventing radicalization, because they see the effects in real life, while others are seeing it online. Often, red-pilled young men are hiding those activities, but their alienation and increasing anger levels also become manifest in their daily workaday and family lives.

"We know that in terrorism cases, for example, when people radicalize, we know that a lot of extremists who may be very deep in their extremist worlds still have so-called bystanders—that is, they have friends, family, people around them, colleagues at school, but most importantly family who still have an influence on them."

Many of these people express shock at the person's radicalization afterward, but many also acknowledge that they saw warning signs. And even after they had fully immersed themselves in their extremist world and embraced Nazism or Islamic State or whatever end the radicalization led to, they would maintain their ties to these bystanders.

"So, even people who went to Syria to join ISIS, we've observed a lot of them, they would still WhatsApp with their mom, because they were missing them, and because for them, their father or their mother was still a figure out of authority, not in all cases, but in some cases they were," Neumann said. "So, that's why a lot of these programs, these countering violent extremism programs are about empowering mothers, empowering parents, etcetera.

"So, I do think that people should take an interest and should be cognizant when suddenly one of their friends or their kids starts saying weird stuff and gets into something that is really problematic, because they all talk about it; we know about this. It's not like they're keeping quiet about it, especially in the early phase when you discover a new paradigm that explains a lot of things that you thought the government was keeping secret. You're very missionary, you're talking about it all the time, and I do think that so-called bystanders, family, friends, people at school should pay attention to that.

"Because it's exactly at that point that you can still intervene and that you still have influence and you can still talk someone out of it or you can engage with them, which at a later point may be much, much more difficult. So, it is really important to pay attention to this and to be ready to engage in a discussion about it for people who are connected to them, at an early point."

———————

The question any investigative reporter worth his or her salt looking at the twisted world of conspiracy theories and its globally toxic effects on every level of society would ask is: who benefits?

Who stands to gain, monetarily and in power, from a phenomenon in which large numbers of people form communities built around non-facts and nonsense that inevitably crumble in fits of extremist rancor and fiduciary miscreancy and, in the process, cut themselves off from their communities and from the political process? Who gains when millions of people dismiss democracy as a delusional joke and abandon what political franchise they possess? Who gains when democracy is debilitated, undermined, hollowed out from within?

Authoritarians do. Certainly authoritarians in government who prefer that every act reflects the instincts of the revered leader atop the heap because they believe that will produce a well-ordered society that also makes them wealthy. But also particularly authoritarians who run corporations that prefer operating without the constraints imposed by democratic government, particularly health, labor, and employment regulations, as well as environmental and workplace safety rules. These are the people who stand to benefit when a democratic society defenestrates itself, unlinks its arms from each other, retreating into survivalist bomb shelters to await the apocalypse or the civil war, whichever comes first.

The world, in truth, has always had a kind of unapologetic conspiracy operating in the open in every nation, under every form of government: namely, the conspiracy of established authority, entrenched wealth, and traditional cultural centers to maintain their positions and enhance and expand them if possible. "He who has the gold, rules" as a cynical but realistic version of the Golden Rule is not a new joke.

Conspiracy theories, sociologist Chip Berlet has long argued, are a kind of wedge between ordinary people and reality whose whole purpose is to distract the public's attention from the very real conspiracy happening before their faces.

"Conspiracism is neither a healthy expression of skepticism nor a valid form of criticism; rather it is a belief system that refuses to obey the rules of logic," he explains. "These theories operate from a pre-existing premise of a conspiracy based upon careless collection of facts and flawed assumptions. What constitutes 'proof' for a conspiracist is often more accurately described as circumstance, rumor, and hearsay; and the allegations often use the tools of fear—dualism, demonization, scapegoating, and aggressively apocalyptic stories—which all too often are commandeered by demagogues.

"Thus conspiracism must be confronted as a flawed analytical model, rather than a legitimate mode of criticism of inequitable systems, structures, and institutions of power. Conspiracism is nearly always a distraction from the work of uprooting hierarchies of unfair power and privilege."[16]

"Conspiracy is really a tool of power," observes Michael Caulfield, who notes that in recent years, academic discourse about conspiracy theories has wandered into discussions of "who gets labeled a conspiracy theorist and who doesn't.

"From my point of view, it's been interesting to see that hit the wall of Internet reality, where we're looking at this massification of conspiracy theory," he says. "Some of that starts to look a little precious in terms of what we're looking at, precisely because of the sorts of violent events which we're talking about, but I think also because more and more people are having this experience of watching people drift, bit by bit, deeper and deeper into these communities."

Kate Starbird first stumbled upon the machinations of foreign authoritarians tampering with the world's media ecosystems when she scientifically examined the spread of misinformation about Black Lives Matter and found clear evidence that Russian intelligence operatives were deliberately sowing racial disharmony on social media. Now, she's finding a variety of strands of authoritarianism woven throughout a number of disinformation campaigns whose data she and her team at University of Washington have gathered.

She believes these campaigns are effective in large part because of the environment in which it's occurring, where more and more people are adopting strong political identities.

"So if that political identity is strong and we're very polarized, we're more susceptible to disinformation," she says. "Disinformation targets political division, and that's also a place where we seem to be psychologically susceptible to it as well."

The work led her to examine Cold War propaganda techniques, where much of the sponsored disinformation originates. "There are some really interesting old books on Russian disinformation, particularly the Vladislav Bitman books," she says. "In one of them, he talks about how really partisan political identities are ones that are easily manipulated in different ways, and they said at the time, the KGB was really focused on targeting the political left, because that aligned with historically their political ideologies.

"But they're saying that there's no reason that these techniques wouldn't also work on the far right, and they'd already seen some instances of this as well, because they said the vulnerabilities themselves aren't about ideology. They're about being so committed to a political identity that you become unable to differentiate truth versus familiarity and what you want to believe."

More current outbreaks of authoritarianism, such as the far-right regime of Rodrigo Duterte in the Philippines, provide even more vivid insights into how the disinformation functions. A recent network disinformation paper was published out of a study in Manila where researchers from the University of Leeds interviewed people who were participating in a government disinformation campaign based on social media, troll accounts that blamed "drug dealers" and liberal elites for all the nation's ills. The result, it found, was a "public sphere filled with information pollution and, consequently, with toxic incivility and polarization.[17]

"We've been trying to figure out, what's the intersection between these populist movements and this disinformation infrastructure," Starbird says. "They intersect, but it's not causal. It seems to be something else. And the rise of these populist movements all over the world, why do they seem to intersect?

"They're authoritarian, because that's their nature," she adds, noting that the populism all seems to be of the right-wing variant. "What we've been seeing in a lot of these recent movements is that the leaders that are able to take advantage of this are ones that are willing to reflect back at the movements what they want to hear, which I guess is the basis of how populism works. It's grievance based, anti-elite based, which feeds into conspiracism.

"But they're able to reflect back some of the nastier parts of mob behavior, which the Internet enables in all sorts of different ways. Then these leaders have been able to take advantage of that in different ways. And you can see the mediascape, the people that have risen in the new media especially, becoming a media player out of doing the same kind of thing, echoing back these kinds of things to the crowd. Finally, political leaders are able to use social media directly to sense what people are talking about and then reflect it right back at them. So we're seeing that en masse."

Formulating an effective response in defense of democracy itself is, in fact, challenging, in large part because so many people living in those democracies haven't recognized that the ground is shifting around them and the landscape with it.

"The hard thing is, there's a really complex set of multiple things happening in concert that are resonating," Starbird says. "It's great to unpack them and understand them, but any one explanation is going to fall short of being complete, because it's such a complex system."

The most essential step in tackling the spread of disinformation and conspiracism on social media, she says, is "to build things that are trustworthy. Not just social media, but all sorts of information ecosystems. Journalism has to figure it out; social media has to figure it out. How do we make trustworthy information-participation systems? There's not an easy answer to that.

"It feels like we're being overwhelmed by something that we don't necessarily have the tools of society to grapple with. That seems to be resonating in ways very quickly and unexpectedly with political conditions and information systems and all of these things are resonating in ways that are just putting us in a really bad place."

The scenario, she says, reminds her of old film footage from 1940 of the Tacoma Narrows Bridge in southern Puget Sound, a suspension bridge that was renowned among drivers for wobbling unsteadily on windy days, earning it the sobriquet "Galloping Gertie." Opening on July 1 that year, it remained up only until November, when a powerful windstorm created such wild oscillations that the bridge came apart and fell into the Sound. Film footage showing the bridge structure warping wildly before its collapse became iconic in the Pacific Northwest.

"Galloping Gertie—I feel like that's what's happening," she says. "It's just hitting us one way and something else is hitting us a different way. It's hitting this resonance, and it's out of control.

"What is it going to take to cut it? Maybe that keeps going until everything just gets shattered to pieces, or maybe we just figure out how to get out of that loop, and we can resolve some of it."

We know what taking the so-called "red pill" looks like. If we *could* devise a "blue pill," what would happen? What would it do to you? To what would you "awaken"?

- First and foremost, it would be about embracing the clear cold light of reality: the workaday world of "normies," based on normative evidence, facts, logic, and reason, one filled with ordinary people doing ordinary things, dispelling the web of dark conspiracism with which the red-pilled cocoon themselves.
- The complexity of modern life would be seen clearly for what it is: a vast web that is connected not at some crude and imaginary dot-to-dot scheme overseen by a nefarious plot, but by the ordinary human connections every person makes in their daily lives—infinitely more complex, infinitely more real, and infinitely beyond any scheme that any radio show host can cook up for gullible audiences.
- You would enjoy facts—the ones established through the reliable sources you enjoy seeking out now. Facts, however, would no longer be based on your sources' conjecture, but on objectively reliable information from well-grounded, verifiable authorities. Science would cease to be a liberal conspiracy.
- Human decency and compassion would cease to be discarded as a liability; we would develop an awareness of how conspiracism destroys relationships, harms innocent people, and, at the horrifying violent end of its funnel, produces death.
- Media consumption would return to the workaday world. That wouldn't mean that you suddenly decide to accept every word published in the *New York Times* or uttered on CNN as unvarnished truth. Rather, you would again clearly see the complex and difficult reality: that corporate ownership has distorted our information diet, that the mainstream media can produce correct

and valuable information, yet it weaves distortions and falsehoods and omissions into its coverage in ways that require constant vigilance by consumers.

- You would cease suspecting that the motives of everyone in your world are connected under the umbrella of a mind-controlling conspiracy and realize that the complex ordinary world is run on billions of individual human motivations, some of them malign, most of them benign and very . . . human.

- Media consumption habits would be affected by the shift in your perceptions of media contents. Toxic places like 4chan and Infowars would lose their appeal, largely because their viciousness and estrangement from factual truth will have lost their appeal. Mainstream media would still, however, be nearly as problematic as it was before—just without the obscuring layer of accusatory hysteria with which their broadcasts are viewed through the prism of the conspiracist worldview.

- The blue pill would eventually induce a kind of mindful empathy or rational compassion, open-minded but not naïve. As you resume relationships with family and connect with old and new friends and expand your horizons to include human generosity, you'll find it increasingly easier to be at relative ease in the world wherever you are and whomever you are with. Like, you know, a normie.

- It would fix what's broken. But not right away. The pill works gradually. It takes time, forbearance, love, patience, compassion. All those old-fashioned words come together in one great and real thing: healing.

It's what we all need right now.

NOTES

Prologue

1. See Robert Evans, "The El Paso Shooting and the Gamification of Terror," *Bellingcat*, August 4, 2019. See also Eliza Mackintosh and Gianluca Mezzofiore, "How the Extreme-Right Gamified Terror," CNN, October 10, 2019.

2. See "The Extremist Medicine Cabinet: A Guide to Online 'Pills,'" Anti-Defamation League, November 6, 2019.

3. See Colette Weeks, "Community Remembers Chuck Davis as Leader, Friend to All," *Skagit Valley Herald*, July 23, 2017, 1B.

4. See Joseph Bernstein, "Alt-Right Troll to Father Killer: The Unraveling of Lane Davis," *Buzzfeed*, July 18, 2018. Bernstein assembled many of Davis's biographical details used here, in conjunction with the author's own research.

5. See David Neiwert, "Alt-Righter 'Seattle4Truth' Charged with Killing Father over Conspiracy Theories," *Hatewatch* (Southern Poverty Law Center), October 23, 2017.

6. See Joseph Bernstein, "Top Conservative Writer Is a Group Effort, Sources Say," *Buzzfeed*, March 31, 2016.

7. See David Neiwert, "'Pizzagate' Theories Inspire D.C. Gunman, but Still Have Defenders in Powerful Places," *Hatewatch* (Southern Poverty Law Center), December 6, 2016.

8. See Davis's YouTube video, "Progressive Ideology's Deep Ties to Pedophilia," April 29, 2017, as well as his older video, "Progress: Pedophilia," September 12, 2015. Davis's YouTube account containing all of these videos remains active.

Chapter 1

1. See, for example, Nelson Blackstock, *COINTELPRO: The FBI's Secret War on Political Freedom* (New York: Pathfinder Press, 1988).

2. See Philip Shenon with Stephen Engelberg, "Eight Important Days in November: Unraveling the Iran-Contra Affair," *New York Times,* July 5, 1987.

3. See, for example, David Neiwert, "'Communist Takeover' Paranoia Gets a Final Resuscitation for Trump's Inauguration," January 17, 2017, *Hatewatch* (Southern Poverty Law Center), and "Far-Right Conspiracists Stir Up Hysteria about Nonexistent 'Civil War' Plot by 'Antifa,'" November 14, 2017, *Hatewatch* (Southern Poverty Law Center).

4. See, for example, Duncan Campbell and Ben Aris, "How Bush's Grandfather Helped Hitler's Rise to Power," *Guardian*, September 25, 2004.

5. See Herbert Parmet, "What Should We Make of the Charge Linking the Bush Family Fortune to Nazism?" *History News Network*, November 17, 2003.

6. See, for example, Joe Conason, "What's Bush Hiding from 9/11 Commission?" *The Observer*, January 26, 2004; also see Thomas Bonsell, "Blame the Leadership Failures," *Seattle PI*, October 7, 2004.

7. See "Kissinger Resigns as Head of 9/11 Commission," CNN, December 13, 2002.

8. See Timothy J. Burger, "9/11 Commission Funding Woes," *Time*, March 26, 2003.

9. See Philip Shenon, "9/11 Commission Says It Needs More Time to Complete Report," *New York Times*, January 28, 2004.

10. National Commission on Terrorist Attacks upon the United States, "The System Was Blinking Red," *The 9/11 Commission Report: Final Report of the National Commission on Terrorist Attacks upon the United States*, 254–66. See also Kurt Eichenwald, "The Bush White House Was Deaf to 9/11 Warnings," *New York Times*, September 10, 2012.

11. See Russell Muirhead and Nancy L. Rosenblum, *A Lot of People Are Saying: The New Conspiracism and the Assault on Democracy* (Princeton, NJ: Princeton University Press, 2019), 19–41.

12. Muirhead and Rosenblum, *A Lot of People Are Saying*, 3.

13. See Chip Berlet, "Holocaust Museum Shooting, Antisemitic Conspiracy Theories, and the Tools of Fear," *Huffington Post*, July 11, 2009.

14. See Chip Berlet and Matthew N. Lyons, "Dynamics of Bigotry," *Political Research Associates*, November 8, 2000.

15. See Chip Berlet, "Dynamics of Right-Wing Populism," *Research for Progress*, August 15, 2016.

16. See Berlet, "Holocaust Museum Shooting."

Chapter 2

1. See Lou Michel and Dan Herbeck, *American Terrorist: Timothy McVeigh and the Oklahoma City Bombing* (New York: Regan Books, 2001), esp. 118–58.

2. See David Neiwert, *Alt-America: The Rise of the Radical Right in the Age of Trump* (New York: Verso, 2017), 49–74.

3. Much of this analysis is based on material provided by former Department of Homeland Security analyst Daryl Johnson.

4. See "Stephen Paddock: Adam Le Fevre Tells of His Time with the Las Vegas Shooter," News Corp Australia Network, October 6, 2017.

5. See Dave Phillips, "Father's History Could Offer Insight into Mind of Las Vegas Gunman," *New York Times*, October 13, 2017.

6. See Itay Hod, "'Math Whiz,' 'Loner,' 'Invisible': Vegas Shooter's Friends Say He Grew Up 'at the Bottom of the Bottom,'" *The Wrap*, October 26, 2017, and Greg Palast, "I Went to School with the Vegas Shooter," GregPalast.com, October 13, 2017.

7. See Doug Poppa, "Stephen Paddock's Brother Eric Called Law Enforcement Dumb Mother*****, Said He and Paddock Were Smarter Than Most," *Baltimore Post-Examiner*, October 19, 2018.

8. See Mark Berman, Sandhya Somashekhar, William Wan, and Matt Zapotosky, "Las Vegas Shooting Motive Eludes Investigators as New Details Emerge about Gunman Stephen Paddock," *Washington Post*, October 5, 2017.

9. See Joshua Robertson and David Smith, "Las Vegas Shooter Recalled as Intelligent Gambler Well-Versed on Gun Rights," *Guardian*, October 4, 2017.

10. See Christal Hayes, "Las Vegas Gunman Was a Trump Supporter, Happy with the President Because Stock Market Was Doing Well," *Newsweek*, November 3, 2017.

11. See Chris Pleasance, "'I Was Born Bad': Las Vegas Prostitute Who Romped with Mass Killer Stephen Paddock Says He Enjoyed Violent Rape Fantasies as She Reveals He Boasted He Had Always Been Evil," *Daily Mail*, October 8, 2017.

12. See Christal Hayes, "Las Vegas Shooting Motive: Gunman Was Narcissistic, Became Depressed after Losing 'Significant Amount of Wealth,'" *Newsweek*, November 2, 2017.

13. See Pleasance, "'I Was Born Bad.'"

14. See Jason Wilson, "New Documents Suggest Las Vegas Shooter Was Conspiracy Theorist—What We Know," *Guardian*, May 19, 2018.

15. See Wilson, "New Documents Suggest Las Vegas Shooter Was Conspiracy Theorist."

16. See Wilson, "New Documents Suggest Las Vegas Shooter Was Conspiracy Theorist."

17. See Kevin Flynn and Gary Gerhardt, *The Silent Brotherhood: Inside America's Racist Underground* (New York: Free Press, 1989), 68–69.

18. See Michel and Herbeck, *American Terrorist*, esp. 118–58.

19. See Henry Schuster with Charles Stone, *Hunting Eric Rudolph: An Insider's Account of the Five-Year Search for the Olympic Bombing Suspect* (New York: Berkley Books, 2005).

20. See Richard Orange, "Anders Behring Breivik's Mother 'Sexualised' Him When He Was Four," *Daily Telegraph*, October 7, 2012.

21. See "Breivik Planned Tagging as a Military Operation," *Dagbladet*, April 2, 2012.

22. See "Anders Behring Gives Evidence," *Guardian*, April 17, 2012.

23. See Matthew Taylor, "Norway Gunman Claims He Had Nine-Year Plan to Finance Attacks," *Guardian*, July 25, 2011.

24. See "The Terrorist and the Arsonists," *Der Spiegel*, January 8, 2012.

25. See Arlid Aspoy, "The Silence of the Shooters," *Dagbladet*, August 29, 2011.

26. Breivik's manifesto is available online as a PDF at a site for researchers.

27. See also Samuel Moyn, "The Alt-Right's Favorite Meme Is 100 Years Old," *New York Times*, November 13, 2018.

28. See Bill Berkowitz, "'Cultural Marxism' Catching On," *Intelligence Report* (Southern Poverty Law Center), August 15, 2003.

29. See Claudio Corredetti, "The Frankfurt School and Critical Theory," *Internet Encyclopedia of Philosophy*, 2015.

30. See Theodor Adorno and Max Horkheimer, "The Culture Industry: Enlightenment as Mass Deception," *Dialectic of Enlightenment* (1940).

31. See Martin Jay, "Dialectic of Counter-Enlightenment: The Frankfurt School as Scapegoat of the Lunatic Fringe," *Salmagundi Magazine*, 2011.

32. See Louis Menand, "How Cultural Anthropologists Redefined Humanity," *New Yorker*, August 19, 2019.

33. See Bill Berkowitz, "'Cultural Marxism' Catching On," *Intelligence Report* (Southern Poverty Law Center), August 15, 2003.

34. See Paul Gottfried, "Yes Virginia [Dare], There Is a 'Cultural Marxism,'" *VDare*, October 15, 2011.

35. See Jacob Siegel, "The Alt-Right's Jewish Godfather," *Tablet Magazine,* November 29, 2016.

36. See Chip Berlet, "Into the Mainstream," *Intelligence Report* (Southern Poverty Law Center), August 15, 2003.

37. See William S. Lind, "What Is Cultural Marxism," *Free Congress Foundation*, 1999; see also Bill Lind, "The Origins of Political Correctness," *Accuracy in Academia*, February 5, 2000.

38. See "Ally of Christian Right Heavyweight Paul Weyrich Addresses Holocaust Denial Conference," *Intelligence Report* (Southern Poverty Law Center), September 20, 2002.

39. See Paul M. Weyrich, "Letter to Conservatives," *Free Congress Foundation*, February 16, 1999.

40. See "1992 Republican National Convention Speech," Patrick J. Buchanan, August 17, 1992.

41. See Patrick J. Buchanan, *The Death of the West: How Dying Populations and Immigrant Invasions Imperil Our Country and Civilization* (New York: St. Martin's Press, 2001). See also "Citing Neo-Nazi and Racist Sources, Buchanan Sounds the Alarm," *Intelligence Report* (Southern Poverty Law Center), June 18, 2002.

42. See "Roger Pearson," *Hatewatch* profile (Southern Poverty Law Center).

43. See Jared Taylor, "Cultural Marxism as Censorship," YouTube, October 9, 2014.

44. See Kevin MacDonald, "Kevin MacDonald on Cultural Marxism," YouTube, September 10, 2010.

45. See Stephen Baskerville, "The Criminalization of Masculinity," *Occidental Observer*, November 18, 2018.

46. See Lydia Brimelow, "Cultural Marxism in Action: Media Matters Engineers Cancellation of VDARE.com Conference," *VDare*, January 24, 2017.

47. See David Neiwert, "'Cultural Marxism': A History of a Far-Right Anti-Semitic Hoax," YouTube, January 22, 2019.

48. See Scott Oliver, "Unwrapping the 'Cultural Marxism' Nonsense the Alt-Right Loves," *Vice*, February 23, 2017.

49. See David Neiwert, "'Cultural Marxism': A History of a Far-Right Anti-Semitic Hoax," YouTube, January 22, 2019.

50. See Anders Breivik, "2083—A European Declaration of Independence," July 2011.

51. See David Neiwert, *Alt-America: The Rise of the Radical Right in the Age of Trump* (New York: Verso, 2017).

52. See Keegan Hankes and Alex Amend, "The Alt-Right Is Killing People," *Hatewatch* (Southern Poverty Law Center), February 5, 2018.

53. See Bill Morlin, "Unrepentant and Radicalized Online: A Look at the Trial of Dylann Roof," *Hatewatch*, December 19, 2016.

54. See Katie Zavadski, "Dylann Roof's Racist Manifesto Is Chilling," *Daily Beast*, July 12, 2017.

55. See Morlin, "Unrepentant and Radicalized Online."

56. See Josh Glasstetter, "Elliot Rodger, Isla Vista Shooting Suspect, Posted Racist Messages on Misogynistic Website," *Hatewatch* (Southern Poverty Law Center), May 24, 2014.

57. See Josh Glasstetter, "Shooting Suspect Elliot Rodger's Misogynistic Posts Point to Motive," *Hatewatch* (Southern Poverty Law Center), May 24, 2014.

58. See Glasstetter, "Elliot Rodger, Isla Vista Shooting Suspect, Posted Racist Messages on Misogynistic Website."

59. See Glasstetter, "Shooting Suspect Elliot Rodger's Misogynistic Posts Point to Motive."

60. See "Elliot Rodger, Isla Vista Shooting Suspect, Posted Misogynistic Video before Attack," YouTube, May 24, 2014.

61. See "Alek Minassian Toronto Van Attack Suspect Praised 'Incel' Killer," BBC News, April 25, 2018.

62. See Katharine Laidlaw, "The Man Behind the Yonge Street Van Attack," *Toronto Life*, April 22, 2019.

63. See Richard Hartley-Parkinson, "Virgin Van Driver 'Killed 10 People Because He Was Sexually Frustrated,'" *Metro UK News*, September 27, 2019.

64. See Amy Dempsey, "Inside the Life of Alek Minassian, the Toronto Van Rampage Suspect No One Thought Capable of Murder," *Hamilton Spectator*, May 14, 2018.

65. See Carli Brosseau and Alan Brettman, "Jeremy Christian's Path from Troubled Youth to TriMet Stabbing Suspect," *Oregonian*, June 11, 2017.

66. See Nicole Chavez, "Accused Portland Stabber Reveals Himself—in His Own Words," CNN, June 7, 2017.

67. See Carli Brosseau and Allan Brettman, "Jeremy Christian's Path from Troubled Youth to TriMet Stabbing Suspect," *Oregonian*, June 11, 2017.

68. See Aimee Green, "What Defenses Could MAX Stabbing Suspect Jeremy Christian Possibly Mount?" *Oregonian*, May 25, 2018.

69. See Lizzy Acker, "Who Is Jeremy Christian? Facebook Shows a Man with Nebulous Political Affiliations Who Hated Circumcision and Hillary Clinton," *Oregonian*, May 30, 2017.

70. See Brosseau and Brettman, "Jeremy Christian's Path from Troubled Youth to TriMet Stabbing Suspect."

71. See Doug Brown, "Suspect in Portland Hate Crime Murders Is a Known White Supremacist," *Portland Mercury*, May 27, 2017.

72. See "Jeremy Christian Marches with Patriot Prayer, Is Asked to Leave: 4-29-17," YouTube, October 1, 2019.

73. See Shane Dixon Kavanaugh, "Watch: MAX Stabbing Survivor Met Suspect at Portland Protest a Month before Attack," *Oregonian*, October 25, 2017.

74. See Conrad Wilson and Amelia Templeton, "Portland Woman Attacked Day before Fatal MAX Stabbings Says Police, TriMet Failed Her," Oregon Public Broadcasting, August 18, 2017.

75. See Kate Williams, "Video: Portland MAX Stabbing Suspect Made Racial Threats Hours before Slayings," *Oregonian*, January 9, 2019.

76. See Will Sommer, "Qanon-Believing Proud Boy Accused of Murdering 'Lizard' Brother with Sword," *Daily Beast*, January 9, 2019. Wolfe's Washington State Militia profile remained online through 2019.

77. King County Prosecutor, "Findings of Fact Conclusion of Law Re: Competency," Case No. 19-1-01395-4 SEA.

78. See Sommer, "Qanon-Believing Proud Boy Accused of Murdering 'Lizard' Brother with Sword."

79. See Andy Campbell, "Proud Boy Allegedly Murders Brother with a Sword Thinking He's Killing a Lizard," *Huffington Post*, January 9, 2019.

80. See Sommer, "Qanon-Believing Proud Boy Accused of Murdering 'Lizard' Brother with Sword."

81. See "Buckey Wolfe: Five Facts You Need to Know," *Heavy*, January 9, 2019.

82. See Sarah Keoghan and Laura Chung, "From Local Gym Trainer to Mosque Shooting: Alleged Christchurch Shooter's Upbringing in Grafton," *Sydney Morning Herald*, March 15, 2019.

83. See Michael Workman, Stephen Hutcheon, and Pat McGrath, "Christchurch Shooter Brenton Tarrant Was a Personal Trainer in Grafton," Australia Broadcasting Corporation, April 4, 2019.

84. See Jovana Gec, "New Zealand Gunman Entranced with Ottoman Sites in Europe," Associated Press, March 16, 2019.

85. See Kim Sengupta, "Brenton Tarrant: Suspected New Zealand Attacker 'Met Extreme Right-Wing Groups' during Europe Visit, According to Security Sources," *Independent*, March 15, 2019.

86. See Victoria Ward, "Brenton Tarrant: The 'Ordinary White Man' Turned Mass Murderer," *Telegraph*, March 20, 2019.

87. See "Who Is Christchurch Mosque Shooting Accused? Brenton Tarrant Member of Bruce Rifle Club in Milton," *New Zealand Herald*, March 16, 2019.

Chapter 3

1. See "LVMPD Preliminary Investigative Report 1 October/Mass Casualty Shooting Event: 171001-3519," Las Vegas Metropolitan Police Department, January 18, 2018.

2. The following section is taken from an interview with a survivor of the massacre. The individual's name has been changed to protect his or her anonymity.

3. See "LVMPD Preliminary Investigative Report 1 October/Mass Casualty Shooting Event: 171001-3519."

4. See "Worker Warned Hotel before Las Vegas Shooter Opened Fire on Crowd," CBS News, October 11, 2017.

5. See Rachel Crosby, "Sheriff Says More Than 1,100 Rounds Fired in Las Vegas Shooting," *Las Vegas Review-Journal*, November 22, 2017.

6. See "LVMPD Preliminary Investigative Report 1 October/Mass Casualty Shooting Event: 171001-3519."

7. See Gerrit De Vynk, "Google Displayed Fake News in Wake of Las Vegas Shooting," Bloomberg News, October 2, 2017.

8. See Bethania Palma, "Did a Second Gunman Shoot from the Fourth Floor of the Mandalay Bay Hotel?" Snopes.com, October 3, 2017.

9. See Kevin Roose, "After Las Vegas Shooting, Fake News Regains Its Megaphone," *New York Times*, October 2, 2017.

10. See Saranac Hale Spencer, "No Evidence Linking Vegas Shooter to Antifa," FactCheck.org, October 5, 2017.

11. See David Neiwert, "In Wake of Las Vegas Massacre, Alex Jones Claims 'Democrats Are Going to Be Killing People,'" *Orcinus*, October 5, 2017.

12. See also "In Wake of Las Vegas Massacre, Alex Jones Claims 'Democrats Are Going to Be Killing People,'" YouTube, October 4, 2017.

13. See Sam Levin, "'I Hope Someone Truly Shoots You': Online Conspiracy Theorists Harass Vegas Victims," *Guardian*, October 26, 2017.

14. See Levin, "'I Hope Someone Truly Shoots You': Online Conspiracy Theorists Harass Vegas Victims."

15. See Jorge L. Ortiz, "Las Vegas Sheriff: Investigation into Mass Shooting Shows No Conspiracy or Second Gunman," *USA Today*, August 3, 2018.

16. See "Norway Camp Shooting: 'As Many as 30 Dead,'" Sky News, July 23, 2011.

17. See Helen Pid, "Anders Behring Breivik Planned to Film Beheading of Former Prime Minister," *Guardian*, April 19, 2012.

18. See Elisa Mala and J. David Goodman, "Big Blast Hits Government Buildings in Central Oslo," *New York Times*, July 23, 2011.

19. See "Norway Attacks: The Victims," BBC News, March 15, 2016.

20. See "Survivors in Norway Describe Scenes of Terror," National Public Radio, July 23, 2011.

21. See Ross Lydall, "Mother of Two Shot Dead for Trying to Stop Norway Gunman," *London Evening Standard*, July 26, 2011.

22. See "Several Young People Shot and Killed on Utøya," NRK News, July 22, 2011.

23. See "Survivors in Norway Describe Scenes of Terror," National Public Radio, July 23, 2011.

24. See Rune Thomas Ege, Tor-Erling Thommet Ruud, and Jarle Brenna, "Doctor: Breivik Used Special Ammunition," VG Net, July 24, 2011.

25. See Aage Borchgrevink and Guy Puzey, *A Norwegian Tragedy: Anders Behring Breivik and the Massacre on Utøya* (London: Polity, 2013), 230–34.

26. Borchgrevink and Puzey, *A Norwegian Tragedy*, 236–37.

27. See "Dylann Roof Almost Backed Out because Parishioners Were 'So Nice,'" *Atlanta Journal-Constitution*, June 19, 2015.

28. See Matthew Weaver, "Charleston Shooting: State Senator Clementa Pinckney among Victims," *Guardian*, June 18, 2015.

29. See Melissa Boughton, "Bishops Bring Together Congregation in North Charleston to Address Police Shootings," *Post and Courier* (Charleston, SC), June 3, 2015.

30. See Nick Corasaniti, Richard Pérez-Peña, and Lizette Alvarez, "Church Massacre Suspect Held as Charleston Grieves," *New York Times*, June 18, 2015.

31. See Wayne Drash, "Inside the Bible Study Massacre: A Mom 'Laid in Her Son's Blood,'" CNN, December 17, 2015.

32. See Jeremy Borden, Sari Horwitz, and Jerry Markon, "Officials: Suspect in Church Slayings Unrepentant Amid Outcry over Racial Hatred," *Washington Post*, June 19, 2015.

33. See Shelby Lin Erdman and Greg Botelho, "Timeline: A Killer's Rampage through a California College Town," CNN, May 27, 2014. See also Oren Dorrell and William M. Welch, "Police Identify Calif. Shooting Suspect as Elliot Rodger," *USA Today*, May 24, 2014.

34. See "Isla Vista Mass Murder—May 23, 2014—Investigative Summary," Santa Barbara County Sheriff's Office, February 18, 2015.

35. See Ian Lovett and Adam Nagourney, "Video Rant, Then Deadly Rampage in California Town," *New York Times*, May 24, 2014.

36. See "Thwarted in His Plan, California Gunman Improvised," CBS News, May 25, 2014.

37. See Bryan Passifume, Kevin Connor, and Jane Stevenson, "10 Dead, 15 Wounded when Van Hits Pedestrians near Yonge and Finch," *Toronto Sun*, April 23, 2018.

38. See Rob Crilly, Christopher Guly, and Mark Molloy, "What Do We Know about Alek Minassian, Arrested after Toronto Van Attack?" *Telegraph*, April 25, 2018.

39. See "'Nobody's Seen Anything Like This': 10 Dead, 15 Injured in North Toronto Van Ramming Attack," CBC News, April 23, 2015.

40. See Tu Thanh Ha, Jeff Grayqueen, and Molly Hayes, "Massive Investigation into Toronto Van Attack Will Shut Down Yonge Street for Days," *Globe and Mail*, April 23, 2018.

41. See Shane Dixon Kavanaugh, "Muslim Teen Targeted before MAX Train Slaying: 'Our Faces Were a Trigger,'" *Oregonian*, August 15, 2018.

42. See Maxine Bernstein, "Portland MAX Hero's Last Words: 'Tell Everyone on This Train I Love Them,'" *Oregonian*, May 29, 2017.

43. See Bernstein, "Portland MAX Hero's Last Words: 'Tell Everyone on This Train I Love Them.'"

44. See Ralph Ellis, Eliott C. McLaughlin, and Madison Park, "Portland Stabbing Suspect Yells in Court: Free Speech or Die," CNN, May 31, 2017.

45. See Sara Jean Green, "'God Told Me He Was a Lizard': Seattle Man Accused of Killing His Brother with a Sword," *Seattle Times*, January 8, 2019.

46. See Linzi Sheldon, "Seattle Man Jailed, Accused of Killing Brother with Sword," KIRO-TV News, January 7, 2019.

47. King County Prosecutor, "Findings of Fact Conclusion of Law Re: Competency," Case No. 19-1-01395-4 SEA.

48. See the Elders, "Buckey Wolfe Was Never a Proud Boy," *Proud Boy Magazine*, January 9, 2019.

49. See Will Sommer, "Qanon-Believing Proud Boy Accused of Murdering 'Lizard' Brother with Sword," *Daily Beast*, January 9, 2019. Wolfe's Washington State Militia profile remained online through 2019.

50. See "Christchurch Mosque Shootings: Gunman Livestreamed 17 Minutes of Shooting Terror," *New Zealand Herald*, March 15, 2019.

51. See Will Sommer and Kelly Weill, "New Zealand Suspect Mixed Death and Disinformation," *Daily Beast*, March 15, 2019.

52. See "'Hello, Brother': Muslim Worshipper's 'Last Words' to Gunman," Al Jazeera, March 15, 2019.

53. See "Christchurch Mosque Shootings: Gunman Livestreamed 17 Minutes of Shooting Terror."

54. See Breanna Barraclough, "Christchurch Mass Shootings: Police 'Strongly Urge' Social Media Users Not to Share 'Disturbing' Video," *Newshub New Zealand*, March 15, 2019.

55. See Sommer and Weill, "New Zealand Suspect Mixed Death and Disinformation."

56. See "Man Who Scared Away Gunman at Christchurch Mosque Hailed a Hero," *Stuff NZ*, March 18, 2019.

57. See Joshua Berlinger and Hilary Whiteman, "New Zealand Terror Suspect Planned Third Attack, Police Chief Says," CNN, March 20, 2019.

58. See "Christchurch Shooting Death Toll Rises to 50 after One More Victim Discovered at Mosque," Australia Broadcasting Corporation, March 16, 2019. See also "Christchurch Mosque Shootings: Gunman Livestreamed 17 Minutes of Shooting Terror."

Chapter 4

1. See "Conspiracists Hype 'Jade Helm' Theory of Yet Another Imminent Martial Law Coup," YouTube, April 28, 2015.

2. See Bill Morlin, "U.S. Military 'Jade Helm' Training Plan Draws Fears from the Antigovernment Right," *Hatewatch* (Southern Poverty Law Center), May 4, 2015.

3. See "Conspiracists Hype 'Jade Helm' Theory of Yet Another Imminent Martial Law Coup," 3:20.

4. See "Conspiracists Hype 'Jade Helm' Theory of Yet Another Imminent Martial Law Coup," 5:40.

5. See "Conspiracists Hype 'Jade Helm' Theory of Yet Another Imminent Martial Law Coup," 7:20.

6. See "Conspiracists Hype 'Jade Helm' Theory of Yet Another Imminent Martial Law Coup," 10:20.

7. See Representative Louie Gohmert, "Gohmert Statement on Jade Helm Exercises," press release, May 5, 2015.

8. See Dylan Baddour, "Ted Cruz, GOP Weigh in on Jade Helm—but Are They Playing to the Alarmists?" *Houston Chronicle*, May 6, 2015.

9. See Justin Miller, "How Greg Abbott Got Played by the Russians during His Jade Helm Freakout," *Texas Observer*, May 3, 2018.

10. See Bill Morlin, "Military Training Exercise Jade Helm Precipitating Fallout," *Hatewatch* (Southern Poverty Law Center), August 5, 2015.

11. See Dan Lamothe, "Remember Jade Helm 15, the Controversial Military Exercise? It's Over," *Washington Post*, September 14, 2015.

12. See Walter Laqueur, *The Changing Face of Antisemitism: From Ancient Times to the Present Day* (Oxford: Oxford University Press, 2006), 56.

13. See Ruth Shuster, "This Day in Jewish History 1189: Richard I Is Crowned and London's Jews Are Massacred," *Haaretz*, September 4, 2013.

14. See E. M. Rose, *The Murder of William of Norwich: The Origins of the Blood Libel in Medieval Europe* (Oxford: Oxford University Press, 2015).

15. See Emmy Stark Zitter, "Anti-Semitism in Chaucer's 'Prioress's Tale,'" *The Chaucer Review* 25, no. 4 (spring 1991): 277–84.

16. See Gavin I. Langmuir, *Toward a Definition of Antisemitism* (Berkeley: University of California Press, 1996), 478–79.

17. See John Pollock, *The Popish Plot: A Study in the History of the Reign of Charles II* (1905; repr., Whitefish, MT: Kessinger Publishing, 2006); see also John Kenyon, *The Popish Plot* (London: Phoenix Books, 2001).

18. See Terry Melanson, *Perfectibilists: The 18th Century Bavarian Order of the Illuminati* (Walterville, OR: Trine Day, 2009).

19. See Lindsay Porter, *Who Are the Illuminati? Exploring the Myth of the Secret Society* (London: Pavilion Books, 2005).

20. See Massimo Introvigne, "Angels & Demons from the Book to the Movie FAQ: Do the Illuminati Really Exist?" *Center for Studies on New Religions*, January 28, 2011.

21. See J. M. Roberts, *The Mythology of Secret Societies* (New York: Charles Scribner's Sons, 1974), 128–29.

22. See Amos Hofman, "Opinion, Illusion, and the Illusion of Opinion: Barruel's Theory of Conspiracy," *Eighteenth Century Studies* 27, no. 1 (1993): 28.

23. See Darrin M. McMahon, *Enemies of the Enlightenment* (New York: Oxford University Press, 2001), 113.

24. See David Simpson, *Romanticism, Nationalism, and the Revolt against Theory* (Chicago: University of Chicago Press, 1993), 88.

25. See Graeme Garrard, *Counter Enlightenments: From the Eighteenth Century to the Present* (London: Routledge, 2006).

26. See Ray A. Billington, "Anti-Catholic Propaganda and the Home Missionary Movement, 1800–1860," *The Mississippi Valley Historical Review* 22, no. 3 (December 1935): 361–84.

27. See Terry Golway, "Return of the Know-Nothings," *America: The National Catholic Weekly*, March 29, 2004.

28. See Amanda Beyer-Purvis, "The Philadelphia Bible Riots of 1844: Contest over the Rights of Citizens," *Pennsylvania History* 83 (summer 2016): 366–93. See also William E. Gienapp, "Nativism and the Creation of a Republican Majority in the North before the Civil War," *Journal of American History* 72, no. 3 (December 1985): 529–59.

29. See Tyler Anbinder, *Nativism and Slavery: The Northern Know Nothings and the Politics of the 1850s* (New York: Oxford University Press, 1992).

30. See Tim Yang, "The Malleable Yet Undying Nature of the Yellow Peril," Dartmouth College (February 19, 2004).

31. See Andrew Gyory, *Closing the Gate: Race, Politics, and the Chinese Exclusion Act* (Chapel Hill: University of North Carolina Press, 1998), 111.

32. Thomas Magee, "China's Menace to the World," Pioneer Laundry Workers Assembly, Knights of Labor, Washington, DC, 1878. The Library of Congress.

33. See Roger Daniels, *The Politics of Prejudice: The Anti-Japanese Movement in California and the Struggle for Japanese Exclusion* (Berkeley: University of California Press, 1999), 3–25.

34. See Daniels, *The Politics of Prejudice*, 76.

35. See Homer Lea, *The Valor of Ignorance* (New York: Harper, 1909).

36. See Daniels, *The Politics of Prejudice*, 70–71.

37. See "Rejoices at the Fall of Schmitz in 'Frisco: Says Jap Trouble Is Only Labor Question, Will Not Tolerate Invasion of California Even if It Is Peaceful," *Boston Herald*, June 16, 1907.

38. See "Asiatic Coolie Invasion," flyer, Official Organ of the State and Local Building Trades Councils of California, San Francisco, April 21, 28, and May 5, 1906. Available online at Virtual Museum of the City of San Francisco.

39. See Daniels, *The Politics of Prejudice*, 25–26.

40. See Madison Grant, *The Passing of the Great Race* (New York: Charles Scribner's Sons, 1916), 263.

41. See Lothrop Stoddard, *The Rising Tide of Color: The Threat against White World-Supremacy* (New York: Charles Scribner's Sons, 1920), 303.

42. See Roger Daniels, *Prisoners without Trial: Japanese Americans in World War II* (New York: Hill and Wang, 2004), 112.

43. See David Neiwert, *Strawberry Days: How Internment Destroyed a Japanese American Community* (New York: Palgrave Macmillan, 2005), 110.

44. See Neiwert, *Strawberry Days*, 110.

45. See Neiwert, *Strawberry Days*, 104–7.

46. See Commission on Wartime Relocation and Internment of Civilians, *Personal Justice Denied* (Seattle: University of Washington Press, 1997), 6 (my italics).

47. See Hadassa Ben-Itto, *The Lie That Wouldn't Die: The Protocols of the Elders of Zion* (New York: Vallentine Mitchell, 2005); see also Binjamin Segel, *A Lie and a Libel: The History of the Protocols of the Elders of Zion* (Lincoln: University of Nebraska Press, 1996).

48. See Anti-Defamation League, "Hoax of Hate: The Protocols of the Learned Elders of Zion"; see also Robert A. Rosenbaum, *Waking to Danger: Americans and Nazi Germany, 1933–1941* (New York: Greenwood Press, 2010), 41.

49. See Randall L. Bytwerk, "Believing in 'Inner Truth': The Protocols of the Elders of Zion in Nazi Propaganda, 1933–1945," *Holocaust and Genocide Studies* 29, no. 2 (fall 2015): 212–29.

50. See David Neiwert, "Anti-Semitism Illustrated: David Duke Working on New 'Protocols of the Elders of Zion,'" *Hatewatch* (Southern Poverty Law Center), May 20, 2014; see also Mike Dash, *Borderlands: The Ultimate Exploration of the Unknown* (Woodstock, NY: Overlook Press, 2000), 131–32.

51. See Ted Bloecher, "Report on the UFO Wave of 1947," National Investigations Committee on Aerial Phenomena, 1967.

52. See Nigel Watson, "Out of This World: 60 Years of Flying Saucers," *Wired*, June 24, 2007; see also Jerome Clark, *The UFO Book: Encyclopedia of the Extraterrestrial* (Detroit: Visible Ink, 1998).

53. See, for example, Henry Hurt, *Reasonable Doubt: An Investigation into the Assassination of John F. Kennedy* (New York: Holt, Rinehart & Winston, 1986); Gerald D. McKnight, *Breach of Trust: How the Warren Commission Failed the Nation and Why* (Lawrence: University of Kansas Press, 2005); and Mark Lane, *Rush to Judgment* (New York: Thunder's Mouth Press, 1992).

54. See Milton William Cooper, *Behold a Pale Horse* (Flagstaff, AZ: Light Technology Publishing, 1991).

55. See Mark Jacobson, "The Granddaddy of American Conspiracy Theorists," *Rolling Stone*, August 22, 2018.

56. See Robert K. Murray, *Red Scare: A Study in National Hysteria, 1919–1920* (Minneapolis: University of Minnesota Press, 1955).

57. See Kenneth D. Ackerman, *Young J. Edgar: Hoover, the Red Scare, and the Assault on Civil Liberties* (New York: Carroll & Graf, 2007).

58. See Landon R. Y. Storrs, "McCarthyism and the Second Red Scare," *Oxford Research Encyclopedia of American History*, July 2, 2015. See also History.com Editors, "Red Scare," History.com.

59. See Albert Fried, *McCarthyism, the Great American Red Scare: A Documentary History* (New York: Oxford University Press, 1997), 40–62; see also Albert Fried, *Nightmare in Red: The McCarthy Era in Perspective* (New York: Oxford University Press, 1990), 119–20.

60. See Robert Griffith, *The Politics of Fear: Joseph R. McCarthy and the Senate* (Amherst: University of Massachusetts Press, 1987), 11.

61. See Griffith, *The Politics of Fear*, 263.

62. See Thomas Doherty, *Cold War, Cool Medium: Television, McCarthyism, and American Culture* (New York: Columbia University Press, 2005), 207.

63. See Jonathan M. Schoenwald, *A Time for Choosing: The Rise of Modern American Conservatism* (New York: Oxford University Press, 2002), 62–99.

64. See William F. Buckley, "Goldwater, the John Birch Society, and Me," *Commentary*, March 2008.

65. See Benjamin R. Epstein and Arnold Forster, *The Radical Right: Report on the John Birch Society and Its Allies* (New York: Vintage Books, 1966), 18–19.

66. See Dion Leffler, "Fluoride Fight Has Long Roots, Passionate Advocates," *Wichita (KS) Eagle*, August 5, 2014; see also William Heisel, "Does Fluoride Have Lessons for the Vaccine Debate?" Center for Health Journalism, November 11, 2016.

67. See Gerald E. Markle, James C. Petersen, and Morton O. Wagenfeld, "Notes from the Cancer Underground: Participation in the Laetrile Movement," *Social Science & Medicine* 12 (January 1978): 31–37. See also Richard D. Lyons, "Rightists Are Linked to Laetrile's Lobby," *New York Times*, July 5, 1977.

68. See Paul Feldman, "Conspiracy Talk a U.S. Tradition," *Los Angeles Times*, May 29, 1995; see also John Færseth, "Militias and Conspiracy Culture," *Hate Speech International*, December 23, 2013.

Chapter 5

1. See David Neiwert, *In God's Country: The Patriot Movement and the Pacific Northwest* (Pullman: Washington State University Press, 1999), 26–29.

2. See Neiwert, *In God's Country*, 27–28.

3. See Neiwert, *In God's Country*, 69–86.

4. See Leonard Zeskind, *Blood and Politics: The History of the White Nationalist Movement from the Margins to the Mainstream* (New York: Farrar, Straus and Giroux, 2009), 399–402.

5. See Daniel Levitas, *The Terrorist Next Door: The Militia Movement and the Radical Right* (New York: Thomas Dunne, 2002), esp. 278–80 and 302–34. See also Neiwert, *In God's Country*, 30 and 69–87.

6. See Alexander Zaitchik, "Meet Alex Jones," *Rolling Stone*, March 2, 2011.

7. See Carey Dunne, "My Month with the Chemtrail Conspiracy Theorists," *Guardian*, May 22, 2017.

8. See Alex Jones, "Alex Jones Gay Frog Press Conference: Big Pharma Chemicals Creating Homosexual Biosphere," *Infowars*, March 17, 2017.

9. See Matt Novak, "Remember That Time Alex Jones Tried to Start a Y2K Riot?" *Gizmodo*, July 16, 2015.

10. See Novak, "Remember That Time Alex Jones Tried to Start a Y2K Riot?"

11. See Joe Hagan, "A Strange Man Is Following You," *New York Magazine*, April 4, 2011.

12. See Alexander Zaitchik, "Meet Alex Jones," *Rolling Stone*, March 2, 2011.

13. See Beau Hodai, "Alex Jones and the Informational Vacuum," *Fairness and Accuracy in Reporting*, February 1, 2011.

14. See Nate Blakeslee, "Alex Jones Is about to Explode," *Texas Monthly*, January 20, 2013.

15. See Tyler Bridges, *The Rise of David Duke* (Oxford: University Press of Mississippi, 1994), 67.

16. See Leonard Zeskind, *Blood and Politics: The History of the White Nationalist Movement from the Margins to the Mainstream* (New York: Farrar, Straus and Giroux, 2009), 34–35.

17. See David Neiwert, *And Hell Followed with Her: Crossing the Dark Side of the American Border* (New York: Nation Books, 2013), 24–26.

18. See Kathleen R. Arnold, *American Immigration after 1996: The Shifting Ground of Political Inclusion* (University Park: Pennsylvania State University Press, 2011), 75.

Also see "The Nativists," *Intelligence Report* (Southern Poverty Law Center), November 2, 2006.

19. See "Anti-Immigration Groups," *Intelligence Report* (Southern Poverty Law Center), March 21, 2001. Also see Kathleen Arnold, editor, *Anti-Immigration in the United States: A Historical Encyclopedia* (Santa Barbara, CA: Greenwood, 2011), 34.

20. See Casey Sanchez, "Glenn Spencer, More Hateful by the Day, Drones On," *Hatewatch* (Southern Poverty Law Center), January 14, 2009.

21. See Bob Moser, "Arizona Extremists Start Anti-Immigrant Citizen Militias," *Hatewatch* (Southern Poverty Law Center), April 15, 2003.

22. See "Paramilitary Compound Goes to SPLC Clients," *Hatewatch* (Southern Poverty Law Center), January 27, 2006; see also "Immigrants Win Arizona Ranch," *Hatewatch* (Southern Poverty Law Center), August 19, 2005.

23. Neiwert, *And Hell Followed with Her*, 44–49.

24. See Susy Buchanan and David Holthouse, "Minuteman Civil Defense Corps Leader Chris Simcox Has Troubled Past," *Intelligence Report* (Southern Poverty Law Center), January 31, 2006. See also Dennis Wagner, "Minuteman Leader Found New Calling after 9/11 Attacks," *Arizona Republic*, June 1, 2006.

25. See Nikolaj Vijborg, *USA under Attack*, 2008.

26. See Neiwert, *And Hell Followed with Her*, 75–80.

27. See David Holthouse, "Minutemen, Other Anti-Immigrant Militia Groups Stake Out Arizona Border," *Intelligence Report* (Southern Poverty Law Center), June 27, 2005.

28. See Hal Bernton, Mike Carter, David Heath, and James Neff, "The Terrorist Within: The Story behind One Man's Holy War against America," *Seattle Times*, June 23-July 7, 2002.

29. See Neiwert, *And Hell Followed with Her*, 159–70.

30. See Neiwert, *And Hell Followed with Her*, 159–72.

31. See Armando Navarro, *The Immigration Crisis: Nativism, Armed Vigilantism, and the Rise of a Countervailing Movement* (Walnut Creek, CA: Altamira Press, 2009), 125–30, 167; Terry Greene Sterling, *Illegal: Life and Death in Arizona's Immigration War Zone* (Guilford, CT: Lyons Press, 2010), x–xiii; United States Government Accountability Office, "GAO-06-770 Illegal Immigration: Border-Crossing Deaths Have Doubled since 1995," August 2006; Karl Eschbach, Jacqueline Hagan, and Nestor Rodriguez, "Causes and Trends in Migrant Deaths along the U.S.-Mexico Border, 1985–1998," Center for Immigration Research, University of Houston, 2001.

32. See Richard Finger, "The Border Fence: Horrible Deal at Cost up to $40,000 per Illegal Immigrant Apprehended," *Forbes*, July 18, 2013.

33. See David Neiwert, "How the Brutal Murders of a Little Girl and Her Father Doomed the Xenophobic Minuteman Movement," *AlterNet*, July 23, 2012.

34. See David Neiwert, "Simcox's Child-Molestation Trial Only the Latest Instance of Minuteman Criminality," *Hatewatch* (Southern Poverty Law Center), March 16, 2015.

35. See David Neiwert, "Chris Simcox's Fall from Minuteman Heights Ends in 19½-Year Sentence for Molesting Girls," *Hatewatch* (Southern Poverty Law Center), July 13, 2016.

36. See Fox News Chicago, "KKK Warns of Death Threat against Obama," May 21, 2007. See also Heidi Beirich and Mark Potok, "Silver Lining: Not All White Supremacists Oppose Black President," *Intelligence Report* (Southern Poverty Law Center), August 29, 2008.

37. See David Neiwert, *Alt-America: The Rise of the Radical Right in the Age of Trump* (New York: Verso, 2017), 96–97. See also Amy Hollyfield, "For True Disbelievers, the Facts Are Just Not Enough," *Tampa Bay Times*, June 28, 2008.

38. See Andy Barr, "Roger Stone Claims Michelle Obama 'Whitey' Video Will Soon Surface," *The Hill*, June 2, 2008.

39. David Weigel, "Change They Can Litigate: The Fringe Movement to Keep Barack Obama from Becoming President," *Slate*, December 4, 2008; Jess Henig with Joe Miller, "Born in the U.S.A.: The Truth about Obama's Birth Certificate," FactCheck .org, August 21, 2008.

40. See Jeff Bercovici, "Who Is Alex Jones, Anyway? Five Fun Factoids," *Forbes*, January 9, 2013. See also Alexander Zaitchik, "Meet Alex Jones," *Rolling Stone*, March 2, 2011.

41. See Neiwert, *Alt-America*, 109–36.

42. See David Neiwert, "'We Are at War': How Militias, Racists and Anti-Semites Found a Home in the Tea Party," AlterNet.org, November 21, 2010.

43. See Neiwert, *Alt-America*, 149–53.

44. See "Active Antigovernment Groups in the United States," Southern Poverty Law Center. Also see Mark Potok, "Rage on the Right," *Intelligence Report* (Southern Poverty Law Center), March 2, 2010.

45. See Daniel Schulman and Rachel Morris, "Meet the Birthers: Who Are These People, Really?" *Mother Jones*, August 10, 2009. See also David Neiwert, "Hannity Gleefully Promotes Birther Soldier's Get-out-of-Service Scam as Legitimate," Crooks AndLiars.com, July 16, 2009.

46. See "Trump Claims Obama Birth Certificate 'Missing,'" CNN, April 25, 2011; also see Ashley Parker and Steve Eder, "Inside the Six Weeks Donald Trump Was a Nonstop 'Birther,'" *New York Times*, July 2, 2016; also see Alana Abramson, "How Donald Trump Perpetuated the 'Birther' Movement for Years," ABC News, September 15, 2016.

47. See Maggie Haberman and Alexander Burns, "Donald Trump's Presidential Run Began in an Effort to Gain Stature," *New York Times*, March 12, 2016; see also Adam Gopnik, "Trump and Obama: A Night to Remember," *New Yorker*, September 12, 2015; also see Amy B. Wang, "'It Was Fantastic': Trump Denies 2011 White House Correspondents' Dinner Spurred Presidential Bid," *Washington Post*, February 28, 2017.

48. See Stephen Lemons, "Joe Arpaio Birther Posse Probes President Obama's Birth Certificate," *Phoenix New Times*, September 19, 2011; also see Sarah Anne Hughes, "Sheriff Joe Arpaio Tasks 'Cold Case Posse' to Investigate Obama's Birth Certificate," *Washington Post*, September 20, 2011.

49. See Sarah Posner and David Neiwert, "How Trump Took Hate Groups Mainstream," *Mother Jones*, October 14, 2016.

50. See Tim Murphy, "How Donald Trump Became Conspiracy Theorist in Chief," *Mother Jones*, November/December 2016.

51. See Liam Stack, "He Calls Hillary Clinton a 'Demon.' Who Is Alex Jones?" *New York Times*, October 13, 2016. Also see "Alex Jones Rants Hysterically That Clinton, Obama Are Actually Demons," YouTube video, April 5, 2017.

52. See Glenn Kessler, "'Pizzagate' Rumors Falsely Link Death of Sex-Worker Advocate to Nonexistent Clinton Probe," *Washington Post*, December 6, 2016.

53. See David Neiwert, "Pizzagate' Theories Inspire D.C. Gunman, but Still Have Defenders in Powerful Place," *Hatewatch* (Southern Poverty Law Center), December 6, 2016.

54. See David Neiwert, "Conspiracy Meta-Theory 'the Storm' Pushes the 'Alternative' Envelope Yet Again," *Hatewatch* (Southern Poverty Law Center), January 17, 2018.

55. See Mark Landler, "What Did President Trump Mean by 'Calm before the Storm'?" *New York Times*, October 6, 2017.

56. See Paris Martineau, "The Storm Is the New Pizzagate—Only Worse," *New York Magazine,* December 19, 2017.

57. See Ben Collins, "NASA Denies That It's Running a Child Slave Colony on Mars," *Daily Beast*, June 29, 2017.

58. See Neiwert, "Conspiracy Meta-Theory 'the Storm' Pushes the 'Alternative' Envelope Yet Again."

59. See Neiwert, "Conspiracy Meta-Theory 'the Storm' Pushes the 'Alternative' Envelope Yet Again."

60. See Kyle Mantyla, "Jerome Corsi Has Uncovered Irrefutable Proof of the Authenticity of 'QAnon,'" Right Wing Watch, January 11, 2018.

61. See Elizabeth Nolan Brown, "Trump's Mythical Crackdown on Sex Trafficking," *Reason*, February 27, 2017.

62. See "Interviewing Liz Crokin on the Storm, QAnon, Pedogate, & Twitter Feuds," YouTube video, January 2, 2018.

63. See Andrea Park, "Chrissy Teigen and John Legend Threaten to Sue Conspiracy Theorist over Pedophilia Allegations," CBS News, January 2, 2018.

64. See "Americans Say Murder More Likely Than Suicide in Epstein Case," *Rasmussen Reports*, August 14, 2019.

65. See "'Epstein Didn't Kill Himself' and the Meme-ing of Conspiracy," *Wired*, November 15, 2019.

66. See Bill Morlin, "Terrorism Suspect Makes Reference to Extremist Conspiracies," *Hatewatch* (Southern Poverty Law Center), July 20, 2018.

67. See Brendan Joel Kelly, "QAnon Conspiracy Increasingly Popular with Antigovernment Extremists," *Hatewatch* (Southern Poverty Law Center), April 23, 2019.

68. See David Weigel, "Conspiracy Theorist Shares Oval Office Photo with Trump," *Washington Post*, August 24, 2018.

69. See Jana Winter and Elias Groll, "Here's the Memo That Blew Up the NSC," *Foreign Policy,* August 10, 2017.

70. See Julie Hirschfield Davis, "White House Aide Forced Out after Claim of Leftist Conspiracy," *New York Times*, August 11, 2017.

71. See James Downie, "This NSC Ex-Staffer's Memo Is Crazy. Trump's Reaction Is More Disturbing," *Washington Post*, August 11, 2017.

72. See Michael D. Shear and Julie Hirschfield Davis, "As Midterm Vote Nears, Trump Reprises a Favorite Message: Fear Immigrants," *New York Times*, November 1, 2018.

73. See Swathi Shanmugasundaram, "Hate Groups and Extremists Cheer President Trump as He Vilifies Migrant Caravan," *Hatewatch* (Southern Poverty Law Center), October 25, 2018.

74. See Avery Anapol, "Fox Business Drops Guest Who Blamed Migrant Caravan on 'Soros-Occupied State Department,'" *The Hill*, October 28, 2018.

75. See "Laura Ingraham Attacks the Media for Not Fearmongering over the Migrant Caravan," Media Matters, October 22, 2018.

76. See Megan Keller, "CNN's Camerota, Matt Schlapp Clash over Migrant Caravan: Will Migrants 'Get a Luxury Car?'" *The Hill*, October 22, 2018.

77. See Donald Trump, October 18, 2018 tweet, 1:04 p.m.

78. See Daniel Politi, "Why Did Synagogue Suspect Believe Migrant Caravan Is Jewish Conspiracy? Maybe He Watched Fox News," *Slate*, October 27, 2018.

79. See Adam Serwer, "Trump's Caravan Hysteria Led to This," *The Atlantic*, October 28, 2018.

80. See Ben Collins, "Pittsburgh Synagogue Shooting Suspect Threatened Jewish Groups, Pushed Migrant Caravan Conspiracies," NBC News, October 27, 2018.

81. See Rita Katz, "Inside the Online Cesspool of Anti-Semitism That Housed Robert Bowers," *Politico*, October 29, 2018. See also "'The Jews Should Count Themselves Lucky': Extremists React to Pittsburgh Synagogue Shooting," Anti-Defamation League, October 27, 2018.

Chapter 6

1. See Belinda Goldsmith, "Is Facebook Envy Making You Miserable?" Reuters, January 22, 2013.

2. From author's interview with Kutner.

3. See Rob Brotherton, *Suspicious Minds: Why We Believe Conspiracy Theories* (London: Bloomsbury, 2017), v.

4. See Sean Illing, "The Trump-Ukraine Story Shows the Power of Conspiracy Theories," *Vox*, October 1, 2019.

5. See Jesse Walker, *The United States of Paranoia: A Conspiracy Theory* (New York: HarperCollins, 2013).

6. See Illing, "The Trump-Ukraine Story Shows the Power of Conspiracy Theories."

7. See Brotherton, *Suspicious Minds*, 105–7.

8. See Brotherton, *Suspicious Minds*, 105–7.

9. See Jennifer A. Whitson and Adam D. Galinsky, "Lacking Control Increases Illusory Pattern Perception," *Science* 322, no. 5898 (October 2008): 115–17.

10. See Joseph E. Uscinski, *Conspiracy Theories and the People Who Believe Them* (New York: Oxford University Press, 2019), 250.

11. See Gwen Snyder, Twitter thread, May 27, 2019.

12. See Uscinski, *Conspiracy Theories and the People Who Believe Them*, 14.

13. See Stephan Lewandowsky, Gilles E. Gignac, and Klaus Oberauer, "The Role of Conspiracist Ideation and Worldviews in Predicting Rejection of Science," *PLoS One* 8, no. 10 (October 2, 2013).

14. See Stephan Lewandowsky, John Cook, Klaus Oberauer, Scott Brophy, Elisabeth A. Lloyd, and Michael Marriott, "Recurrent Fury: Conspiratorial Discourse in the Blogosphere Triggered by Research on the Role of Conspiracist Ideation in Climate Denial," *Journal of Social and Political Philosophy* 3, no. 1 (2015).

15. See Michael Wood and Karen M. Douglas, "Conspiracy Theory Psychology: Individual Differences, Worldviews, and States of Mind," in *Conspiracy Theories and the People Who Believe Them*, ed. Joseph E. Uscinski (New York: Oxford University Press, 2019), 245–56.

16. See Brotherton, *Suspicious Minds*, 110.

17. See Andrew K. Przybylski, Kou Murayama, Cody R. DeHaan, and Valerie Gladwell, "Motivational, Emotional, and Behavioral Correlates of Fear of Missing Out," *Computers in Human Behavior* 29, no. 4 (July 2013): 1841–8. Also see John M. Grohol, "FOMO Addiction: The Fear of Missing Out," *Psych Central*, July 8, 2018.

18. Author's interview with Lewandowsky.

19. See Wood and Douglas, "Conspiracy Theory Psychology," 245–56.

20. See Brotherton, *Suspicious Minds*, 67.

21. See Illing, "The Trump-Ukraine Story Shows the Power of Conspiracy Theories."

22. See A. Cichocka, M. Marchlewska, and A. Golec de Zavala, "Does Self-Love or Self-Hate Predict Conspiracy Beliefs? Narcissism, Self-Esteem, and the Endorsement of Conspiracy Theories," *Social Psychological and Personality Science* 7, no. 2 (2016): 157–66.

23. See Kelly Weill, "Christmas Is the Loneliest Time for QAnon Fans," *Daily Beast*, December 23, 2018.

24. See Renee Diresta, "Online Conspiracy Groups Are a Lot Like Cults," *Wired*, November 13, 2018.

25. See Weill, "Christmas Is the Loneliest Time for QAnon Fans."

26. See Wood and Douglas, "Conspiracy Theory Psychology," 245–56.

27. See Weill, "Christmas Is the Loneliest Time for QAnon Fans."

28. See Leanne Naramore, "Sandy Hook Families Are Suing Alex Jones. This Is What He Said about the Shooting," Media Matters, April 17, 2018.

29. See Bob Cesca, "Alex Jones Is Actually Dangerous: Why We Have to Start Taking His Paranoid Worldview Seriously," *Salon*, May 15, 2015. Also see "Mystic Playground Sign Thief Gets Jail Time in Virginia," *Westerly (RI) Sun*, November 30, 2017.

30. See Reeves Wiedeman, "The Sandy Hook Hoax," *New York Magazine*, September 2016. Also see Paula McMahon, "Fired FAU Prof James Tracy Testifies about Feud with Sandy Hook Victim's Parents," *Orlando Sun-Sentinel*, December 1, 2017.

31. See Emily Shugerman, "US Shock Jock Alex Jones Sued by Six More Families of Sandy Hook Victims," *Independent*, May 25, 2018. See also "Infowars' Alex Jones Blames 'Psychosis' for His Sandy Hook Hoax Claim," Associated Press, March 30, 2019.

32. See "Infowars' Alex Jones Blames 'Psychosis' for His Sandy Hook Hoax Claim."

33. See Will Sommer, "Jack Posobiec and Laura Loomer Fight for Credit over Vegas Shooting Conspiracy Theory," *Daily Beast*, June 27, 2018.

34. See Dan Friedman, "Inside the Crazy and Vicious Feud between Roger Stone and Jerome Corsi—and Why It Matters," *Mother Jones*, January 31, 2009.

35. See David Neiwert, "Portland Far-Right 'Patriot' Street Brawlers in Disarray as Proud Boys Part Ways amid Violent Talk," *Daily Kos*, February 11, 2019.

36. See David Neiwert, "Defiant Alt-Right 'Patriots' Encounter Portland's Simmering Anger after Train Killings," *Hatewatch* (Southern Poverty Law Center), June 6, 2017.

37. See David Neiwert, "What You Need to Know about Saturday's 'Patriot' Rally in San Francisco," *Hatewatch* (Southern Poverty Law Center), August 25, 2017.

38. See David Neiwert, "Portland Far-Right Rally once Again Quickly Turns Violent as March Becomes a Riot," *Hatewatch* (Southern Poverty Law Center), July 3, 2018.

39. See Neiwert, "Portland Far-Right 'Patriot' Street Brawlers in Disarray as Proud Boys Part Ways amid Violent Talk."

40. See Neiwert, "Portland Far-Right 'Patriot' Street Brawlers in Disarray as Proud Boys Part Ways amid Violent Talk."

41. See Illing, "The Trump-Ukraine Story Shows the Power of Conspiracy Theories."

42. See Uscinski, *Conspiracy Theories and the People Who Believe Them*, 13.

Chapter 7

1. See Zeynep Tufekci, "We're Building a Dystopia Just to Make People Click on Ads," TED Talk, September 2017.

2. For more on this subject, see Zeynep Tufekci, "It's the (Democracy-Poisoning) Golden Age of Free Speech," *Wired*, August 16, 2018.

3. See David Neiwert, "Good Intentions on Extremism at YouTube, Facebook Hit the Wall of Profitability," *Daily Kos*, April 3, 2019.

4. See Mark Bergen, "YouTube Executives Ignored Warnings, Letting Toxic Videos Run Rampant," *Bloomberg News*, April 2, 2019.

5. See Alexis Madrigal, "The Reason Conspiracy Videos Work So Well on You-Tube," *The Atlantic*, February 21, 2019.

6. See Jane Coaston, "YouTube, Facebook, and Apple's Ban on Alex Jones, Explained," *Vox*, August 6, 2018. Also see Neiwert, "Good Intentions on Extremism at YouTube, Facebook Hit the Wall of Profitability."

7. See Timothy Johnson, "Despite Ban, Alex Jones' Infowars Appears to be Operating Yet Another Youtube Channel," Media Matters, March 25, 2019.

8. See Kelly Weill, "How YouTube Built a Radicalization Machine for the Far-Right," *Daily Beast*, December 17, 2018.

9. See Bergen, "YouTube Executives Ignored Warnings, Letting Toxic Videos Run Rampant."

10. See Safiya Umoja Noble, *Algorithms of Oppression: How Search Engines Reinforce Racism* (New York: New York University Press, 2018), 185.

11. See Rebecca Hersher, "What Happened When Dylann Roof Asked Google for Information about Race?" National Public Radio, January 10, 2017.

12. See Mike Caulfield, "The Curation/Search Radicalization Spiral," *Hapgood*, May 7, 2019. Also see Mike Caulfield, "Info-Environmentalism: An Introduction," *New Horizons*, October 23, 2017.

13. See Noble, *Algorithms of Oppression*, 116.

14. See Weill, "How YouTube Built a Radicalization Machine for the Far-Right."

15. See Caulfield, "The Curation/Search Radicalization Spiral."

16. See Peter Neumann, "Options and Strategies for Countering Online Radicalization in the United States," *Studies in Conflict & Terrorism* 36, no. 6 (2013).

17. See Neumann, "Options and Strategies for Countering Online Radicalization in the United States."

18. See Neumann, "Options and Strategies for Countering Online Radicalization in the United States."

19. Author's interview with Caulfield, April 2019.

20. Author's interview with Caulfield, April 2019.

21. Author's interview with Caulfield, April 2019.

22. See "Understanding Fake News and Misinformation," *Trends and Issues in Higher Ed*, University of Washington, May 29, 2018.

23. See Kate Starbird, "The Surprising Nuance behind the Russian Troll Strategy," *Medium*, October 20, 2018.

24. See Kate Starbird, "Muddied Waters: Online Disinformation during Crisis Events," University of Washington lecture series, Vimeo video, April 18, 2018.

25. See "Understanding Fake News and Misinformation."

26. See Starbird, "The Surprising Nuance behind the Russian Troll Strategy."

27. See Kate Starbird, "Examining the Alternative Media Ecosystem through the Production of Alternative Narratives of Mass Shooting Events on Twitter," International AAAI Conference on Web and Social Media, 2017.

28. See Starbird, "Examining the Alternative Media Ecosystem through the Production of Alternative Narratives of Mass Shooting Events on Twitter."

29. Author's interview with Starbird, April 2019.

30. Author's interview with Starbird, April 2019.

31. See Michael Edison Hayden, "Neo-Nazi Website Daily Stormer Is 'Designed to Target Children' as Young as 11 for Radicalization, Editor Claims," *Newsweek*, January 16, 2018.

32. See Jared Holt, "At AmRen 2018, White Nationalists Boast about Grooming the Next Generation of Racists," *Right Wing Watch*, May 2, 2018.

33. See J. M. Berger, "Nazis vs. ISIS on Twitter: A Comparative Study of White Nationalist and ISIS Online Social Media Networks," George Washington University Program on Extremism, September 2016.

34. See David Neiwert, "Meet 'Patriot Front': Neo-Nazi Network Aims to Blur Lines with Militiamen, the Alt-Right," *Hatewatch* (Southern Poverty Law Center), December 12, 2017.

35. See Hatewatch Staff, "Donning the Mask: Presenting 'The Face of 21st Century Fascism,'" *Hatewatch* (Southern Poverty Law Center), June 20, 2017.

36. See Lynsi Burton, "Theater Poster-Plastering Latest in String of UW Nazi Recruitment Propaganda," *Seattle PI*, February 16, 2017.

37. See Dan Sullivan, "National Guard 'Neo-Nazi' Aimed to Hit Miami Nuclear Plant, Roommate Says," *Tampa Bay Times*, June 14, 2017.

38. See "Vanguard America," Anti-Defamation League (profile), 2017.

39. See Hatewatch Staff, "Alleged Charlottesville Driver Who Killed One Rallied with Alt-Right Vanguard America Group," *Hatewatch* (Southern Poverty Law Center), August 13, 2017.

40. See Neiwert, "Meet 'Patriot Front': Neo-Nazi Network Aims to Blur Lines with Militiamen, the Alt-Right."

41. See Neiwert, "Meet 'Patriot Front': Neo-Nazi Network Aims to Blur Lines with Militiamen, the Alt-Right."

42. See Neiwert, "Meet 'Patriot Front': Neo-Nazi Network Aims to Blur Lines with Militiamen, the Alt-Right."

43. See A. C. Thompson, Ali Winston, and Jake Hanrahan, "Inside Atomwaffen as It Celebrates a Member for Allegedly Killing a Gay Jewish College Student," *Pro Publica*, February 23, 2018.

44. See Robert Evans, "From Memes to Infowars: How 75 Fascist Activists Were 'Red-Pilled,'" Bellingcat, October 11, 2018.

45. See Evans, "From Memes to Infowars: How 75 Fascist Activists Were 'Red-Pilled.'"

46. See Evans, "From Memes to Infowars: How 75 Fascist Activists Were 'Red-Pilled.'"

47. See Evans, "From Memes to Infowars: How 75 Fascist Activists Were 'Red-Pilled.'"

48. See Evans, "From Memes to Infowars: How 75 Fascist Activists Were 'Red-Pilled.'"

49. See Evans, "From Memes to Infowars: How 75 Fascist Activists Were 'Red-Pilled.'"

50. See Evans, "From Memes to Infowars: How 75 Fascist Activists Were 'Red-Pilled.'"

51. See Evans, "From Memes to Infowars: How 75 Fascist Activists Were 'Red-Pilled.'"

52. See David Neiwert, "What the Kek: Explaining the Alt-Right 'Deity' behind Their 'Meme Magic,'" *Hatewatch* (Southern Poverty Law Center), May 9, 2017.

53. See "Kek," Know Your Meme, January 2014.

54. See Neiwert, "What the Kek: Explaining the Alt-Right 'Deity' behind Their 'Meme Magic.'"

55. See Neiwert, "What the Kek: Explaining the Alt-Right 'Deity' behind Their 'Meme Magic.'"

56. Neiwert, "What the Kek: Explaining the Alt-Right 'Deity' behind Their 'Meme Magic.'"

57. See Neiwert, "What the Kek: Explaining the Alt-Right 'Deity' behind Their 'Meme Magic.'"

58. See Evans, "From Memes to Infowars: How 75 Fascist Activists Were 'Red-Pilled.'"

Chapter 8

1. See Zeynep Tufekci, "We're Building a Dystopia Just to Make People Click on Ads," TED Talk, September 2017.

2. See especially Theodor Adorno, *The Authoritarian Personality* (New York: Harper and Brothers, 1950).

3. See Robert Altemeyer, *The Authoritarians* (Ramona, CA: Cherry Hill Publishing, 2006); and Marc J. Hetherington and Jonathan D. Weiler, *Authoritarianism and Polarization in American Politics* (Cambridge: Cambridge University Press, 2009).

4. See Amanda Taub, "The Rise of American Authoritarianism," *Vox*, March 1, 2016.

5. See Altemeyer, *The Authoritarians*, 27.

6. See Altemeyer, *The Authoritarians*, 75–95.

7. See Maggie Koerth-Baker, "Why Rational People Buy into Conspiracy Theories," *New York Times Magazine*, May 21, 2013.

8. Sinclair's quote—"It is difficult to get a man to understand something, when his salary depends upon his not understanding it!"—can be found in his book *I, Candidate for Governor: And How I Got Licked* (1935; repr., Berkeley: University of California Press, 1994), 109.

9. See David Neiwert, "The Far Right's Hate-Spewing Trolls Come Crawling Out to Celebrate Christchurch Massacre," *Daily Kos*, March 26, 2019.

10. See John Wagner, "'So Ridiculous!': Trump Accuses the Media of Trying to Blame Him for New Zealand Shootings," *Washington Post*, March 18, 2019.

11. See Colby Itkowitz and John Wagner, "Trump Says White Nationalism Is Not a Rising Threat after New Zealand Attacks: 'It's a Small Group of People,'" *Washington Post*, March 15, 2019.

12. See Jim Sidanius and Felicia Pratto, *Social Dominance: An Intergroup Theory of Social Hierarchy and Oppression* (Cambridge: Cambridge University Press, 2001).

13. See Bart Duriez and Alain Van Hiel, "The March of Modern Fascism: A Comparison of Social Dominance Orientation and Authoritarianism," *Personality and Individual Differences* 32, no. 7 (2002): 1199–1213.

14. See Jordan Peterson, "The Gulag Archipelago: A New Foreword by Jordan B. Peterson," in *The Gulag Archipelago*, by Aleksander Solzhenitsyn (New York: Penguin Books, 2018).

15. See Samantha K. Stanley, Taciano L. Milfont, Marc S. Wilson, and Chris G. Sibley, "The Influence of Social Dominance Orientation and Right-Wing Authoritarianism on Environmentalism: A Five-Year Cross-Lagged Analysis," PLoS One, July 10, 2019.

16. Although the quote is frequently attributed to John Steinbeck, it is not a direct citation of anything he wrote, but rather a paraphrase attributed to Ronald Wright, *A Short History of Progress* (Toronto: House of Anansi Press, 2004), 124.

17. See Ledyard King, Bill Theobald, Kevin McCoy, Brett Murphy, and Ali Schmitz, "What We Know about Cesar Sayoc, the Florida Man Suspected of Mailing More Than a Dozen Bombs," *USA Today*, October 26, 2018.

18. See Kevin McCoy, "Pipe Bomb Suspect Cesar Sayoc Pleads Guilty in Spree Aimed at Trump Critics, Including Obama, Biden," *USA Today*, March 21, 2019.

19. See Chip Berlet, "Heroes Know Which Villains to Kill: How Coded Rhetoric Incites Scripted Violence," *Research for Progress*, January 2014.

20. See Xeni Jardin, "'MAGA Mail-Bomber' Cesar Sayoc: Trump Was 'My New Found Drug' and I Was Also on Steroids," *Boing Boing*, April 23, 2019.

21. See Ayal Feinberg, Regina Branton, and Valerie Martinez-Ebers, "Counties That Hosted a 2016 Trump Rally Saw a 226 Percent Increase in Hate Crimes," *Washington Post*, March 22, 2019.

22. See Justin Wm. Moyer, "Trump Says Fans Are 'Very Passionate' after Hearing One of Them Allegedly Assaulted Hispanic Man," *Washington Post*, August 20, 2015.

23. See Chip Berlet, "Heroes Know Which Villains to Kill: How Coded Rhetoric Incites Scripted Violence."

24. See David Neiwert, "The American Right Hankers for a Civil War: A History in Four Videos," *Daily Kos*, February 25, 2019.

25. See Glenn Thrush and Maggie Haberman, "Trump's N.F.L. Critique a Calculated Attempt to Shore Up His Base," *New York Times*, September 25, 2017.

26. See Inae Oh, "Trump Defends Claim That There Were 'Very Fine People on Both Sides' of White Supremacist Rally," *Mother Jones*, April 26, 2019.

27. See David Neiwert, "Christopher Hasson Is Just the Latest Sign of America's Rising Far-Right Domestic Terrorist Tide," *Daily Kos*, February 21, 2019.

28. See Charles P. Pierce, "A Coast Guard Officer Was Just Found Plotting to Murder Democrats and Media Personalities 'On a Scale Rarely Seen,'" *Esquire*, February 20, 2019.

29. See Neiwert, "The American Right Hankers for a Civil War: A History in Four Videos."

30. See Jason Wilson, "Are Rightwing Pundits Right That America Is on the Brink of a Civil War?" *Guardian*, June 22, 2017.

31. See David Neiwert, "'Communist Takeover' Paranoia Gets a Final Resuscitation for Trump's Inauguration," *Hatewatch* (Southern Poverty Law Center), January 17, 2017.

32. See Abby Ohlheiser, "A Short History of Alex Jones Claiming That the Left Is about to Start a Second Civil War," *Washington Post*, July 3, 2018.

33. See David Neiwert, "Far-Right Conspiracists Stir Up Hysteria about Nonexistent 'Civil War' Plot by 'Antifa,'" *Hatewatch* (Southern Poverty Law Center), November 14, 2017.

34. See "Cohen: Fears No 'Peaceful Transition' if Trump Loses in 2020," Reuters, February 27, 2019.

35. See Libby Nelson, "Donald Trump Just Said He Might Not Concede the Election if Clinton Wins," *Vox*, October 19, 2016.

36. See Chris Cilizza, "Donald Trump Is Setting the Stage to Never Concede the 2016 Election," *Washington Post*, October 14, 2016.

37. See Jenna Johnson, "Donald Trump Says He Will Accept Results of Election—'If I Win,'" *Washington Post*, October 20, 2016.

38. See Jack Shafer, "Trump's Final Days," *Politico*, September 19, 2018.

39. See Aaron Blake, "The Most Ominous Thing Michael Cohen Said about Trump This Week," *Washington Post*, February 28, 2019.

Chapter 9

1. See Robert Jay Lifton, *Destroying the World to Save It: Aum Shinrikyo, Apocalyptic Violence, and the New Global Terrorism* (New York: Henry Holt, 1999), 340.

2. See Joseph Bernstein, "Alt-Right Troll to Father Killer: The Unraveling of Lane Davis," *BuzzFeed*, July 18, 2018.

3. See Joseph Bernstein, "The Unsatisfying Truth about Hateful Online Rhetoric and Violence," *BuzzFeed*, November 24, 2018.

4. See Bernstein, "Alt-Right Troll to Father Killer: The Unraveling of Lane Davis."

5. See Bernstein, "The Unsatisfying Truth about Hateful Online Rhetoric and Violence."

6. See Bernstein, "The Unsatisfying Truth about Hateful Online Rhetoric and Violence."

7. The remainder of this chapter is constructed from advice and insight provided by a team of experts with backgrounds in extremism, radicalization, disinformation, and rehabilitation/recovery, to whom I am eternally grateful for the extensive time they provided through interviews:

- Dr. Peter Neumann, founding director of the International Centre for the Study of Radicalisation and Political Violence as well as professor of security studies at the War Studies Department of King's College London.
- Dr. Stephan Lewandowsky, chair of cognitive psychology at the School of Experimental Psychology, University of Bristol, and a longtime professor at the University of Western Australia.
- Kate Starbird, associate professor in the Department of Human Centered Design and Engineering (HCDE) and director of the Emerging Capacities of Mass Participation (emCOMP) Laboratory at the University of Washington. She is also adjunct faculty in the Paul G. Allen School of Computer Science and Engineering and the Information School.
- Michael Caulfield, the director of blended and networked learning at Washington State University–Vancouver.
- Samantha Kutner, a researcher on far-right Proud Boys organizing with the anti-extremist organization Light upon Light.
- C. V. Vitolo, professor of debate at University of Wisconsin–Madison, an anti-racist activist with a track record of successful deradicalization.

8. Author's interview with Peter Neumann, April 2019.

9. Author's interview with Stephan Lewandowsky, April 2019.

10. Author's interview with Michael Caulfield, April 2019.

11. See Noah Berlatsky, "The Case against Empathizing with Trump Supporters," *Medium*, May 2, 2019.

12. See especially Carl Rogers, *Client-Centered Therapy: Its Current Practice, Implications, and Theory* (Boston: Houghton Mifflin, 1951).

13. See Anonymous, "What Happened after My 13-Year-Old Son Joined the Alt-Right," *Washingtonian*, May 5, 2019.

14. See Paol Hergert, "How Tangible Is Cyberspace?" *Digital Culturist*, March 15, 2017.

15. See Tim Stevens and Peter Neumann, "Countering Online Radicalisation: A Strategy for Action," The International Centre for the Study of Radicalisation and Political Violence, December 7, 2017.

16. See Chip Berlet, "Toxic to Democracy: Conspiracy Theories, Demonization, and Scapegoating," Political Research Associates, 2009.

17. See Jonathan Corpus Ong and Jason Vincent Cabanes, "Architects of Networked Disinformation: Behind the Scenes of Troll Accounts and Fake News Production in the Philippines," Newton Tech4Dev Network, University of Leeds, 2017.

INDEX

4chan, vi, 22, 36, 82, 87, 180; and alt-right, 123; Bowers and, 94; and immersion, 98; QAnon and, 84–85; and radicalization, 127
8chan, 85, 87, 98

Abbott, Greg, 51–52
activities, real-world, and deradicalization, 168–169
Adams, Haley, 109
addictive nature of conspiracy theories, 96, 99
Affleck, Ben, 117
Affordable Care Act, 80
agency, lack of: and authoritarianism, 136; conspiracy theories and, 101–102, 104, 166
aggression, authoritarian, 135
Akerlund, Ebba, 28
Aldean, Jason, 29–30
Alexander, Raymond, 24
algorithms: and extremism, 113, 115–116; and grooming, 153; and radicalization, 116–120
alienation: and conspiracy theories, 96, 105; as end point, 110–111
Alien Land Laws, 58
aliens, theories on, 27, 46, 63, 104
Al-Noor mosque, 46–47

Altemeyer, Robert, 134–135, 145
alt-lite, 26, 108
alt-right, 122–126; and birtherism, 82; and immersion, 98; and Kek, 128–132; term, 15
American Border Patrol, 75
American Nazi Party, 61
American Party, 56
American Patrol, 74
Americans for Intelligence Reform, 108
American Vanguard, 123
Anglin, Andrew, 122, 131–132
anomie, 105
antifa, 24, 28, 45, 142–143
anti-Semitism, 60–61, 161; blood libel, 54; Bowers and, 93; conspiracy theories and, vii; Davis and, ix; The Order and, 12; and radicalization, 127; Roof and, 19; white nationalists and, 122–126. *See also* globalist plots
anti-tax movement, 10–11
anti-vaccination movement, and disinformation, 121
Army-McCarthy hearings, 65
Arnold, Kenneth, 62
Arpaio, Joe, 82
Aryan Nations, 61, 164
Asian immigrants, theories on, 56–60
Asiatic Exclusion League, 58

assault-weapon ban, 9
Atlanta Olympics bombings, 12, 70
Atlantic Centurion, 131–132
Atomwaffen Division, 123, 126
authenticity, and deradicalization,
    167–168
authoritarianism, 133–146; conspiracy
    theories and, 176–177; leaders of,
    137–139; personality types and,
    134–137, 156; support for, 133–134;
    Trump refusal to leave office, 143–145
Avallone, Hunter, 26

Baker, Christopher James, 53
Bannon, Steve, 98, 130–131
Barruel, Augustin, 55
Barry, Steven, 75
Bavarian Illuminati, 55–56
Behold a Pale Horse, 63
beliefs, underlying, challenges to, 165–166
Bell, Art, 63
Bellingcat, 126, 128, 132
Bergen, Mark, 114
Berger, J. M., 122–123
Berlatsky, Noah, 159
Berlet, Chip, 7–8, 140–141, 176
Bernstein, Joseph, x, 147–149
Bernstein, Rachel, 104
Berntsen, Trond, 41
Best, Rick, 45
bias(es): cognitive, 101, 120; empathy,
    159
bin Laden, Osama, 3
Birch (John) Society, 13, 65–66
birther theories, 2, 80–81
Bitman, Vladislav, 177
black helicopters, 68
blacklist, 65
Black Lives Matter, 135
Black Pidgeon Speaks, 128
black-pilling, vii
Blake, Aaron, 144
blood libel, 54
Bloom, Paul, 159

blue pill (antidote to conspiracy theories),
    147–180; issues with, 148
Boas, Franz, 15
book discussions, and deradicalization,
    169
border security, 71, 74–79; Trump and,
    82, 91–92
Bøsei, Monica, 41
Bowers, Robert, 93–94, 140
Brachmann, Jaret, 118
Bracken, Matt, 138
brain: conspiracy theories and, 95–96;
    hate and, 169
bread pill, viii
Breitbart, Andrew, 17
Breitbart News, x, 17, 98, 137
Breivik, Anders, 13–14, 17–18, 40–42,
    142
Brimelow, Peter, 16–17
Brotherton, Rob, 96–97, 101
Brundtland, Gro Harlem, 40
Bryant, Phil, 53
bubble (alternate reality), 168; and
    authoritarianism, 135–136
Buchanan, Patrick, 16
Buckley, William F., 65
Burke, Kenneth, 157
Bush, George W., 2, 73

Camerota, Alisyn, 93
Campbell, Christopher Todd, 53
Campos, Jesus, 34
Canada, 77–78
cancer cures, 66, 71
caravans of migrants, theories on, 92–93
Catholics, theories on, 54–56
Caulfield, Michael: on algorithms,
    116–117; on authenticity, 167; on
    deradicalization, 164–165; on digital
    literacy, 118–120; on immunization,
    152–155; on power issues, 177
challenges: with facts, timing of,
    170–171; to non-core issues, 167; to
    underlying beliefs, 165–166

chaos, Kek and, 129–132
Charles II, king of England, 54–55
Charles Theodore, elector of Bavaria, 55
Charleston massacre, 19–20, 42–43, 116–117
Charlottesville, VA, 124, 141
chat rooms, 20; immunization and, 153; and radicalization process, 123
Chaucer, Geoffrey, 54
chemtrails, 63, 71
Chen, George, 43
Chenoweth, Helen, 69
children, alt-right and, 122
China, 76, 133
Chinese Exclusion Act, 56–57
Chinese immigrants, theories on, 56–57
Christchurch mosque shootings, 27–28, 46–47, 115, 140; reactions to, 137–138
Christian, Jeremy, 23–26, 44–45
Christian Identity movement, 13, 93–94
circumcision, Christian and, 24
civil war, 141, 143; Trump and, 143–145. See also culture war; race war
Clarke, Richard, 4
clinical approach, for deradicalization, 157
Clinton, Bill, 9, 67, 88–89, 139
Clinton, Hillary, 37, 113, 144; Christian and, 23; Jones and, 93; militia movement and, 69; QAnon and, 27, 83, 98; Sayoc and, 139
cognitive biases, 101, 120
cognitive dissonance, 136
Cohen, Michael, 143–144
Cohn, Roy, 64
Communism, theories on, 63–66
community of conspiracists, 103–104; and deradicalization, 156; feuds in, 107–111, 123–124
complexity, acceptance of, 179–180
concentration camps: Jones and, 71–72; militia movement and, 68
Conservative Tribune, 98

conspiracies, real, characteristics of, 2, 5, 160
conspiracism, vi–vii, 144–145; and division, 176–177; effects of, vii–viii, 5–7; new, 6; personality traits and, 135–136
conspiracist ideation, 100–101
conspiracy theories, 1–8; beneficiaries of, 176; characteristics of, versus real conspiracies, 5–6; clusters of, 155; and domestic terrorism, 12–18; history of, 18, 49–94; immersion process, 95–111; and need to push envelope, 85; rejection of, 179–180; rules of, 100; term, 1; and violent incidents, 29–47
contact hypothesis, 172
control, conspiracy theories and, 97–98, 163
conventionalism, and authoritarianism, 135
Cooper, William, 63
Corsi, Jerome, 86–87, 108
Council of Conservative Citizens, 19–20, 116–117
countermessaging, 150, 174. See also deradicalization
coworkers. See relationships
credulity, selective, 70
crisis actors, 38–39, 106
Critical Theory, 14, 16. See also cultural Marxism
critical thinking: versus authoritarian tendencies, 134; recommendations for, 118–120; weaponization of, 161–162
Crokin, Liz, 84, 87–88
Crowder, Steven, 26, 128
Cruz, Ted, 51
Cuellar, Henry, 78
cultural Marxism, 14–17; Breivik and, 14, 41; conspiracy theories and, vii; Davis and, ix–x; Higgins and, 90–91
culture war, 16; Trump and, 141. See also civil war; race war
curation, 116–117, 119

Daily Stormer, 19, 122, 131
data void, 117
Davis, Charles "Chuck," ix
Davis, Lane, viii–xi, 147–148
death panels theory, 80
death threats, survivors and, 38
deep state, 2, 85–86, 88, 90–92
dehumanization, 118, 168–169
democracy: authoritarianism and, 139; conspiracy theories and, 5–6; immersion and, 103
demographic change: border movement and, 75; Tarrant and, 28
demonization, 93, 137
De Niro, Robert, 139
depression, and conspiracism, 166
deradicalization, 147–180; precautions with, 160–162; risks and costs of, 150–151; scale of, 158; timing of, 150, 158, 175
DeWitt, John L., 60
Dick, Philip K., 1, 4, 7
diGenova, Joseph, 142
digital literacy: and immunization, 153–154; promotion of, 174–175; recommendations for, 118–120, 162
Discord, 127–128
disinformation, 120–122, 177; function of, 177–178. *See also* misinformation
disinhibition, online, 118
Dobbs, Lou, 92
Dr. Strangelove, 66
domestic terrorism, 71; conspiracy theories and, 12–18
dopamine, 96
doubts, 103; and deradicalization, 162–163, 165
Douglas, Karen M., 101–102, 105, 152
doxxing, x, 123
Duke, David, 61, 74, 128

eco-fascism, viii
education: and deradicalization, 151; and immunization, 175–176

ego: conspiracy theories and, 166; and immersion, 95
Eisenhower, Dwight D., 65
Ellis, Frank, 16
Emanuel, Rahm, 140
Emanuel AME Church, 42–43
empathy, 179–180; versus authoritarian tendencies, 134; and deradicalization, 149, 158–159
empowerment: conspiracy theories and, 95–96, 164; and deradicalization, 167–168; of family/friends, and prevention, 175
Endresen, Hanna, 40
enemy, identification of, 102
engagement, social media and, 115
Enlightenment ideals, 55
epistemology, 99, 159
Epstein, Jeffrey, 88–89
ethnocentrism, and authoritarianism, 135
eugenics, 16, 59
evangelical Christians, and conspiracy theories, 80
evidence, changing role in conspiracy theories, 6, 53, 70, 100
executive orders, militia movement and, 68
extremist content: reducing demand for, 173–174; reducing supply of, 173–174

Facebook: Christchurch mosque shootings and, 46–47; and extremism, 114; Minassian and, 22–23, 44; and regulation, 174
facts: acceptance of, 180; for deradicalization, issues with, 150, 170–171
Fairbanks, Cassandra, 131
fake news, 2–3
false-flag operations, ix, 87; Las Vegas as, 36–37; 9/11 as, 73; Oklahoma bombing as, 71; Tree of Life massacre as, 94

family(/ies): versus conspiracy
community, 105; and survivors,
38; trolls and, 105–107. *See also*
relationships
far-left conspiracy theories, 73; and
disinformation, 122
Farrell, Chris, 92
fascists, versus alt-right, 128. *See also*
white nationalists/supremacists
fear: and authoritarianism, 135; of
missing out, and conspiracy theories,
101
Federal Reserve Bank, militia movement
and, 69
FEMA, Jones and, 71–72
feuds within conspiracy community,
107–111; white nationalists and,
123–124
Fields, James Alex, 124
financial issues: community and, 107; and
extremism on social media, 114–116
Fletcher, Bob, 69
Fletcher, Micah David-Cole, 25, 45
fluoridation, 63, 66
flying saucers, 62–63
FOMO, and conspiracy theories, 101
Ford, Henry, 60–61
Forde, Shawna, 78–79
Fox News, 17, 80, 93, 142; and caravans
of migrants, 92; and disinformation
campaigns, 121; and Epstein death,
89; and immersion, 98; and Jade
Helm, 50
Frankfurt School, 14. *See also* cultural
Marxism
Freemasons, 55–56
free speech issues, 173–174; Christian
and, 45
friends. *See* relationships
Furie, Matt, 129

Gab, 93
Gadsden flags, 24, 80
Gaetz, Matt, 93

Galinsky, Adam, 97–98
Gamergate, Davis and, ix–x
gaming. *See* video games
gay frogs, Jones and, 71
gender issues: and authoritarianism,
135; and conspiracy theories, 166;
Gamergate and, ix–x; Kek and, 131;
and radicalization, 127–128; Rodger
and, 20–22, 43–44. *See also* misogyny
Gibney, E. J., 137
Gibson, Joey, 24, 108–109
Gilchrist, Jim, 77
globalist plots, 18; border movement
and, 75–76; Las Vegas massacre as,
38; QAnon and, 85. *See also* anti-
Semitism
Gohmert, Louie, 51
Google, 114, 116, 119
Gottfried, Paul, 15
government agencies, and control of
extremist content, 174
Grant, Madison, 58
Great Awakening, 89
green pill, viii
grooming, 117–118, 153, 165
gun control: Jones and, 37; militia
movement and, 68
gun culture: border movement and,
76; Breivik and, 13–14; diGenova
and, 142; Paddock and, 9–12; and
violence, 111; white nationalists and,
124
gun-related violence, vii, 29–47;
Charleston massacre, 19–20, 42–43,
116–117; Christchurch mosque
shootings, 27–28, 46–47, 115,
137–138, 140; Las Vegas massacre, v,
vii, 9–12; Norway shootings, 13–14,
17–18, 40–42; personal experience of,
29–36; Tree of Life massacre, 94

HAARP, 68, 71
Halbig, Wolfgang, 106
Hannity, Sean, 17

Hasson, Christopher, 142–143
hate crimes, 7; heroic ideal and, 164;
    increase in, 140
hate groups, 82
hate residuals, 169
Hate Tracker, 85
Hauge, Kai, 40
healing, 147–180; elements of, 179–180;
    support for, 172–173
health-related conspiracies, 66, 71, 104,
    121
Hearst, William Randolph, 57
Hebrew Immigrant Aid Society, 93–94
Heller, Brittan, 115
heroic ideal, 141, 149; alternative
    approaches to, 163–164
Hester, Demetria, 25
Hetherington, Marc, 134
Heyer, Heather, 124
hierarchy, authoritarian leaders and,
    138–139
Higgins, Rich, 90–91
Hill, Ida Marie, 40
Hispanics, theories on, 74–79
Hiss, Alger, 64
Hitler, Adolf, 61
Hollywood: and blacklist, 65; and UFOs,
    62
Holocaust denial, 15
Holter, Anne Lise, 40
Homulos, Amanda, 38
Hong, Cheng Yuan "James," 43
Hoover, J. Edgar, 63
Hopper, Dillon, 123–124
Horowitz, David, 128
House Un-American Activities
    Committee, 64–65
Hugh of Lincoln, 54
humor: alt-right and, 125; and
    deradicalization, 157

Icke, David, 27
identification, and deradicalization, 157
Identity Evropa, 123
Illing, Sean, 102

Illuminati, 55–56, 63
immersion, 95–111; avoiding, during
    deradicalization, 160–162; end point
    of, 110–111; personal experience of,
    95. See also radicalization
immigration: conspiracy theories and, 28,
    56, 74–79; Trump and, 82, 91–92
immunization to extremism, 149;
    and deradicalization, 160–162;
    recommendations for, 151–155
impeachment, and violence, 142
incels, vi; Minassian and, 22–23, 44;
    nature of, 20; Rodger, 20–22, 43–44
inequality, authoritarian leaders and,
    138–139
information: addiction to, 96; evaluation
    of, 4; recommendations for, 155–156
informational literacy: and
    immunization, 153–154; promotion
    of, 174–175; recommendations for,
    118–120, 162
Infowars, xi, 26, 73, 128, 180; and
    community, 103–104; and immersion,
    117; and Jade Helm, 50–52; and Las
    Vegas massacre, 36–37; and Obama,
    79–80; and platforms, 114–115; and
    Sandy Hook families, 105–107. See
    also Jones, Alex
Ingraham, Laura, 92, 142
intelligence, and conspiracism, 10
intention, conspiracy theories and, 100
Internet: and community, 156;
    emotional effects of, 96; and growth
    of conspiracism, 18; misinformation
    on, 113–132; positive uses of, 173;
    regulation of, 173–174
internment of Japanese Americans, 60
Irizarry, Dillon, 123–124
IronMarch, 123, 125
irony, alt-right and, 125, 128
Islam: Breivik and, 14; Canada and, 77;
    Christchurch mosque shootings and,
    27–28, 46–47; Christian and, 44–45;
    conspiracy theories and, vii; Obama
    and, 79–80; and radicalization, 122

isolation: approaches to, 157; as end point, 110–111

Jackson, Susie, 42
Jade Helm, 49–53, 82
Japanese immigrants, theories on, 57–60
Jenna (Las Vegas witness), 29–36, 39
Jews. *See* anti-Semitism
Joly, Maurice, 60
Jones, Alex, xi, 18, 26, 71–74, 128; and assault-weapon ban, 9; and Christchurch mosque shootings, 137; and civil war, 143; and community, 103–104; and cultural Marxism, 17; and demonization, 137; and Jade Helm, 50–52; and Las Vegas massacre, 36–37; and 9/11, 3; and Obama, 79–81; and platforms, 114–115; and QAnon, 84, 86–87; and Sandy Hook, 105–108; and scams, 107; and Trump, 82–83
journalism: and disinformation campaigns, 121; and trust issues, 2, 178
journals, and deradicalization, 169
Judicial Watch, 92

Kek, 128–132
Kelly, Megyn, 50
Kelzel, Harleen, 127
Kennedy assassination, theories on, 62–63
Kissinger, Henry, 3
Knights Templar, 18, 28
Know Nothing Party, 56
Knutsen, Tove Ashill, 40
Koernke, Mark, 69, 71
Kowalski, Chase, 106
Kubrick, Stanley, 66
Ku Klux Klan, 18, 61, 74
Kutner, Samantha, 96; on deradicalization, 157–158, 160, 166–167, 169–170, 172

laetrile, 66
Lanza, Adam, 105

Larsen, Ray, 79
Lastoria, Mark, 49, 52
Las Vegas massacre, v, vii, 29–36; conspiracy theories on, 36–40, 108; disinformation on, 120; QAnon and, 87
Latinos, theories on, 74–79
Lea, Homer, 57
leaders, authoritarian, 137–139
Lebron, Michael Lionel, 89–90
Lee, Robert E., 124
Le Fevre, Adam, 10
legal issues: border movement and, 75–76; Sandy Hook lawsuit, 106–107, 114
Legend, John, 88
Le Pen, Marine, 98
Lervag, Jon Vegard, 40
Levine, Alex, 118
Lewandowsky, Stephan: on heroic ideal, 164; on ideation, 100–101; on immunization, 152; on motives, 163; on preparation, 155–156; on psychology, 101–102; on real conspiracies, 160–161; on replacement narratives, 170–171; on targets, 162
Lewis, Becca, 115
Lifton, Robert Jay, 147
Limbaugh, Rush, 73
Lind, William S., 15
Linwood Islamic Centre, 47
listening, and deradicalization, 158–159, 170; strategies for, 160
Litteral, Walter Eugene, 53
lizard people, theories on, 27, 46, 63
Loevlie, Hanne Ekroll, 40
logic, 99; and immunization, 152
Lombardo, Joe, 11
Lone Wolf, definition of, 141
Loomer, Laura, 108
Loy, Railston, 79

MacDonald, Kevin, 16
Madrigal, Alexis, 114
#MAGAbomber, 139–142

magic, Kek and, 129–132

Magnum, Destinee, 44

Maher, Bill, 117

manifestos: Breivik and, 14; Patriot
Front, 125–126; Rodger and, 22, 43;
Roof and, 20; Tarrant and, 27–28

Mars colony, QAnon and, 85

Martin, Trayvon, 19–20, 116

Martineau, Paris, 84

Marxism. *See* cultural Marxism

masculinity, toxic, 166; Kek and, 131;
Rodger and, 21–22. *See also* gender
issues; misogyny

mass shootings, vii; Charleston massacre,
19–20, 42–43, 116–117; Las Vegas,
9–12, 29–36; Norway, 13–14, 17–18,
40–42; Pittsburgh, 94

Matejka, Braden, 38

Matejka, Taylor, 38

The Matrix, vi

McCain, John, 85

McCann, Betina, 75

McCarthy, Joe, 63–65

McDonnell, Grace, 106

McInnes, Gavin, 26

McIntosh, Rob, 38

McMaster, H. R., 91

McVeigh, Timothy, 9, 12, 70, 164

Mead, Margaret, 15

meaning making, conspiracy theories and,
96–97

media: and anti-Semitism, 61;
consumption of, 103, 179–180;
and disinformation campaigns,
121, 177; fake news and, 2–3; and
misinformation, 32–34; Sayoc and,
139; and trust issues, 2; and Yellow
Peril theories, 57, 59–60

Media Matters, 115

meme magick, 130–132

men in black, 62–63

mental illness: and community, 107; and
conspiracy theories, 4, 166; Wolfe
and, 26

Metzger, Tom, 74

Mexico, theories on, 74–79

militia movement, 9–11, 63; history of,
67–94; structure of, 74; and white
supremacists, 124; Wolfe and, 26

Militia of Montana, 67–70

Miller, Stephen, 87

Minassian, Alek, 22–23, 44

Minuteman Civil Defense Corps, 76–79

mirror sites, 115

misinformation, 113–132; in active-
shooter situation, 32–34; on Las Vegas
massacre, 36. *See also* disinformation

misogyny: alt-right and, 122–126; Kek
and, 131; motives for, 162–163;
Rodger and, 18–22. *See also* gender
issues

Molyneux, Stefan, 127

moral boundaries, and deradicalization,
158–159

Morse, Samuel F. B., 56

mortality salience, 118

motives, for conspiracism, 162–163;
alternative approaches to, 163–165

Mueller, Robert, 27, 84, 108

Muirhead, Russell, 6

multiculturalism, 14–15; and
authoritarianism, 135. *See also* cultural
Marxism

Muslims. *See* Islam

Namkai-Meche, Taliesin Myrddin, 45

narcissism, authoritarian leaders and,
138–139

National Alliance, 61

national security issues, and control of
extremist content, 174

nativism, 56, 74–79; and border security,
71; Trump and, 82, 91–92

natural disasters, militia movement and,
68–69

needs, alternative approaches to, and
deradicalization, 163–165

neo-Confederates, 71

neo-Nazis, 12, 61, 82, 122–126. *See also* white nationalists/supremacists
Nethercott, Casey, 75–76
Neumann, Peter, 118, 150–151, 171–173, 175
new conspiracism, 6
NewsMax, 98
New World Order, 10, 12, 66–70, 72
Next News Network, 51
NFL, 141
Nichols, Terry, 164
Nixon, Richard, 64
Noble, Safiya Umoja, 115–117
nondirective approaches, and deradicalization, 158
normies, 179; term, 95
Norway shootings, 13–14, 17–18, 40–42

Oates, Titus, 54–55
Oath Keepers, 80, 137
Obama, Barack, 2, 79–82, 84, 139
Obama, Michelle, 37, 79
Oklahoma City bombings, ix, 9, 11–12, 70–71, 164
The Order, 12
O'Reilly, Bill, 73
outrage: and manipulation, 120; and social media models, 115

Paddock, Stephen, v, 9–12, 29–36, 39–40; disinformation on, 120; theories on, 108
Palin, Sarah, 80
Palmer Raids, 64
partisanship, and conspiracy theories, 2
Patriot Front, 123–125
Patriot movement, 10–11, 63; history of, 67–94
Patriot Prayer, 24–25, 108–109
Pearl Harbor attack, 59
Pearson, Roger, 16
pedophilia, theories on: Davis and, xi; Pizzagate and, 93; QAnon and, 27, 84, 87–88; Simcox and, 79

Peinovich, Mike, 138
Pepe the Frog, 128–132
persecution, conspiracy theories and, 100
personality types: and authoritarianism, 134–137, 156; and credulity, 155. *See also* psychological tendencies
persuasion, approaches to, 157
Peterson, Jordan, 138–139
PewDiePie, 127
Phelan, James, 57
Pinckney, Clementa, 42
pink pill, vi
Pirro, Jeanine, 98
Pittsburgh Tree of Life massacre, 94
Pizzagate, xi, 93
Planned Parenthood, militia movement and, 69
Podesta, John, 93
political correctness, 15, 127; Kek and, 129–132; Trump and, 141. *See also* cultural Marxism
pop culture, alt-right and, 125
Popish Plot, 54–55
populist movements, and disinformation, 178
Portland incidents, Christian and, 23–26, 44–45
Posobiec, Jack, 108
postmodernism, 14–15
posttraumatic stress disorder, 35–36
power, conspiracy theories and, 101–102
problem solving, 101–102
The Protocols of the Elders of Zion, 60–61
Proud Boys, 26; and feuds, 108–110; and immersion, 98; Wolfe and, 26–27, 46
psychological tendencies, 101; and community, 107; and violence, 148–149. *See also* personality types
psyops, 52
purple pill, vi
Putin, Vladimir, 72

QAnon: and community, 104; and disinformation, 121; and immersion,

98; Storm theory of, 83–90; Wolfe and, 26–27
quantum physics, ix
questions, for deradicalization, 159–160, 166; on deeper motives, 162–163

rabbit hole, going down, 95–111; avoiding, during deradicalization, 160–162; end point of, 110–111; personal experience of, 95. *See also* radicalization
race war: Atomwaffen Division and, 126; Jones on, 37. *See also* civil war; culture war
racism, viii; border movement and, 74–79; Roof and, 19, 42–43. *See also* white nationalists/supremacists
radicalization: algorithms and, 116–120; as incremental, 117; personal experience of, 117; prevention of, recommendations for, 151–155; process of, 123, 126–128, 150; social media and, 113–114; speed of, 123
Ralph, Ethan, x
The Ralph Retort, x
Ranch Rescue, 75–76
reactance, 150
Reaction America, 123
reality: acceptance of, 179–180; alternate, 135–136, 168; versus conspiracism, vi–vii
real-world activities, and deradicalization, 168–169
reason, 99; and immunization, 152
recruitment, 13; alt-right and, 122; Birchers and, 66
Reddit, vi, 22, 82, 127
red-pilling, vi, 9–28, 145–146; personal experience of, v–vi, 127–128; selective, 127; term, 126
Red Scare, 63–66
relationships: conspiracy theories and, 4–5, 149–150; and deradicalization, 149, 156–158, 171–172; immersion

and, 102–105; and prevention, 175; real-world activities and, 168–169; restoring, 272; Wolfe and, 27
religion, Church of Kek, 128–132
repetition, and deradicalization, 158
replacement narratives, 170–171
Republican Party: and authoritarianism, 134; and conspiracy theories, 80
researchers, 99–100
resilience, and deradicalization, 160
respect, intellectual, 164
Ressam, Ahmed, 77
Rhodes, Stewart, 137–138
Rich, Seth, xi
right-wing authoritarian (RWA) personalities, 135–137
right-wing domestic terrorism, 12–18
right-wing populism, and disinformation, 177
Robison, John, 55
Rodger, Elliot, 19–23, 43–44
Rogan, Joe, 108
Rogers, Carl, 158, 160
Roma people, 61
Roof, Dylann, 19–20, 42–43, 116–117
Rosenberg, Ethel and Julius, 64
Rosenblum, Nancy, 6, 96–97, 110–111
Rosicrucians, 55
Rousseau, Thomas, 124–125
Route 91 massacre, 29–36; conspiracy theories on, 36–40; disinformation on, 120; theories on, 108
Ruby Ridge standoff: militia movement and, 68; Paddock and, 11
Rudolph, Eric, 12, 70
Russia: and disinformation, 121–122, 177; and election interference, 2; and Jade Helm, 51–52; Jones and, 72; and misinformation, 36
Russo-Japanese War, 57
RWA. *See* right-wing authoritarian personalities

sacrifices. *See* casualties
Sageman, Marc, 118
Samish Island murders, viii–xi, 147–148
Sand, Kjersti Berg, 40
Sanders, Bernie, 23, 113
Sanders, Sarah, 89
Sanders, Tywanza, 42
Sandy Hook massacre, 39; conspiracies on, 105–107
Sargon of Akkad, 26
Savage, Michael, 128, 143
Sayoc, Cesar, 139–142
scams, 1, 69, 107
scapegoating, 7, 54–55, 101–102
Schlapp, Matt, 92–93
Schuck, Steve, 34
Schultz, Russell, 109–110
science-related conspiracies, ix; Wolfe and, 26
SDO. *See* social dominance orientation
search engines, 115–116
Seattle4Truth, ix
Second Amendment, militia movement and, 68
secrecy, and conspiracy theories, 3
Sedition Act, 64
selective credulity, 70
selective skepticism, conspiracy theories and, 100
self-reflexivity, and deradicalization, 169
self-worth: and authoritarianism, 136; conspiracy theories and, 96, 104
September 11, 2001: and authoritarianism, 135; conspiracy theories on, 3–4; Davis and, ix; Jones and, 73; Paddock and, 11
Shafer, Jack, 144
shame, approaches to, and deradicalization, 169–170
Shapiro, Ben, 98, 128
sheeple: term, 29. *See also* normies
SIFT model, 154–155
Simcox, Chris, 76, 79
SJWs. *See* social justice warriors

skepticism, selective, conspiracy theories and, 100
Slavros, Alexander, 123
Snyder, Gwen, 98
social dominance orientation (SDO), 138–139
social justice warriors (SJWs), 26, 127
social media: and conspiracy theories, 85–86; emotional effects of, 96; lack of regulation of, 114–115; misinformation on, 113–132; and trust issues, 178. *See also specific platform*
Soros, George, xi, 84, 92–93, 139
Southern Poverty Law Center, 76, 80, 82, 85
Spencer, Glenn, 74–75
Sputnik, 36
Starbird, Kate, 120–122, 161–162, 177–179
status, 101, 165
Steele dossier, 87
Steinbeck, John, 139
stigma, approaches to, and deradicalization, 169
stochastic terrorism, 139–142
Stoddard, Lothrop, 59
Stoltenberg, Jens, 40
Stone, Roger, 108
The Storm, 83–90
Stormfront, 18, 82, 123
submission, authoritarian, 135
suicide, of perpetrators: Paddock and, 34; Rodger and, 43
supplements, 1, 63, 107
surveillance, 133
survival gear, 69
survivors: experience of, 29–36; treatment of, 36–40

Tarrant, Brenton, 27–28, 46–47, 137–138
tax issues, 10–11
Taylor, Jared, 16

Tea Party, 80
Teigen, Chrissy, 83, 88
terrorism: prevention of, family/friends and, 175; stochastic, 139–142
Three Percenters, 98
time: and deradicalization, 170–172, 180; of exposure, and desensitization, 118; on social media, 115
Toese, Tusitala "Tiny," 108–109
Tombstone Militia, 76
totalitarianism. *See* authoritarianism
Tracy, James, 106
Tree of Life massacre, 94
Trochmann, John, 67–71
trolls: and disinformation, 121; Jones and, 103–104; and Kek, 130–131; pro-social, 157; and Sandy Hook families, 105–107
Truelove, Andrew David, 106
Trump, Donald: and authoritarianism, 134, 137; and border security, 78; Christian and, 23; clinging to office, 143–145; and conspiracy theories, 2, 81–93; and extremism, 113; and immersion, 98, 127; Paddock and, 11; QAnon and, 27; Sayoc and, 139–142; Tarrant and, 138; and violence, 140, 142; and weaponization of empathy, 159
trust issues, 2; and community, 107–111; and disinformation campaigns, 121; and immersion, 101; recommendations for, 178
truth: conspiracy theories and, 7; uncertainty and, 39
Truthers, 73
Tufekci, Zeynep, 113–114, 133
The Turner Diaries, 9
Twitter, 85, 174

UFOs, 62–63, 104
uncertainty, 163
underlying beliefs, challenges to, 165–166

unhinging effect, 7; Bernstein on, 147–148; process of, 95–111; QAnon and, 89
United Nations, 66–67, 71
United States, division in: conspiracism and, 176–177; disinformation and, 120–122
"Unite the Right" rally, 124; Trump and, 141
Uscinski, Joseph, 99, 111

Vanguard America, 123–124
VDare, 16
video games: Breivik and, 14; Christchurch mosque shootings and, 46–47; immunization and, 153; and Kek, 129; and radicalization, 118, 123; Roof and, 19
View, Travis, 104
violence, vii, 7, 29–47; authoritarianism and, 137, 139; isolation and, 111; Pizzagate and, 93; predicting, 148–149; scripted, 139–142; speed of radicalization and, 123; Trump and, 140, 142
Vitolo, C. V., 158–160, 163
Voices of Citizens Together, 75
voting: conspiracy involvement and, 5; immersion and, 103

Waco siege: militia movement and, 68; Paddock and, 11
Wahabzada, Abdul Aziz, 47
Walker, Jesse, 97
Wall (border), 92
Wang, Weihann "David," 43
Washington, George, 55–56
watch time, social media and, 115
water supply, theories on, ix, 63, 66
Watson, Paul Joseph, 117, 128
weaponization: of critical thinking, 161–162; of empathy, 159
weather control: Jones and, 71; militia movement and, 68–70

Weiler, Jonathan, 134
Weill, Kelly, 105, 117
Weishaupt, Adam, 55
Welch, Joseph, 65
Welch, Robert, 65–66
Weyrich, Paul, 15–16
white nationalists/supremacists, 16, 122–126; and birtherism, 82; and disinformation, 121–122; and immigrants, 56–60; multiculturalism and, 15; and Obama, 79–81; Roof, 19, 42–43; Trump and, 138, 141
white pill, viii
whitey tape, 79
Whitson, Jennifer, 97–98
Wolfe, Buckey, 26–27, 46
Wolfe, James, 26, 46

Wood, Michael, 101–102, 105
World of Warcraft, 129
Wright, Matthew P., 89
#WWG1WGA, 89

Y2K bug, Jones and, 71–72
Yellow Peril theories, 56–60
Yiannopoulos, Milo, x, 26, 128, 147
Your News Wire, 36
YouTube: Breivik and, 14; and extremism, 113–115, 117, 128; and growth of conspiracism, 18–19; and regulation, 114, 174; Rodger and, 22, 43; Wolfe and, 26

ZOG, 12
Zublick, David, 84